A Guide to Hellenistic Lite

BLACKWELL GUIDES TO CLASSICAL LITERATURE

Each volume offers coverage of political and cultural context, brief essays on key authors, historical figures, and the most important literary works, and a survey of crucial themes. The series provides the necessary background to read classical literature with confidence.

Published

A Guide to Hellenistic Literature
Kathryn Gutzwiller

A Guide to Ancient Greek Drama
Ian C. Storey and Arlene Allan

In preparation

A Guide to Epic Poetry
Brendon Reay and Timothy Hampton

A Guide to
Hellenistic Literature

Kathryn Gutzwiller

Blackwell
Publishing

BLACKWELL PUBLISHING
350 Main Street, Malden, MA 02148-5020, USA
9600 Garsington Road, Oxford OX4 2DQ, UK
550 Swanston Street, Carlton, Victoria 3053, Australia

First published 2007 by Blackwell Publishing Ltd

1   2007

Library of Congress Cataloging-in-Publication Data

Gutzwiller, Kathryn J.
A guide to Hellenistic literature / Kathryn Gutzwiller.
p. cm.—(Blackwell guides to classical literature)
Includes bibliographical references and index.
ISBN-13: 978-0-631-23321-3 (hardcover: alk. paper)
ISBN-13: 978-0-631-23322-0 (pbk.: alk. paper)
1. Greek literature, Hellenistic—History and criticism. I. Title.

PA3081.G88 2007
880.9′001–dc22
2006025004

A catalogue record for this title is available from the British Library.

Set in 10/12.5 Calisto
by SPi Publisher Services, Pondicherry, India
Printed and bound in Singapore
by COS Printers Pte Ltd

The publisher's policy is to use permanent paper from mills that operate a sustainable forestry
policy, and which has been manufactured from pulp processed using acid-free and elementary chlorine-free practices. Furthermore, the publisher ensures that the text paper and cover
board used have met acceptable environmental accreditation standards.

For further information on
Blackwell Publishing, visit our website:
www.blackwellpublishing.com

To Louise Price Hoy
and
In Memory of Barbara Hughes Fowler

Contents

Figures

Maps

Preface

This Guide is intended to serve as an introduction to the literature of the Hellenistic age for students of classics and for general readers with an interest in the ancient world. Other books on the subject tend to focus on poetry and offer literary interpretation of major authors, together with a small number of more minor ones. This study covers a broader range of literature, so that, although poetry is treated most fully, prose texts, even those of a technical nature, receive some attention; an emphasis is placed on similarities and connections between literary texts within and across genres, and some attempt is made to set these works within their historical and cultural contexts. My goal is to inform rather than to argue positions or develop interpretations. The extant texts from the three centuries following the death of Alexander have been my main subject, but certain crucial works of Hellenistic literature, known only in fragmentary form, have been discussed as well. I also include a selection of other fragmentary texts and authors, in order to give a more rounded picture of genres and literary trends.

The book begins with a chapter on history and culture, which focuses on the formation of the Hellenistic kingdoms and briefly discusses historical, cultural, and literary developments in the territories belonging to the Antigonids, Seleucids, Attalids, and Ptolemies. The second chapter provides basic information about the new aesthetics that informed Hellenistic literature. It includes a section on style, meter, and diction, and concludes with an overview of the physical nature of Hellenistic bookrolls.

The third chapter is organized into sections on major authors and on selected generic types. Each section includes brief biographical

information, information about the literary forms being used, summary of
the contents of texts, and brief interpretive remarks. The sections on
generic types and multiple authors are designed to give a sense of the
range of (often lost) Hellenistic literature and to suggest what cultural and
aesthetic impulses produced the variety of literary forms found during the
period.

The last chapter treats major topics in Hellenistic literature. The interpretive trends presented here often overlap with more general approaches
in literary criticism, even though scholars of Hellenistic literature tend not
to fall into theoretical camps. Here I attempt to show how the philological
approaches of nineteenth-century scholarship have shaped basic ideas
about the learnedness of Hellenistic literature and its innovative features
and how a growing awareness of the social background for the literature
has produced a set of new, broader questions about such matters as the
nature of reading and the role of performance, the interaction of authors
with patrons, and methods of establishing identity within the complex
world created in the aftermath of Alexander. In addition, I suggest some
of the developing trends in scholarship, such as parallels between literature
and art, the influence of philosophical criticism on literary practice, and
the importance of technical and scientific prose for the new poetics.
Lastly, some brief remarks are provided about the reception of Hellenistic
literature in Rome, or perhaps better, the way Hellenistic literature was
rewritten in Latin form for a Roman audience.

Greek names, both for historical figures and literary characters, have
been given a Latinized spelling. I have chosen to write, for instance,
Cnemon rather than Knemon or Chrysippus rather than Khrusippos, in
order to preserve the most familiar spelling for well-known persons and
places and to provide consistency with the less-familiar proper nouns.
Unless otherwise stated, all dates are BC (or BCE).

This book is dedicated to two of my teachers – to Louise Price Hoy, who
once suggested in the margins of an exam that Hellenistic literature might
be more interesting than the handbooks allowed, and to the late Barbara
Hughes Fowler, who showed me just what the handbooks had missed.
Two of my own students, Joel Hatch and Valentina Popescu, gave me
advice on the manuscript and helped me find errors; I am deeply grateful to
both. I am also indebted to Sophie Gibson, my patient and inspiring editor,
who helped shape the book in ways that I did not foresee. John Wallrodt,
our technical wizard, has been invaluable in constructing the maps. Peter
Bing took time from his year of residency as a Tytus Fellow at the
University of Cincinnati to read the whole manuscript and offer many
valuable suggestions. My thanks are due as well to Marco Fantuzzi and to
Dee Clayman, who wrote a generous and encouraging report for the press.

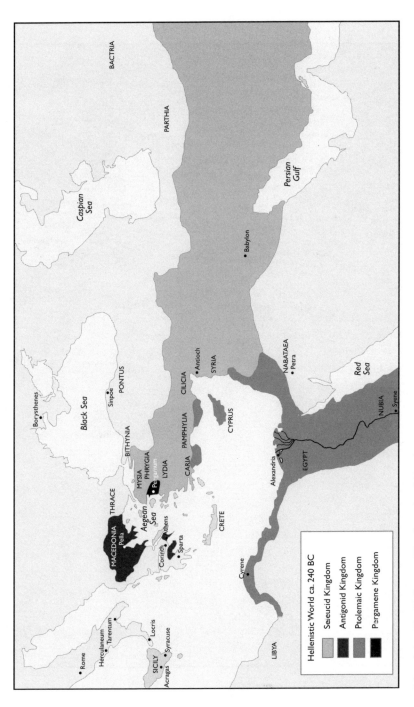

Map 0.1 *The Hellenistic Kingdoms (ca. 240 BC).*

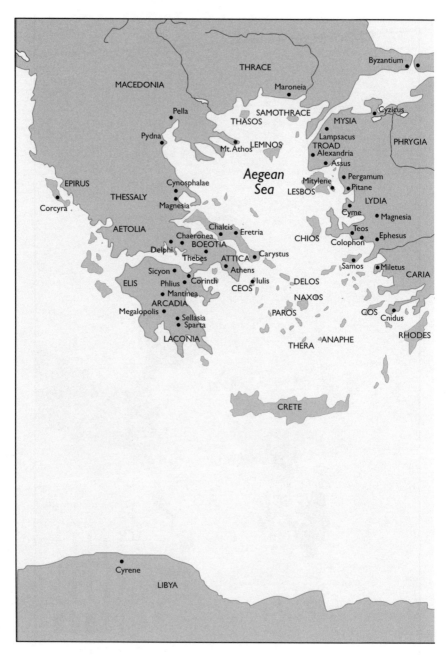

Map 0.2 *Greece, Egypt, and Asia Minor.*

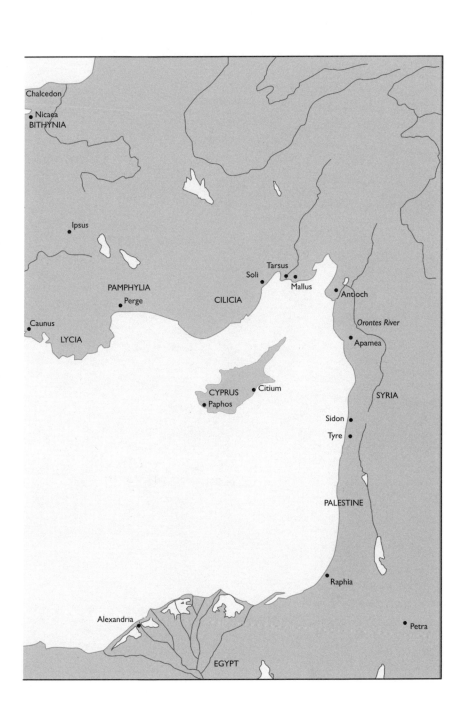

Chalcedon

Nicaea
BITHYNIA

Ipsus

PAMPHYLIA
Perge

Caunus
LYCIA

Soli Tarsus
Mallus
CILICIA

Antioch

Orontes River

Apamea

CYPRUS Citium
Paphos

SYRIA

Sidon
Tyre

PALESTINE

Raphia

Alexandria

Petra

EGYPT

1

History and Culture

The Hellenistic age is generally defined as the period from the death of Alexander the Great in 323 BC to Octavian's defeat of Mark Antony and Cleopatra VII at Actium in 31 BC. During a short but brilliant career, Alexander had extended his father's consolidation of Macedonian political power over mainland Greece through an extraordinary military campaign that brought under his control Syria and Palestine, Egypt, and the old Persian empire. His march to the east ended only within the borders of India. The geographical, political, social, and economic changes that took place as a result of these conquests profoundly affected the intellectual and literary production of the following era. Despite much cultural continuity in non-Greek areas, the elite members of the new multiethnic kingdoms developed a shared identity as Hellenes, based on an attachment to earlier Greek culture that was now viewed as a fixed element of a bygone era. After the first quarter of the third century BC political stability, coupled with unprecedented wealth for Greek rulers from the vast material resources of their kingdoms, produced a remarkable period of innovative literary activity. Although Athens remained the center for philosophical thought, the courts of the monarchs served as magnets for aspiring and talented authors. The most spectacular of these was the court of the Ptolemaic rulers of Egypt, who established poets and scholars alike in the Museum and Library complex that graced their new capital at Alexandria.

1.1   The Successors

After a period of illness and heavy drinking, Alexander died unexpectedly at Babylon at the age of only 34. With his Macedonian forces he had acquired a vast empire, but the task of consolidating political power and establishing administrative structures had scarcely begun at the time of his death. Lacking the tradition of constitutionally established government prevailing in most Greek city-states (*poleis*), the Macedonian kings held power through military conquest and personal excellence. Alexander, the last of the Argead dynasty, left no heir capable of securing the succession. His half-brother, Philip III Arrhidaeus, was considered mentally deficient, and his only child, Alexander IV, was born posthumously to his Bactrian wife Rhoxane. These young "kings" eventually fell victim to the ambitions of those claiming regency, while the Macedonian army was prepared to accept as leader whoever exerted power at a given moment. As a result, a long period of struggle ensued among Alexander's commanders, known as the Diadochs, "Successors," before geographical and political stability set in about 276 BC.

The seeds for the division of Alexander's empire into separate kingdoms were planted shortly after his death, when the empire was parceled out among members of his high command. Antigonus the One-Eyed, one of the older generation of generals, received parts of Asia Minor; Lysimachus, a member of Alexander's personal bodyguard, took over Thrace; and Ptolemy, a Macedonian aristocrat with kinship ties to Alexander, was awarded Egypt. As a result of disagreements that quickly followed, the elderly general Antipater became regent of the young "kings" in Macedonia, and Seleucus, another of Alexander's former commanders, acquired the administration of Babylonia. Nearly a half-century of military conflict, shifting alliances, and assassinations intervened before relative stability was achieved.

Antipater's son Cassander, rejected as his father's successor in Macedonia, allied himself with Antigonus the One-Eyed and in 317 won the support of Eurydice, who had married Philip Arrhidaeus. Alexander's mother Olympias, returning to Macedonia from exile, then murdered Eurydice and her weak husband; Olympias in turn was condemned and put to death. Unlike the secluded women at Athens and in many parts of Greece, Macedonian royal women often played significant roles in dynastic politics, and so set the pattern for the influential queens of the Hellenistic kingdoms. The Macedonian practice of polygamy – serial marriage to form connections to other powerful families – often resulted in multiple sons by different wives and so disputed successions. The pattern of assassination even of close relatives, characteristic of all the Hellenistic kingdoms, is related in part to rivalries among royal wives supporting the interests of their sons. Alexander's posthumous son by Rhoxane survived until 310 when Cassander, his regent, had him killed.

The one successor who most clearly aimed at controlling a reunited empire was Antigonus the One-Eyed, who sought to extend his territorial position in Syria by fighting Seleucus. In 306 his son Demetrius, later called Poliorcetes, "Besieger," established Macedonian naval power by defeating Ptolemy, commander in Egypt, at sea. Antigonus and his son were pronounced kings (*basileis*), in an apparent claim to replace the Argeads. But shortly after, other Successors also accepted the title of king; overlordship of a *division* of Alexander's empire rather than the whole was now the reality, if not the intention. Antigonus' son Demetrius also partially restored the democracy in Athens and was fulsomely praised as liberator in a hymn that survives (Powell p. 174):[1]

> Oh son of the most powerful god Poseidon
>   and Aphrodite, hail.
> The other gods are far away,
>   do not lend us an ear,
> do not exist, or pay us no heed,
>   but we see you present here,
> not made of wood or stone, but real.
>   So we pray to you.

This hymn, together with the cult honors granted by the Athenians to Demetrius and his father as "Savior Gods," was a harbinger of the dynastic worship to come in the Hellenistic kingdoms. Demetrius acquired the epithet Poliorcetes as a result of an eventually unsuccessful siege of Rhodes, which lasted over a year (305–304). To commemorate their deliverance, the Rhodians constructed the famous Colossus, a bronze statue of the god Helius (32 meters in height) that became one of the Seven Wonders of the World; unfortunately, it lasted only until the 220s when it was destroyed in an earthquake. Antigonus' ambition of reuniting Alexander's empire ended in 301 at the battle of Ipsus in Phrygia, where he was trampled to death by war elephants and his son routed by the combined forces of Cassander, Lysimachus, and Seleucus.

By the end of the first quarter of the third century, three of Alexander's commanders had proved successful in establishing for their heirs kingdoms with permanent geographical centers and stable administrations: the Antigonids in Macedonia and parts of Greece, the Seleucids in Asia, and the Ptolemies in Egypt. Another culturally important kingdom, which gradually seceded from the Seleucids during the middle decades of the third century, was that of the Attalids at Pergamum, a city of Mysia in western Asia Minor. For all these kingdoms the period of greatest brilliance was the third century and the earlier part of the second (map 0.1). The principal story of later Hellenistic history is the growing dominance of Rome. To name only key events, the Romans abolished the Macedonian monarchy in 168, sacked and destroyed Corinth in 146, received Pergamum by the bequest of Attalus III in 133, and made Egypt a Roman province in 30 after the death of Cleopatra VII.

1.2 Macedonia and Greece

In the fourth century the mountainous region of Macedonia, located in northern Greece between Thrace to the northeast and the Illyrians to the northwest, was considered a fringe area of Hellenic society. But as recent archaeological discoveries have shown, the Macedonian aristocracy was not only fully hellenized but also had sophisticated tastes in art, architecture, literature, and philosophy. Philip II (382–336), the father of Alexander the Great, was a strong ruler who set the stage for his son's conquests. He brought the Macedonian hinterland under monarchic control, developed hugely successful military techniques with long spears and phalanx formations, urbanized much of the population, and increased trade. He also extended Macedonian domination over Greece with a decisive defeat of Thebes and Athens at Chaeronea in 338. Philip's capital city of Pella, adorned with a large palace complex serving as the kingdom's administrative center, has produced some of the best mosaics surviving from the Hellenistic period, some featuring the hunts favored by the Macedonian aristocrats and some with Dionysiac themes. The royal tombs at Vergina provide astounding artefactual evidence for the opulent lifestyle of the Argeads, foreshadowing the ostentatious displays of later Hellenistic monarchs. An undisturbed tomb, perhaps that of Philip II himself, has provided grave goods in ivory, silver, and gold of the finest artistic workmanship, while tomb paintings, such as that of Hades carrying off Persephone, offer unique examples of Greek fresco technique. The earliest surviving Greek literary papyrus, containing a philosophical text on Orphic cosmology, was found in a tomb of about 340–330 at Derveni in Macedonia. Perhaps related were the mysteries of Dionysus, involving promises of an afterlife, which were popular among the Macedonians.

The Hellenistic kingdom of Macedonia dominated Greece north of the Isthmus, partially by garrisoning key ports including the Piraeus at Athens, but the Peloponnese remained largely outside of its direct control (map 0.2). Antigonus Gonatas (ruled ca. 276–239) was an energetic king who resisted the opulent trappings adopted by his counterparts in Asia and Egypt. His court was a cultured one, filled with poets, philosophers, and historians, and apparently dominated by his personal interests in Stoic philosophy. A precedent had been set by Philip II, who attracted Aristotle from Athens to tutor the young Alexander in Macedonia. Antigonus, in turn, had studied in Athens with Zeno of Citium (335–263), the founder of Stoicism, and two of Zeno's disciples lived with the king to guide him in his desire to find true happiness and to be a virtuous ruler. Aratus of Soli (see Ch. 3.5), whose astronomical poem entitled *Phaenomena* has Stoic underpinnings, also dwelled at Antigonus' court. The king was interested in other philosophical approaches as well. Among the visitors at his court were, apparently, the Skeptic poet Timon of Phlius, who wrote *Silli*, "*Lampoons*," in which he satirized earlier philosophers by making snide or witty comments about their beliefs (Ch. 3.8), the popular philosopher Bion of Borysthenes, known for his caustic wit and theatrical displays, and Menedemus of Eretria, who founded the Eretrian school concerned with ethical philosophy. Other visitors included the epic poet Antagoras of Rhodes, who wrote a lost epic *Thebaid*, and Alexander of Aetolia, a playwright and scholar who also worked in Ptolemaic Alexandria.

During his reign Antigonus strengthened Macedonian control over Greece, which increased resentment among cities hoping to maintain their liberty, and ended Ptolemaic naval expansion in the Aegean. His most energetic successor was Philip V (ruled 221–179). He attempted to expand his domain against the Illyrians and eventually came into disastrous conflict with the Romans. As a result of a decisive defeat at Cynoscephalae in Thessaly in 197, Philip was restricted to Macedonia and forced to become an ally of Rome. His son Perseus (ruled 179–168) engaged in campaigns in northern Greece until overthrown by the Romans. The kingship abolished, Macedonia was divided into four republics and in 146 became a Roman province.

Throughout this period "freedom," from the overlordship of Macedon and later of others, was the watchword of the Greek *poleis*. The right to conduct foreign affairs as they pleased existed at times for some cities, while internal self-governance remained fairly common on the mainland and among Aegean islands. Athens, the example of most interest, had possessed a radical democracy during most of the fifth and fourth centuries. With democratic institutions suppressed after the defeat by Philip II at Chaeronea in 338, an authoritarian oligarchy was put in effect in 322 by Antipater, who brought about the death of the anti-Macedonian orator Demosthenes. Cassander put in charge Demetrius of Phalerum, whose philosophically based government was conservative, slanted toward the aristocratic elite, and known for its legislative curtailment of luxury. Liberation at the hands of Demetrius Poliorcetes in 307 led to the reestablishment of some democratic forms, but Athens remained within the Macedonian sphere of influence throughout the third century. The garrison at the Piraeus was one of the four "fetters of Greece" upon which Macedonian naval power depended. In addition, Demetrius Poliorcetes took advantage of his position of power in Athens to engage in riotous and disrespectful behavior. His taking up residence in the Parthenon, with his favorite prostitutes, stood as a symbol of the untrammeled mode of living that could be adopted by the monarchic figures of the post-Alexander age. Toward the close of the fourth century, the Athenian tradition of great dramatic poetry, produced for consumption by the populace at large, had one last notable practitioner, the comic poet Menander. With his reworking of earlier tragic and comic plots to form comedies of manners, focusing on familial relationships and romance, Menander foreshadows the more personal orientation of much Hellenistic literature.

Although Athens ceased to be on the cutting edge of poetic production, it continued as an intellectual center. Throughout the Hellenistic period larger questions about the physical universe, knowledge, government, and ethics continued to find their home in the Athenian philosophical schools, where individuals were free to talk rather than do. The schools founded in the fourth century by Plato (the Academy) and by Aristotle (the Peripatetic Lyceum) provided models for communities of thinkers working on fundamental questions from a given set of principles. The Lyceum, headed after the death of Alexander by Aristotle's successor Theophrastus (ca. 371–287), provided the model, through investigation into many areas of science and social life, for the expansion of knowledge that characterized Hellenistic intellectual life. Toward the end of the fourth century several new philosophies arose. Cynicism was more a way of life than a formal school; its adherents were named after Diogenes of Sinope (ca. 403–321), who was called "doggish" (*kynikos*) because of his shameless flouting of all convention. Skepticism, usually traced back to the oral teachings of Pyrrho of Elis (ca. 365–275), who traveled with Alexander the Great, raised a serious challenge to the theories of knowledge advanced by Plato and Aristotle. Partially in response to Skepticism, the founders of Epicureanism, Epicurus of Samos, and of Stoicism, Zeno of Citium, produced full-service philosophies with integrated theories about the physical universe and human psychology. The writings of the major philosophical schools have, for the most part, been reduced to fragments and summaries, and only three short treatises and a kind of catechism by Epicurus survive in complete form from the extensive philosophical literature associated with Hellenistic Athens (Ch. 3.8).

In the new political and social climate that focused people away from public action to private life, it is understandable that the fundamental goal behind Hellenistic philosophy was ethical. All the schools asked the same basic question – "What is the nature of happiness (*eudaimonia*)?" – and gave the same answer – "peace of mind" (*ataraxia*). The word *eudaimonia* refers not to a transitory emotional state, as the translation "happiness" suggests, but to generalized and lasting wellbeing in the world. The differences between the schools, however, lay in how they thought peace of mind could be achieved. The goal of the Cynic way of life, often demonstrated theatrically, was to shake off the tyranny of social conformity and to live naturally. Diogenes, for instance, took as his possessions only a coarse cloak, walking staff, and wallet for provisions, performed sexual and other natural functions in public, and was fearlessly disrespectful to the powerful, including Alexander the Great, who seems to have admired his Cynic ways. For the Skeptics emotional balance lay in "suspension of belief," a kind of agnosticism that focused on the search for truth rather than finding it. For the followers of Epicurus, happiness was defined as freedom from fear and pain, and the method of achieving this equanimity was to understand the atomistic nature of the universe and the indifference of the gods. For the Stoics, however, happiness resulted from the virtuous life, and virtue was predicated on an intellectual understanding in accord with the rational principles of the universe. By offering internal tranquility as the goal of the reflective life, all the Hellenistic philosophical schools, despite their differences, acknowledged the limitations on the politically active life in the world as now constituted. For the most part (though not exclusively), the philosophers of these schools preferred the quieter intellectual atmosphere of Athens to the wealth and fanfare of the royal courts, and well into the imperial period upper-class Romans finished off their elite educations by studying there.

The Athenians came to recognize that what freedom remained to them was due to the protection of benefactors elsewhere, who were rewarded with honors for contributing to the embellishment of the city. Examples of such civic adornments are the Stoa of Attalus, built by the second Pergamene king of that name near the agora and now visible in restoration, and a series of statues set up on the Acropolis (partially surviving in copies) that represented mythological and historical victories over forces of chaos (including the Giants, the Amazons, the Persians, and the Gauls), also contributed by an Attalus of Pergamum. In line with acknowledgments of their political dependency was the Athenian decision to act as loyal supporters of Rome, initially in resistance to Macedonian expansion under Philip V. As a result, the city enjoyed a period of peace during the Roman advance in the second century. But when Mithradates VI of Pontus (ruled 120–63) attempted to drive the Romans from Asia Minor and Greece, Athens eagerly joined the revolt. In 87–86 the Roman general Sulla besieged and sacked the city.

Other Greek *poleis* developed the defensive strategy of forming confederacies for military purposes. The two principal alliances of this type were the Aetolian League in west-central Greece and the Achaean League, originally centered in the northwestern Peloponnese. The earlier history and ethnography of these allied areas were written up by epic poets of the era, such as Rhianus of Crete, whose works included *Achaica*, *Eliaca*, *Thessalica* (in at least sixteen books), and *Messeniaca* (in at least six books). Nicander wrote a long poem on the topography and unusual natural features of Aetolia. The historian Polybius was the son of a commander of the Achaean League and provides invaluable information about the league's formation in the middle of the third century, its initial purpose in protecting the Peloponnese against Macedon, and its conflict with a resurgent Sparta. In the second half of the third century, two Spartan kings (a constitutional office of long standing in Sparta), Agis and then Cleomenes, attempted to institute social and political reforms by canceling debt and redistributing land. Cleomenes, who was guided by the Stoic philosopher Sphaerus of Borysthenes, in this way extended the dwindling citizen base and trained the newly enfranchised in Spartan fighting. After suffering military defeats, the Achaean League, with the guidance of the Cynic poet Cercidas of Megalopolis (Ch. 3.8), invited their former Macedonian adversary, Antigonus Doson, into the Peloponnese. He defeated the Spartans at Sellasia in 222 and reversed the reforms. Cleomenes escaped to Egypt, where he committed suicide after attempting to arouse the Alexandrians to revolt against Ptolemy IV. After additional attempts at land reform by another king, Nabis (ruled 207–192), were aborted through the intervention of the Romans, Sparta was incorporated into the Achaean League and so ended its independent history. A final effort by the League to resist Roman dominance in 146 failed miserably. The result was the sack of Corinth by Lucius Mummius, who destroyed or carried off its priceless works of art.

1.3   Seleucid Asia

Seleucus I left to his son and co-regent Antiochus I (ruled 281–261) an immense empire, extending from Bactria in the east to Asia Minor in the west. To a much greater extent than the Antigonids or even the Ptolemies, the Seleucids ruled a multiethnic realm, diverse in its languages and cultures. Their ability to govern this complex territory was made possible by adapting the communication system and administrative structures of the Persian Achaemenids. The empire was parceled out to satraps, who administrated with a relatively free hand as long as revenues and loyalty were provided the king. Military intervention occurred only when local governors became seriously in arrears or openly declared independence. The geography of the empire was never stable, and the Seleucids struggled, through military campaigns that usually had only temporary success, to hold on to the outer territories. Bactria broke away under Seleucus II (ruled 246–225), and the third century also witnessed the formation of the Parthian state, which in the second century expanded westward to occupy Mesopotamia. Southern Syria and Palestine were disputed with the Ptolemies and not under Seleucid control during much of the third century. The Attalids in Pergamum, as allies of the Romans, succeeded in expanding eastward into Seleucid satrapies in Asia Minor in the early second century. One important effect of Seleucid domination was a process of hellenization, which took place even in the distant eastern territories. Spreading Hellenic culture may not, as such, have been a primary goal of the Seleucids, and certainly local customs and non-Greek languages were maintained as well, particularly among nonelites. But especially in many western areas Greek influence had been strong before Alexander's campaigns, and in the Hellenistic period privileged members of society, including eventually the Romans, eagerly took up a Hellenic style of life as a mark of their status. A cultured life was defined by knowledge of Greek language, literature, and traditions.

Whether due to the personal tastes of the dynasty or the exigencies of controlling such an empire, the Seleucids were not as interested in philosophy as was Antigonus Gonatas, nor did they invest in literature and scholarship as seriously as the Ptolemies and Attalids. There is no evidence, for instance, that a trio of authors from Syrian Gadara who span the third to first centuries BC – the Cynic satirist Menippus, the erotic epigrammatist Meleager, and the Epicurean philosopher Philodemus – had any direct connections with the Seleucid court. But sponsorship of literary or intellectual culture was not altogether lacking, especially when it supported dynastic interests. Berossus of Babylon composed for Antiochus I a (now fragmentary) cultural history of Babylonia, which began with creation, described the great flood, and traced the kings down to Alexander. Simonides Magnes wrote a (lost) epic poem celebrating the same king's victory over the Gauls with war elephants, and the didactic poet Aratus, who also lived with Antigonus Gonatas, visited Antiochus' court in Syria. Ruler cults were first established by cities to honor Seleucus I, and there survive lines from a hymn composed to glorify him as the reputed son of Apollo (Powell p. 140). Inscriptions give evidence for civic cults honoring Laodice, the wife of Antiochus III (ruled 223–187), who was the first Seleucid to institute state worship for living monarchs and their royal ancestors. Like other Hellenistic dynasties, the Seleucids promoted themselves in the popular imagination through stories of their divine ancestors and wondrous deeds, by setting up their images as statues and on coins, and by founding cities that were given politically crafted traditions.

An outstanding example of such a new settlement is Antioch, one of several Seleucid capital cities. Seleucus I founded the great Antioch, laid out on an axial-grid plan, a few miles inland on the river Orontes in northern Syria. As the protecting Fortune of the city, a statue of the goddess Tyche was commissioned from the sculptor Eutychides, who depicted her seated on a nearby mountain, above a swimming figure of the Orontes, and wearing the city's turrets in her crown (figure 1.1). While the traditional deities of Zeus and Apollo protected the city as well, this figure of Tyche heralds the Hellenistic awareness that the future is controlled as much by

Figure 1.1   *Tyche of Antioch (ca. 300), Roman copy. Photo Vatican Museums.*

Lady Luck as by the gods of Olympus. Rivaled only by Alexandria, Antioch became a large, ethnically diverse urban center, including among its citizens Macedonians, Athenian settlers, Jews from nearby Palestine, and local Syrians. A library was founded there on the Ptolemaic model, and Antiochus III appointed as its head Euphorion of Chalcis (Ch. 4.5), a scholar and learned poet whose verse strongly influenced the "neoteric" Latin literature of the next century. In 166 Antiochus IV Epiphanes (ruled 175–164) chose the city as the site for an ostentatious display of Seleucid wealth. An enormous procession included thousands of soldiers and chariots, many decked with gold and silver, masses of statues illustrating gods and traditional stories, hundreds of slaves with gold vessels, and richly dressed women riding in litters or sprinkling perfume from golden urns.[2] By the first century BC Cicero could describe Antioch, the home of the poet Archias, as "a populous and rich city overflowing with learned men and excellent scholarship" (*For Archias* 4). For its luxurious style of living, its allegiance to a great monarch, and its diversity, Antioch was more like the cities of old Persia than earlier Greek *poleis*.

Antiochus III "the Great," son of Seleucus II, was one of the most successful of the Seleucid monarchs. He earned his epithet from his long and profitable eastern campaign, during which he reestablished Seleucid control over Parthia and Bactria. Later, after an initial defeat by Ptolemy IV at Raphia, he also regained Syria, Phoenicia, and Palestine. But attempted expansion into Thrace brought him into conflict with Rome and, after a disastrous defeat at Magnesia in Lydia in 189, he was forced to give up territory in Asia Minor. After the assassination of an elder son, his second son, Antiochus IV Epiphanes (ruled 175–164), a former political hostage in Rome, acceded to the throne. He successfully invaded Egypt in 168 but was prevented from taking control by a Roman commander, fresh from defeating the Macedonian king Perseus. Antiochus IV is known to history for his dealings with the Jews, events best recorded in *Maccabees* 1 and 2. In support of Jewish aristocrats who wished to hellenize by establishing a gymnasium in Jerusalem and training youths there in Greek athletics and culture, Antiochus banned many Jewish religious practices. Armed resistance led to a rescinding of such an extreme order and eventually, in 142, to the establishment of an independent Jewish state under the Hasmoneans. This episode, a relatively minor one from the perspective of the kingdom as a whole, was symptomatic of the gradual weakening of Seleucid rule. After the death of Antiochus IV, dynastic succession destabilized through assassination by family members and Roman interference. The Seleucid empire began to disintegrate, despite military campaigns that attempted to recover lost territory. The Pontic king Mithradates took Babylonia, the Nabataeans, who had a flourishing capital city at Petra, gained territory in the Arabian peninsula, and in the first century the Armenians occupied Syria itself. The final suppression of the dynasty was the act of the Roman general Pompey in 63.

1.4 Attalid Pergamum

Pergamum, a city in Mysia in northwestern Asia Minor, became the center of an independent kingdom during the third century. The Attalid kings who ruled there are important as rivals to the Ptolemies in intellectual and scholarly pursuits, for their development of a baroque style in art, and for their transmission of Hellenistic culture to Rome.

From 302 Pergamum was administered for Lysimachus by the eunuch Philetaerus, who was entrusted with the Diadoch's treasury. Shrewdly defecting to Seleucus I in 283, Philetaerus became a Seleucid vassal after Lysimachus' death in battle in 281 but retained his treasury as the basis of Pergamene wealth. His descendants received their dynastic name because Philetaerus' father, apparently a Macedonian, was called Attalus. Although Attalid rule in Pergamum was backdated to 283, the process of breaking away from the Seleucids occurred gradually over a period of time. Philetaerus' nephew and adopted son Eumenes I (ruled 263–241) put the image of his predecessor rather than Seleucus on his coinage and supported a declaration of independence after victory over Antiochus I. But Attalus I (ruled 241–197) was the first to proclaim himself king and, in the course of his long rule, to win recognition of Pergamum's independent status from the Seleucids. The self-identity of the Attalid dynasts was strongly associated with a series of victories over the Gauls. These barbarian groups, which had invaded Macedonia in 279 and were stopped only at Delphi, routinely received protection money from the smaller rulers in Asia Minor. In the 230s Attalus I refused their demands and defeated them in Mysia. In 229–228 he turned back, only at the very walls of Pergamum, a larger force of Gallic mercenaries and later expanded Attalid territory in Asia Minor at Seleucid expense. Attalus' support of Rome in the first Macedonian war was the beginning of a long and friendly association, extending through the reigns of his two sons, Eumenes II (ruled 197–158) and Attalus II (ruled 158–138). Even so, Attalid rule ended in 133 when Attalus III (ruled 138–133), bowing to the inevitable, left his kingdom to Rome in his will.

Their defeat of the Gauls seems to have given the Attalids a sense of pride as the preservers of Greek culture against forces of chaos and barbarism, the role played by Athens in the fifth century. Designed on the Athenian model, though visually quite different, the Attalid building program on the citadel at Pergamum, with structures ascending on different levels, made dramatic use of the commanding position of the Acropolis to create what has been called "the greatest city plan of Antiquity."[3] At the highest point was the temple of Athena with the great Pergamene library, a shrine to intellectual culture. Within this sacred complex Attalus I dedicated a series of statues of dying Gauls, remarkable for the dramatic and pathetic treatment given a noble enemy. Just below, Eumenes II placed the great Altar of Zeus (now reconstructed in the Berlin Pergamum Museum), which was decorated on the outside with a frieze depicting the battle of the gods and Giants (figure 1.2). This series of about 100 figures, symbolizing Pergamene victory over forces that would destroy political and cultural order, exemplifies the theatricality and extreme emotional expressiveness of large-scale Hellenistic baroque sculptures. On the inside was a smaller frieze illustrating, in continuous narrative, the life story of Telephus, a Mysian king at the time of the Trojan War, whom the Attalids adopted as their mythical ancestor. A poetic fragment addressed to one of the kings named Attalus, composed by Nicander of Colophon (Ch. 3.5), celebrates their ancestral connection through Telephus to the Greek heroes Heracles and Pelops.[4] This imaginative construction of a heroic heritage parallels the Roman connection to Troy through the figure of Aeneas.

The Pergamene rulers conceived their city as a cultural repository for the Greek heritage they claimed. Their interest in education and intellectual life was apparently genuine, passed from Philetaerus to his successors.

Figure 1.2 *Altar of Zeus at Pergamum, as restored in Berlin. Johannes Laurentius, Bildarchiv Preussischer Kulturbesitz / Art Resource, NY.*

The Attalids of the third century generously supported philosophers of the Academy and the Lyceum in Athens, and as a young man Attalus II studied there with Carneades, the most brilliant Academic philosopher of the second century. Among scholars who came to live at the Attalid court were Antigonus of Carystus, a biographer of philosophers and an art historian, and Apollodorus of Athens, who dedicated to Attalus II his influential *Chronica*, a didactic poem covering intellectual and historical events from the Trojan War to his own day (Ch. 4.1). The library, constructed by Eumenes II, had grown to 200,000 volumes by the time it was presented to Cleopatra by Mark Antony to replace losses sustained by the Alexandrian library in a fire. It was not just a collection of texts but an active center for literary scholarship and criticism. Material for the copying of texts was plentiful, since an important local product, made from animal skins, was what the Romans called *charta pergamena* ("Pergamene paper"), from which our word *parchment* derives. The most famous scholar at Pergamum was Crates of Mallus, who was sent by Attalus II as an envoy to Rome in 159 and gave lectures that introduced the Romans to scholarship. In his allegorical method of interpreting Homer and the grammatical principles he applied to editing, he was the rival of the great Alexandrian scholar Aristarchus of Samothrace, who was his contemporary. Crates called himself a *kritikos* ("critic") rather than a *grammatikos* ("scholar"), so indicating his interest in literary criticism and in the broader usefulness of literature within society. His interpretation of the shield of Achilles in the *Iliad* as an emblem of the cosmos (see Ch. 4.4) seems to mirror the Pergameme artistic taste in baroque grandeur. A dedicatory epigram (Merkelbach and Strauber 06/02/05), once inscribed beneath a statue of a Satyr (cf. figure 1.3) in Pergamum, illustrates how the monarchs also sought to commemorate the heritage of Athenian literature in a Pergamene context. The dedicator, in setting up this gift for both Dionysus and one of the Attalids, surely expected the king to appreciate the artfulness of his epigram, as well as the importation of this spirit of the boisterous satyr drama developed on the fifth-century Athenian stage. In their self-appointed role as the saviors of Greek culture, the Attalids were also generous in their benefactions abroad. For instance, Philetaerus constructed a shrine of the Muses at Helicon in Boeotia, and Athens benefited from two stoas, one built by Eumenes II on the Acropolis slope and one by Attalus II in the agora. These two rulers, who were brothers, also constructed a temple for the cult of their mother Apollonis in her hometown of Cyzicus and decorated it with art depicting mythical stories of filial devotion.

The rulers of Pergamum differed from other Hellenistic monarchs in a number of ways. While they succeeded in defending themselves against

Figure 1.3 *Dancing Satyr, Roman copy of Hellenistic original, ca. 200 BC. Naples, Museo Nazionale.*

the Gauls, in maintaining independence from the Seleucids, and in expanding their territory eastward, they did not administer a geographically and ethnically diverse empire. Succession was effected without familial bloodshed, often through adoption of a relative, and the Attalids seem to have placed loyalty and affection for family members above dynastic ambitions, a rarity in the Hellenistic world. Apollonis, wife of the long-ruling Attalus I and mother of the two succeeding kings, looms suggestively behind the period of greatest brilliance for the kingdom. In imitation of Periclean Athens after the defeat of the Persians, the Attalids made their city an architectural and artistic showplace. Their sculptural program, with its themes of cosmic strife and human suffering, acts as a

transition into the Ptolemaic

counterweight to the more subtle and personal themes characteristic of Alexandrian tastes. A rivalry between Pergamum and the Ptolemaic court, in scholarship, literature, and art, seems by the second century to have coalesced into somewhat different aesthetic standards, and the tension between them continued to shape the Roman adaptation of Hellenistic culture.

1.5   Ptolemaic Egypt

Of the three Diadochs who succeeded in establishing dynastic rule, only Ptolemy of Egypt died peacefully in his kingdom. This happy fortune was partially due to the remoteness of his allotted territory and partially to his cautious involvement in the struggles among the Successors. Though schooled in military affairs, this first Ptolemy, who wrote a lost history of Alexander's campaign, had a love of learning that strongly affected the character of the dynasty he founded. The intellectual and literary culture developed at the court of the early Ptolemies was so influential throughout the Greek world that the term *Alexandrian*, reflecting Ptolemy's capital city of Alexandria, often connotes a style and attitude characteristic of the entire Hellenistic period.

During his long rule (323–282) Ptolemy I Soter ("Savior") attended to the dual tasks of securing his position as ruler of Egypt and promoting his

Figure 1.4 *Coin portrait of Ptolemy I Soter and Berenice I. American Numismatic Society, New York.*

interests in the broader Hellenic world (figure 1.4). The wealthy land of Egypt, with its population clustered along the strip made arable by the annual flooding of the Nile, was an ancient, hierarchical kingdom with powerful priesthoods and a tradition of pharaohs who ruled as gods incarnate. Soter successfully adapted preexisting administrative structures to keep the resources of Egypt flowing into his treasury while leaving daily life among the native population largely unchanged. In their self-presentations the Ptolemies early learned how to appeal to dual Greek and Egyptian audiences. Ptolemaic brother–sister marriage, first practiced by Soter's children Ptolemy II Philadelphus ("Sister-loving") (ruled 282–246) and Arsinoe II Philadelphus ("Brother-loving"), followed the model of the pharaohs and was justified to the Greeks by the example of Zeus and Hera. Another example of Soter's creation of new amalgamations of Greek and Egyptian cultural ideas was his support for the kindly deity Serapis, a combination of the Apis bull and the god Osiris, fundamental elements in Egyptian religious belief, in a form that eventually appealed to Greek speakers throughout the world. In praise of Soter's new kingdom, Hecataeus of Abdera wrote *Aegyptiaca*, an ethnographical account that drew parallels between Egyptian and Greek culture (paraphrased in Diodorus Siculus Book 1), and somewhat later, perhaps under Ptolemy II, an Egyptian high priest named Manetho composed another *Aegyptiaca*, in three books, which drew upon Egyptian archives to chronicle the history and religious customs of Egypt down to the middle of the fourth century.

At the same time, Ptolemaic interest in the larger Greco-Macedonian arena is shown by the expansionist ambitions they maintained throughout the third century. Their navy was a potent force in the Aegean, and key islands, especially Samos, Cos, and Cyprus, as well as parts of Asia Minor, were at times Ptolemaic possessions. There were a number of military conflicts with the Seleucids over Syria, which was sometimes under Ptolemaic control. Cyrene, which lay to the west of Egypt in Libya and had been founded as a Greek colony in the archaic period, was brought under Ptolemaic protection early in Soter's rule. It was fully annexed by the time Ptolemy III Euergetes ("Benefactor") (ruled 246–221) married Berenice II, the daughter of king Magas of Cyrene.

The city of Alexandria, which had been founded by Alexander at a harbor site near where the western branch of the Nile entered the Mediterranean, was the center of Ptolemaic culture (map 1.1). Because of continuous habitation and changing sea levels, little remains of this most brilliant of Hellenistic urban centers, although excavated tombs and underwater exploration have enhanced what we know from texts. The most elaborate tombs, with central chambers for sacrifice, were constructed, apparently, for royal burials and as places of dynastic worship.

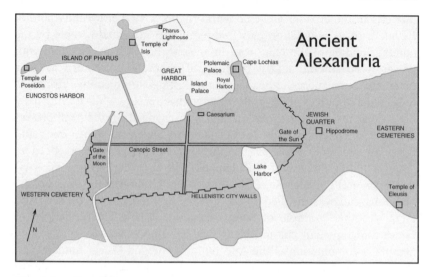

Map 1.1   *Alexandria.*

One extraordinary antechamber, made entirely of alabaster, just possibly
led to the final resting place for the body of Alexander the Great, which
Soter had shrewdly carried off to Egypt. Statues of monarchs depicted in
the manner of Egyptian pharaohs have been recently raised from the
harbor; it is believed that they may have fallen from the famous lighthouse
on the Pharus island, which was classed as one of the Seven Wonders of
the Ancient World. With its beacon amplified by mirrors, the Pharus
lighthouse offered ship passengers a concrete emblem of Ptolemaic influence shining far out from Egypt into the Hellenic world. Physically and
culturally distinct from the rest of Egypt, Alexandria was a cosmopolitan
city, the largest in the world by the early Roman period. In addition to the
Macedonians who functioned as its ruling and military class, it attracted
Greeks from many locations, like the Syracusan women in Theocritus'
Idyll 15 whose Doric accents are noticed by strangers in the streets
(figure 1.5). Egyptian natives and various ethnic minorities, including a
large Jewish contingent, rounded out the diverse population. Herodas
(Ch. 3.7), a writer of mimes, lists the attractions found in Egypt during
the reign of Ptolemy II: "Wealth, wrestling grounds, power, peace,
renown, spectacles, philosophers, money, young men, the precinct of the
Brother–Sister Gods [that is, deified Ptolemy and Arsinoe], a good king,
the Museum, wine, everything good you might want, women as numerous
as the stars that the sky boasts to bear and in appearance like the goddesses
who once rushed to be judged for their beauty by Paris" (*Mimiambi*
1.28–35). The Ptolemies were, in fact, the wealthiest of the Hellenistic

Figure 1.5   *Terracotta figurine of a young woman, bearing traces of paint, from a grave, Ptolemaic era. Graeco-Roman Museum, Alexandria.*

monarchs, as shown by an incredibly sumptuous procession filled with commissioned works of art and objects of precious metal that Ptolemy II put on in 274.[5]

Importantly, Ptolemy I decided to adorn his new capital with a Museum and Library, which were apparently part of the royal complex. In doing so, he may have been influenced by two Peripatetic philosophers living in Alexandria, Demetrius of Phalerum, who had been driven out of Athens in 307 and who was initially in charge of setting up the Library, and Strato of Lampsacus, who was recalled to Athens from Alexandria in 287 to head the Lyceum, an institution that may have offered the model for the Museum. Not an art gallery as the word might suggest today, the Museum ("place of the Muses") was a center of learning where scholars lived and worked in a community supported by the monarchs and devoted to the study and preservation of earlier Greek culture. The goal for the Library was to collect all works written in Greek, including multiple copies or versions of the same work. The Ptolemies sometimes purchased books and at other times took them from ships that docked at Alexandria, had them copied, and returned the copies rather than the originals. The story, told in the so-called *Letter of Aristeas* (Ch. 4.3), that Ptolemy II commissioned seventy-two Jewish scholars to produce the first Greek version of the Old Testament, called the Septuagint, indicates that translations into Greek from other languages were included as well. The Library reportedly contained nearly 500,000 volumes when in 47 BC a great fire caused significant damage, if not wholesale destruction.

The reign of Soter's son Ptolemy II Philadelphus and his sister Arsinoe II brought with it the flowering of Alexandrian artistic creativity (figure 1.6). Arsinoe, who had earlier been married to Lysimachus of Thrace, was queen only a few years, from 278 to 270 or 268, but she seems to have played an important part in setting the tone for the innovative literature produced in Alexandria. While alive, she received cult

Figure 1.6 *Gold octodrachm, with portrait of Ptolemy II and Arsinoe II. American Numismatic Society, New York.*

worship as Arsinoe-Aphrodite at the seaside site of Zephyrium, where she had the dual role of protecting Ptolemaic maritime interests and fostering happy marriages for young women; after her death an important civic cult was set up in her honor. The best and most famous Hellenistic poets worked in Alexandria during the second quarter of the third century, and all wrote poetry flattering to the monarchs. For instance, Callimachus, a native of neighboring Cyrene, celebrated the apotheosis of Arsinoe in a lyric poem and later in his *Aetia* praised Berenice II as loving wife of Ptolemy III and owner of victorious racing horses. Theocritus, a native of Sicily, wrote an *Encomium for Ptolemy* (*Idyll* 17) and depicted an elaborate festival honoring Aphrodite and Adonis, for which Arsinoe II invited the people of Alexandria into her palace (*Idyll* 15). The *Argonautica* of Apollonius, a royal tutor and second head of the Library, obliquely connects the voyage of Jason and the Argonauts to future Greek settlements in northern Africa. Even a poet from the Antigonid capital of Pella, the epigrammatist Posidippus (Ch. 3.6), praised the Ptolemies as the legitimate heirs to the Persian empire of Alexander in an epigram collection recently recovered on a papyrus bookroll. The character of this Alexandrian poetry is closely related to the aesthetic tastes of the court for which it was created, while other writings reveal the interests of the Ptolemies in scientific and scholarly pursuits. For instance, Eratosthenes of Cyrene (Ch. 3.10, 4.1), the tutor of the young Ptolemy IV Philopator, addressed a letter containing his solution for a long-standing mathematical problem to his pupil's father, and Agatharchides of Cnidus (Ch. 3.10) composed his geographical work on the territory bordering the Red Sea from court archives reporting the discoveries of explorers sent by the Ptolemies to explore the lands to the south. The crossing of the scientific and poetic in the interest of pseudo-science is shown by epigrams concerning creatures thought to emerge from the corpses of animals, written by Archelaus of Egypt for one of the Ptolemaic kings (125–9 Lloyd-Jones and Parsons).

Literary scholarship, as we understand the activity today, is in origin largely a product of the Alexandrian Museum and Library. Desiring to preserve inherited Greek culture, the early Ptolemies used the immense wealth of Egypt to support the systematic collection, cataloguing, and study of literary texts. The learned men who gathered at the Museum in Alexandria produced the first scholarly editions of earlier authors, studied the meanings and forms of words, wrote running commentaries on important works, and composed treatises on literary problems. Their selection of authors worthy of editions and commentaries set the literary canons for each genre and determined to a large degree the pre-Hellenistic works that have survived for us. Callimachus in *Iambus* 1 complains about the quarreling among scholarly "lovers of words" (*philologoi*) in the Museum, and the Cynic Timon of Phlius (Ch. 3.8) directed his most famous lampoon to the bickering scholars there: "Many cloistered pedants feed in the ethnic mix of Egypt, quarreling endlessly in the Muses' work basket" (786 Lloyd-Jones and Parsons).

Philitas of Cos, who served as tutor of the young Ptolemy II Philadelphus, provides one key to the link between poetry, scholarship, and patronage in the early Alexandrian age. A poet much admired by the next generation, Philitas produced a famous scholarly work called *Miscellanea* or *Glosses*, which consisted of an explanatory list of rare words, namely, dialectical forms, technical terms, and problematic words in Homer. We now know, from the new Posidippus collection, that Ptolemy II set up, perhaps in the Museum, a bronze statue of his tutor, who was depicted realistically as an old man thinking deep thoughts. The poet Callimachus played a crucial role in the development of the Library by creating vast lists, called *Pinaces*, of all the different works held there. The task of creating this first comprehensive catalogue of Greek literature from the myriad bookrolls in the Library must have been incredibly difficult, and the method of cataloguing that Callimachus developed became the standard format for later antiquity. He first arranged authors by literary class and subclass, and then for each author he gave brief biographical information, the title of the works by genre, and the first words of each work. Other poets participated in the scholarship of the Museum as well; for instance, the playwright Alexander of Aetolia edited tragedies and another playwright Lycophron edited comedies.

The primary energies of the Alexandrian scholars were directed, however, to the epic poems of Homer, as texts that had long formed the basis of Greek education. Zenodotus of Ephesus, a student of Philitas and the first librarian at Alexandria, is generally credited as the first scholarly editor of Homer. The many copies of the *Iliad* and *Odyssey* collected for the Library differed one from the other; they had significant variations in wording within lines and some contained whole lines not in other copies. Textual variation was a much greater problem for the Homeric poems than for other literary works because these epics were products of oral composition practiced during the Dark Age and performed in later times by rhapsodes who worked from memory to produce dramatic renditions. The task of Zenodotus and his successors was to compare these variant copies and to decide upon the "correct" text of Homer. Modern scholars disagree about whether this task was possible, since some believe that the *Iliad* and *Odyssey* were given an authoritative written form by a master epic poet in the seventh century BC, while others believe that the epics were transmitted in the archaic period primarily through memory and performance. What is clear is that the Alexandrians eventually achieved a text of Homer that became widely accepted as authoritative and forms the basis of our medieval manuscripts. Their scholarly opinions and explanations have survived only indirectly, being known primarily from marginal notes, called scholia, in manuscripts.

Other scholars who served as librarians, and also acted as tutors to the young princes of the Ptolemaic courts, included the epic poet Apollonius of Rhodes, the scientist and poet Eratosthenes of Cyrene, the textual editor Aristophanes of Byzantium, and the greatest of all textual scholars, Aristarchus of Samothrace. Eratosthenes (ca. 285–194) called himself a "philologist" because of his diverse scholarly interests including astronomy, geography, and historical chronology. In his important *Geography*, in which he worked out by mathematical and astronomical means the distance between localities, he expressed the opinion that Homer's geography was largely imaginary, not a beginning point for the kind of rationalistic study that he was undertaking. Aristophanes (ca. 257–180) produced authoritative editions in the fields of epic, lyric, and dramatic poetry. He advanced the use of punctuation in texts, added accents to his editions of Homer, and invented the system of colometry that still shapes our textual presentation of lyric poetry. His student Aristarchus (ca. 216–144) was famous for his detailed running commentaries on Homer, Hesiod, lyric poetry, tragedy and comedy, and (for the first time) a prose author, Herodotus. In opposition to the allegorizing interpretation of the Pergamene Crates, he followed the practice of "clarifying Homer from Homer," meaning that he based his interpretations on the poet's own usage. In the area of grammatical theory, Aristarchus used the principle of analogy, namely, that similar words should be the model for determining a correct form, while Crates was an adherent of anomaly, the principle that language is arbitrary and usage should determine form. The rival view of how to conduct scholarship that developed at Pergamum underlies later criticism of Callimachus and his followers and of Alexandrian scholars like Aristarchus for their pedantic interest in words and obscure mythical or scientific problems.[6]

Scientific and mathematical research also took place in Alexandria. It is uncertain how actively the Ptolemies supported pure research of this nature, since evidence is lacking that the Museum functioned as a research center for theoretical science, as it did for humanistic scholarship and creative writing. But the atmosphere of curiosity about the world, coupled with royal interest in practical applications of new scientific knowledge, certainly created an environment conducive to the expansion of scientific and technical knowledge. The followers of Euclid, if not the geometer himself, were resident in Alexandria, as was the mathematician

Apollonius of Perge. The advances in anatomy made by the physician Herophilus resulted from dissection of corpses supplied by the Ptolemies, who even allowed vivisection as a means of executing condemned criminals. Eratosthenes' calculation of the circumference of the earth was made possible by extrapolation from precise measurements made by royal survey expeditions into southern Egypt and Nubia. The astronomer Conon of Samos, much respected by the great mathematician Archimedes of Syracuse, had a court connection, and on one occasion practiced the astronomical hoax of "discovering" a new constellation, the Coma Berenices, to please the monarchs. Ctesibius, an inventor in the area of pneumatic devices, was a native Alexandrian, and the automated figures that appeared in the grand Ptolemaic procession seem to have resulted from advances in pneumatics and other technologies from the early Hellenistic period.

The Ptolemaic dynasty began to destabilize with the accession of Ptolemy IV Philopator ("father-loving") in 221. We know from documentary papyri, which have survived for Egypt as they have not for the other kingdoms, that there were tensions between the ethnic Macedonians, who had a privileged position in Ptolemaic society, and native Egyptians. From the late third century unrest among the Egyptians, leading to a series of revolts, became increasingly common. The Rosetta Stone, which provided the key to decipherment of Egyptian hieroglyphs, contains a trilingual inscription (in hieroglyphic and demotic Egyptian and in Greek) that concerns one of these rebellions. During this time as well, Ptolemaic power in the Aegean and in Syria began to fade. Ptolemy IV was murdered in 205 by two courtiers, who tried to hold on to power under the young Ptolemy V Epiphanes ("God Manifest") partly by murdering his mother Arsinoe III. Dynastic intrigue of this type dominates the sad history of the later Ptolemies. Ptolemy VIII (ruled 170–163, 145–116), nicknamed "Physcon" ("Potbelly"), upon regaining his throne through dynastic murder after years of exile, drove out of the country the intellectuals working in the Museum, including Aristarchus. Scholarship on earlier Greek literature did not stop as a result, but it did disperse, to the detriment of Alexandria. Despite such political troubles, records of business and personal activities on documentary papyri indicate that the daily lives of ordinary people, especially in the rural areas of Egypt, continued much as before. Intermarriage between those of Hellenic origin and native Egyptians became increasingly common, to the point that Greek or Egyptian names on documents were no longer a good indicator of ethnicity.

The only worthy descendant of the early Ptolemies was the last of the dynasty, Cleopatra VII. She was a brilliant woman, who reportedly spoke nine languages and was the only Ptolemaic monarch to learn Egyptian.

Politically savvy as well, she turned her romantic relationships with Roman leaders into intrigues aimed at nothing less than mastery of the civilized world. Cleopatra is said to have presented herself to Julius Caesar rolled in a carpet, and their liaison led to the birth of a son called Caesarion. Living in Rome with Caesar at the time of his assassination in 44, she quickly withdrew to Egypt to consolidate her power by murdering her younger brother and consort. She developed an even stronger hold on Mark Antony, with whom she began a decade-long relationship in 41. She presented him with three children, and he eventually divorced his Roman wife for her. But his infatuation with the Egyptian queen, and perhaps with the glorious Greek past she represented, was a distraction from the serious business of assembling eastern forces sufficient to defeat Caesar's heir Octavian. In 31, in a naval battle at Actium on the northwestern coast of Greece, Antony and Cleopatra were decisively defeated and, after a failed defense of Egypt, committed suicide. No real threat but too royal to survive, Caesarion was slaughtered as well. Egypt became a Roman province, the private reserve of the new emperor. As a sign of the times, the poetic accounts we have of Cleopatra come from a hostile Roman perspective; any works composed at her own court have vanished without a trace.

2

Aesthetics and Style

The social and political changes that took place in the aftermath of Alexander's conquests were accompanied by new aesthetic sensibilities, which led in the early third century to a remarkable period of literary innovation. While the Greek poetry of the archaic and classical eras fascinates and thrills with its depth and grandeur, Hellenistic literature charms and challenges with its more modern realism and intricacy. A complex interaction between specialized poetic expertise and depiction of commonplace human experience is the hallmark of the best and most innovative poetry produced in the courts of Hellenistic kings and queens. Of course the nature of Greek poetry was not suddenly transformed, and certain literary works from the late fifth and fourth centuries, as well as critical writings, foreshadowed the characteristics associated with Hellenistic literature. But we are justified to speak of a new literary era because of fundamental changes in subject matter, generic forms, reception of literature, and understanding of purpose.

In analyzing the relationship of subject matter to genre, Aristotle (*Poetics* 2) famously states that the characters depicted in literature are distinguished by their moral qualities as either good persons, who are "better than ourselves," or low persons, who are "worse than ourselves." The former are found in tragedy and the latter in comedy, but in epic, as in painting, Aristotle allows for a third possibility of persons just like ourselves. This intermediate group, who share with most of humanity a mixture of virtue and vice, receives increased attention from Hellenistic writers. Figures formerly present only on the margins of literature – workmen and slaves, middle-class citizens, children, women, and the elderly, even animals (see the cover illustration) – now move to the center. The traditional subjects of serious poetry – heroes and gods – remain, but they are often deflated, not to the level of parody but to ordinary status, as if they were no different from commonplace individuals in Hellenistic society. So too those "worse than ourselves," such as the economically destitute or monstrous villains, are typically elevated, not to heroic status but by behaving, in their emotions and desires, just like us. This leveling of status, foreshadowed in Euripides and realized in the New Comedy of Menander, becomes the preferred method for depicting the post-Alexander world. Cultural changes demand it. Gods now live on earth in the form of monarchs or their immediate ancestors, while the shifting of political power from the polis with its homogeneous citizenry to the monarchic kingdoms with their ethnic diversity brings in its wake a greater appreciation for the commonality of humankind.

While traditional performance genres such as lyric and the dramatic forms of tragedy and comedy continue throughout the Hellenistic age, the most innovative poets experimented with generic forms, often by giving minor or subliterary types a more sophisticated treatment. Mime, a form of popular entertainment that involved dramatization of character, became formalized as the genre of choice for realistic depictions of contemporary life, as in Herodas' *Mimiambi* (Ch. 3.7) and Theocritus' *Idylls*. The *Idylls* concerning herdsmen and countryfolk were conceived as the new genre of bucolic poetry, which through its adaptation in Vergil's *Eclogues* developed into one of the major genres of European literature, called pastoral from the Latin translation of the Greek word *bucolic*. While long epics on mythical topics, such as Apollonius' *Argonautica*, or on local history, such as Rhianus' *Messeniaca*, continued to be written, short epic narratives, conventionally called "epyllia," rose to a new prominence as a vehicle for the humanization of the heroic. From the epitaphs and inscriptions on dedicated objects, there developed another new genre, that of literary epigram. These short poems could be adapted to treat almost any subject matter, including the erotic, and women poets of the third century, prominently Anyte and Nossis, composed epigrams, a form that suited the contemporary taste for variety and discontinuity. Almost every major poet of the era composed epigrams, and some, like Posidippus, specialized in the genre. Much of the writing of the period consisted of prose treatises on scientific or technical subjects, which developed their own aestheticized format involving the interrelationship of text and illustration. Certain poets, like Aratus and Nicander of Colophon, took a new interest in developing stylistic excellence in the genre of didactic poetry, earlier practiced by Hesiod as well as by philosophical poets of the classical era;

the goal was to marry the informational purpose of scientific or technical writing with the attractiveness of poetic form.

In earlier Greek culture poets had composed their poetry for performance either in aristocratic households, as depicted in the Homeric epics, or at public festivals, mostly local ones, though some were Panhellenic in scope. This poetry was preserved in written copies, primarily as an aid to reperformance, either at symposia, where men drank and dined together, or sometimes at public events. The court poets of the Hellenistic era also seem to have written poetry for recitation at private gatherings or for performance at festivals; for instance, the fragmentary ending to *Idyll* 24 on the young Heracles indicates that Theocritus performed that poem in a competition, likely at a celebration for the Ptolemies who claimed descent from Heracles. But it was also in the first half of the third century that poets began to plan for the continuing reception of their poetry in book format. Hellenistic poets, some of whom were also editors of earlier authors, invented what are commonly called poetry books, by collecting and artistically arranging their own verse on papyrus rolls. The best surviving examples are Callimachus' *Iambi*, Herodas' *Mimiambi*, and the newly discovered epigram collection apparently by Posidippus, all known from papyri. It is first in this era, then, that we can be confident poets expected their poems to be read, not just heard in performance, and this new manner of reception surely had an effect on the nature of the compositions. Just as arrangement of poems in groups enhances meaning, so, too, leisurely perusal of a composition grants the reader a greater opportunity to appreciate complicated allusions and subtleties of style. The two most important writers of New Comedy differed in just this way; Menander, we are told, was popular with actors because his disjointed syntax was more dramatic, whereas his contemporary Philemon, who composed in a tighter, more involved style, was better liked by readers.[1]

In addition to subject matter, generic form, and manner of reception, the perceived purpose of poetry also underwent transformation in the Hellenistic period. Poets were traditionally the preservers of knowledge and wisdom in Greek culture, and their function was to teach, although sensual enjoyment was also recognized as part of the poetic experience. But Plato, especially in the *Republic*, took a highly critical view of the literary enterprise. He held that traditional poetry, including Homer, often depicted heroes and gods behaving in an immoral manner; he believed that, as an imitative art, poetry offers only a pale reflection of universal truth and so is a poor method of instruction, stimulating the audience to emotional weakness. Philosophical discussion that appeals to reason, rather than poetry or rhetoric that both appeal to the emotions, was for Plato the path to true understanding. In his *Poetics* Aristotle attempted to defend the value of the imitative arts, in particular tragedy, by finding its "special pleasure" in a catharsis, or purging, of the negative emotions of pity and fear. Lively discussion on the nature and value of poetry ensued between the Peripatetics and followers of other Hellenistic philosophies, especially Stoicism. But Plato's view that only philosophical reflection, not poetry or rhetoric, could lead to the truth seems to have had a strong influence on the way in which the most influential Hellenistic poets conceived the nature and purpose of their art. As shown by Aratus' verse rendering of an astronomical treatise, the content of poetry could be scientifically or philosophically "true," independent of its nature as poetry. The author's claim to literary excellence lies elsewhere, in the *techne*, "art," of the composition, based on a different kind of knowledge, that of how to compose verse. The view that a poet is to be judged good or bad on the basis of technical poetic skill and attention to detail of language, rather than the contents of the poetry, was contested among critical thinkers of the era, but it seems to have had a profound effect on those literary practitioners who created the new aesthetic standards of the third century. The literary qualities of verse consist of sound, imagery, style, proper diction, use of dialectal forms, and metrical smoothness; thus the appeal to the audience is through the pleasures of hearing and imaginative visualization. The poet's truthfulness seems now to derive from expert scholarly knowledge, obtained either through consultation of an authoritative technical treatise or through accurate personal observation.

2.1 Aesthetic Principles

Beginning in the late fifth century and continuing throughout the Hellenistic period, philosophical thinkers composed treatises, mostly lost, on poetic criticism, prose style, and the art of rhetoric. The leading poets were acutely aware of these discussions and in many instances contributed to them. In this section we will examine a selection of passages in which Hellenistic poets asserted their allegiance to certain aesthetic principles through key images and metaphors.

A recently discovered papyrus bookroll preserving a collection of epigrams by Posidippus of Pella contains a section of poems on statues, which is designed to reveal Posidippus' standards for art.[2] In the first epigram the principles of the "old art" that produced rigid statues are contrasted with the "new art" of statue-making, in which Lysippus occupies first place (62 Austin and Bastianini). Lysippus was the favorite sculptor of Alexander, and he was famed for his detailed naturalism and the appealing slenderness of his figures.[3] Posidippus' epigram provides

proof that the poets of the third century saw themselves as part of a
modernist movement that had its beginnings in the retinue of artists and
intellectuals attached to Alexander.

The next epigram in Posidippus' section on statues makes it clear that
sculpture functions as a parallel, and metaphor, for poetry. This poem
concerns a statue made by a student of Lysippus, which depicts Philitas
of Cos, the intellectual and literary forerunner of the Alexandrian poets
gathered at the court of Ptolemy II Philadelphus (63 Austin and Bastianini):

> The equivalent of Philitas is this bronze statue, molded
>   With precision by Hecataeus even to the nails.
> He pursued a standard of humanness in size and skin texture
>   and mixed in no element from heroic form.
> He rather showed, with all possible art, this old man thinking
>   With precision, and his canon of truth was straight.
> The elder appears on the verge of speaking, his character is so carefully
>   Depicted, a living being, though made of bronze.
> On the command of Ptolemy, both god and king, this man of Cos
>   is here dedicated, for the sake of the Muses.

While only a few fragments of Philitas' verse survive, he was praised as a
poet by both Callimachus (fr. 1.9–10, with scholia) and Theocritus (*Idyll*
7.39–41) and is often cited as the earliest of the *poetae docti*, or "learned
poets."[4] It seems reasonable to conclude, therefore, that his poetry and
teachings were, at least in part, the source for the stylistic terminology,
aesthetic principles, and accompanying system of imagery espoused by the
Alexandrian poets. If so, then certain elements of it are, in all likelihood,
present in Posidippus' description of the statue: the detailed accuracy of
the image, the use of humanity as the model without heroic idealization,
the portraitlike representation of Philitas' elderly appearance and scholarly *ēthos*, "character," and the illusionistic effect of the realistic depiction.
A key repetition of the word *akribēs*, here rendered "with precision,"
connects the qualities of Hecataeus' statue as a work of art with the
qualities of its subject as a thinker. In fact, that seems the point of the
epigram: to parallel Philitas' contribution to the new taste for realism,
erudition, and precision in literature (the new "canon of truth") with the
similar achievement of Lysippus in sculpture.

Another celebrated forerunner of the Alexandrians was Erinna, a
fourth-century poet perhaps from the Aegean island of Teos, who reportedly died unmarried at the age of nineteen. Her *Distaff*, a poem of three
hundred lines known only in fragments (401–2 Lloyd-Jones and Parsons),
remodeled the epic meter of Homer to convey the personal voice of a
young woman lamenting the death of a childhood friend, named Baucis.

The qualities that attracted Hellenistic poets to Erinna's work are suggested by the early third-century epigrammatist Asclepiades of Samos (*Palatine Anthology* 7.11):

> Sweet is this labor of Erinna, and not at all verbose,
> As is fitting for a maiden of nineteen,
> Yet more compelling than many other works. If Hades had not come
> Quickly to me, whose name would be as great as mine?

The epigram takes the form of a label attached to a bookroll to identify the author and work. But the fictitiousness of that function is shown when, in the second couplet, it appears that the author herself has composed the epigram, though she speaks of her own untimely death. The real point is to comment, cleverly, on the style that has resulted in fame for this most unlikely of authors. Asclepiades celebrates not only the sweetness and directness of Erinna's writing, but also the hard work (*ponos*) expended upon her poem. Elsewhere the word *ponos* signifies the technical skill and erudition held up by Hellenistic poets as the hallmark of their craft.

Another epigram by Asclepiades, perhaps set as a companion piece in his poetry book, contrasts with Erinna's sweet, simple style the more dignified or elevated (*semnos*) style of Antimachus. This author of the early fourth century, who came from Colophon in Asia Minor, wrote a long elegiac poem called *Lyde*, now lost, in which he catalogued various mythical stories in order to console himself for the death of his beloved. Plato adored Antimachus' poetry, which included an epic *Thebaid*, but his studied style, marked by tireless prolixity and seriousness of tone, never had broad appeal.[5] In Asclepiades' epigram Lyde herself speaks in the dual role of Antimachus' beloved, here posing as a grand lady descended from the city's founder, and as title for the famed poem (*Palatine Anthology* 9.63):

> I am Lyde (or Lydian) in both race and name, and I am the most dignified
> Of all the women from Codrus because of Antimachus.
> Who has not sung of me? Who has not read the *Lyde*,
> The joint composition of the Muses and Antimachus?

In these two epigrams Asclepiades has chosen female literary figures of the previous century to represent a binary system for classification of style current from the late classical period; the two styles recognized in this system were the elevated, marked by circumlocutions and tragic grandness, and the plain, marked by conciseness and clarity.

An early description of this stylistic dichotomy animates the debate between Aeschylus and Euripides in Aristophanes' *Frogs*. There "loud-roaring" (814) Aeschylus represents old-fashioned *semnotēs*, "dignity," while the more intellectually subtle, plain-speaking Euripides represents the alternative style. On the subject of his characters, Euripides is accused of subverting tragic form by bringing on stage heroes dressed in rags, fallen women, and noble slaves. This greater accessibility of Euripidean drama in terms of characterization and style is yet married to a subtle intellec-tualism, and Euripides, in the manner of the new rationalism of the sophistic movement, is accused of dicing up, through minute analysis (*kataleptolegēsei*, 828), the traditional value system and style of Aeschylus. Euripides calls Aeschylus' art "swollen with boasts and ponderous words" and claims that he "has put it on a diet (*ischnana*) and eliminated its weight with small words, vigorous discussion, and clarifying beets, and by giving it a tonic consisting of regular talk derived from books" (940–2). The *Frogs* begins with Dionysus traveling to the underworld to retrieve Euripides, although in the end he takes a victorious Aeschylus back to Athens, as the better choice to preserve the city through his dignified (*semnoisin*, 1496) talk. The debate between these two modes of discourse, metaphorically identified as large/small or fat/thin, became the under-lying pattern that dominated rhetorical and literary criticism into the Hellenistic period and beyond.

The epigrams on Erinna and Antimachus' *Lyde*, taken as a pair, cele-brate a representative of each style, as if Asclepiades recognized the value and appeal of both. Callimachus, however, parodies the *Lyde* epigram to convey a negative assessment of Antimachus: "The *Lyde* is a fat (*pachu*) composition and not clear" (fr. 398). He favored the opposite style, called slender (*ischnos*) in manuals on oratorical modes of speech. In an epigram that reworks the diet image from the Euripides' speech in the *Frogs*, Callimachus declares that not only can the Muses "reduce"/"make thin" (*katischnainonti*) love longing, but so can hunger, and both charms against love's wound are in residence with him (*Palatine Anthology* 12.150). This concept of stylistic thinness extended beyond the literary to other arts as well, since, as we have seen, Lysippus was known for the charm and slenderness of his statues. In addition, anecdotes about the scholar-poet Philitas, perhaps descending from New Comedy, joke about his extreme thinness. It was said, in fact, that he became so emaciated from the hard work of composing his scholarly works that he had to wear lead shoes to avoid being blown away by the wind. Another elegiac poet, Hermesianax, refers to a bronze statue of Philitas, this one set up by his fellow Coans, which depicted him singing of his beloved Bittis (or Battis?) and wearing himself out in his researches on diction (fr. 7.75–8 Powell, p. 100). Here we have a remarkable combination of the images we have been tracing – the statue so realistic it represents the scholar-poet in his essential activity of thought, the female beloved who was apparently a subject of his poetry and perhaps also a metaphorical embodiment of it, and the scholar-poet's excessive, even unhealthy dedication to his erudition.

While *ischnos*, "slender," became the most common technical term for the plain prose style, also associated with Attic clarity, Callimachus and other early Hellenistic poets chose another adjective, *leptos*, to convey the essential qualities of their poetry. This term, used in the *Frogs* with reference to Euripides, meant, etymologically, "peeled," "stripped off," and then "delicate" and "thin," and in the anecdotal tradition Philitas' excessive thinness is called *leptotēs* (Aelian, *Varia Historia* 10.6). In Callimachus the meaning of the term is closer to "refined," in the sense of minutely sifted, so that what remains is accurate, delicate, and choice. An important example of this usage appears in Callimachus' epigram about Aratus of Soli's *Phaenomena*, modeled in part on Hesiod (*Palatine Anthology* 9.507):

> Hesiodic is the song and the manner. Not the ultimate of poets,
> but, I dare to say, the sweetest of verses
> has the poet of Soli stripped off to copy. Hail words of
> refinement, symbol of Aratus' wakefulness.

Callimachus makes it clear that Aratus' words are refined (*leptai*) not only because they imitate Hesiod selectively, choosing only what is sweet, but also because they result from the hard work of a scholar. The Greek word translated "wakefulness" plays beautifully on the nighttime observations required for Aratus' astronomical poem and on the midnight hours of labor that went into its composition.

Callimachus' fullest presentation of his stylistic preferences appears in the prologue to his *Aetia* (fr. 1), which is perhaps the single most important passage in Hellenistic poetry. He begins by paraphrasing criticism made of his poetry by his detractors, whom he calls Telchines. The Telchines were primeval magicians and metal-workers associated with the island of Rhodes, who had come to stand for malicious jealousy. The type of poetry that they, in their ignorance, accuse him of avoiding – "one continuous song" "in many thousands [of lines]," concerning "kings and heroes of old" – could be the cyclic epics that second-rate poets composed from the archaic period forward but might also be long elegies or even lyric poems on heroic themes, as are known to have been written by earlier poets like Archilochus, Stesichorus, and Simonides. The Telchines, whether or not they represent historically real critics of Callimachus (and the scholiast

believes Asclepiades and Posidippus among their number), fit the category
of those with old-fashioned tastes, like the sculptors of rigid statues
rejected by Posidippus. Callimachus begins his defense by naming the
good poet as one who speaks in "but a few lines." As examples of such
poetry and its opposite, he cites, first, Philitas' *Demeter*, apparently a
relatively short elegiac poem, which far outweighs the "tall woman,"
apparently another Philitan poem longer and heavier in style (though
some think Antimachus' *Lyde* is meant). Here, again, poems are characterized as women, and size or weight is the metaphorical criterion to
determine their value. The same judgment is made of the archaic elegist
Mimnermus, whose short disconnected elegies, rather than the "large
lady," meaning, apparently, his *Smyrneis* on the history of his hometown
of Smyrna, teach that he is "sweet." Sweetness is, for Callimachus, the
essential quality of poetry. After two images involving great distance,
the cranes that migrate from Egypt to Thrace and the Scythian Massagetae
who attacked the Persians with bows from afar, he offers in contrast
the sweet song of the nightingale, an emblem for himself as poet. The
Telchines have made the mistake of judging poetry by the Persian chain, a
unit of measure used in Egyptian surveying, rather than by art (*technē*).
Turning from the length, size, and weight of bad poetry to its sound, he
then asserts that he produces no "loud-sounding" poetry – thunder is
the prerogative of Zeus.[6]

Callimachus next turns to the advice that Apollo, the god of song, gave
to him as a youth: nurture your sacrificial victim to be as fat as possible,
but keep your Muse thin. The Greek word for "thin" is here the variant
form *leptaleēn*, which Callimachus uses elsewhere for the clear, delicate
sound of the panpipe (*Hymn to Artemis* 243). Apollo continues with a
different image, by advising the young poet to drive his chariot along
the narrow, untrodden path, preferable to the busy road cut into ruts by
many wagons. The road image is an old one, used already by Pindar in his
Paean to Apollo, where the god urges singers not to follow in the worn
wagon roads of Homer (fr. 52h.10–12). Callimachus explains his obedi-
ence to the god's commands, by an oblique compliment to his patrons,
who appreciate the "clear sound of the cicada, not the braying of asses."
Already in Homer the "lily voices" of cicadas stand for the speech of the
Trojan elders (*Iliad* 3.150–3), and in Plato's *Phaedrus* cicadas become the
spies of the Muses, once men who loved song so much that they neglected
to eat and so wasted away, now magical creatures who watch for truth in
the noontime discussion of Socrates and his companion (259). Contrari-
wise, the harsh-sounding braying (*ongkēsaito*) of asses recalls a standard
term for stylistic heaviness (*ongkos*). Once again, Callimachus evokes a
combination of poetic elements – sound, manner of expression, and

subject matter – through skillful use of imagery. He ends by praying to become a cicada, the light one, the winged one, who can feed on dew and can cast off the weight of old age, which has become to the aged poet oppressive as the weight of an island. It appears that Callimachus here alludes to a lyric poem by Sappho, newly discovered on papyrus, a poem in which she compares her aging self to the mythical Tithonus, the handsome lover of the Dawn goddess who gained immortality but wasted away with aging.[7] Though Sappho does not mention the fact, we know from other sources for the myth that Dawn eventually gave her aged lover continued life as a cicada. When Callimachus closes with the statement that since the Muses favored him in youth, they will not abandon him at the end of his life, he casts himself in a poetic stance as old as Sappho. While scholars debate much about Callimachus' complex text, known primarily from a torn papyrus, it can scarcely be doubted that it was intended as both statement and illustration of his poetics, and as such it had enormous influence on later Greek and Latin poetry.

While interpretation of Callimachus' dense and allusive system of imagery has dominated scholarship on Hellenistic poetics, other poets as well employed special metaphors to enunciate their aesthetic preferences. Certain Hellenistic thinkers, including the Alexandrian scholar Eratosthenes, maintained that the purpose of poetry was enchantment (*psychagōgia*) rather than instruction (*didaskalia*), a position vigorously opposed by the Stoics (Strabo 1.1.10, 1.2.3). This radical reworking of the traditional view about the purpose of poetry ironically accepts Plato's argument that poetry has nothing to do with teaching moral behavior, while positively revaluing its ability to produce pleasure (*hēdonē*) through its appeal to the emotions. Such privileging of the emotional persuasiveness of poetry was related to a strong critical trend that emphasized euphony, or pleasant sound, above all else in verse. These views seem to inform the system of imagery developed in Theocritus' pastoral *Idylls*. Theocritus offers the simple music-making of herdsmen to illustrate that the essential quality of poetry is its pleasant sound. The opening of *Idyll* 1, for instance, reproduces the sweet sounds (*hadu...hadu*) of a rustling pine tree to which a herdsman's piping is compared, and later a shepherd's song is praised as like the taste of honey or sweet dried figs, and better than the piercing (but pleasing) tone of the cicada. As the bucolic genre was later developed by Moschus and Bion, the cowherd (*boukolos*) became the emblem of the poet who composed in this sweet, musical style. The qualities that Theocritus had granted to the herdsman – his devotion to leisure, music, and nature and his strong focus on the personal emotion of love – were associated with a certain philosophy of life, which rejects ambition and the striving after wealth or power. Because of this

combination of specific subject matter, meaningful imagery, and underlying philosophical model, bucolic poetry evolved into the long-product-
ive genre of pastoral.

In the later Hellenistic period poets and editors adapted earlier images
to model the new phenomenon of collecting poetry by multiple authors
into anthologies. In the early first century BC, an editor of bucolic poetry,
Artemidorus of Tarsus, composed an introductory epigram in which he
claimed that the Bucolic Muses, once scattered, were now all gathered
into one fold, one herd (*Palatine Anthology* 9.205). About the same time
Meleager of Gadara made an important collection of Hellenistic epigrams
that he called the *Garland*. The image of poems as flowers was as old as
Sappho and Pindar. But Meleager's conceit, worked out in a long introductory poem (*Palatine Anthology* 4.1), was to figure his multiple-book
edition as a complex, colorful garland plaited from flowers or plants
symbolizing the epigrammatists included in his collection. Although
Meleager does not use the word itself, his *Garland* is thus an *anthology*, in
the etymological sense of a "gathering of flowers." But again the image
points to a certain poetic style and aesthetic choice. By emphasizing
the interweaving of many different plants into a discontinuous whole,
Meleager highlights his innovative use of editorial technique to produce an
anthology poetically pleasing in the complex arrangement of its epigrams
as well as in the quality of the poems selected. In doing so, he illustrates how
one of the most important critical categories of the age, *sunthesis*, meaning
"composition" in the literal sense of "placing together,"[8] could play itself
out in the new arena of multi-authored anthologies.

2.2   Meter, Dialect, and Diction

The metrical system used for ancient Greek was very different from the
system for English. Ancient Greek was a pitch language, not a stress
language like English or even Latin. As a result, an accented syllable
was distinguished from an unaccented one by a rising tone, not by stress,
and the metrical pattern was independent of the accent. It was rather
based on the sequence of long versus short syllables in a word, and syllable
length was determined by the quantity of the vowels and diphthongs or by
the number of consonants following the vowel. The details of this system
need to be known only to those who wish to read ancient Greek poetry in
the original, and our discussion here will focus on how Hellenistic poets
adapted the metrical system, in order to place themselves within a certain
poetic tradition, to set themselves apart as innovative in poetic usage, or to
signal the artful refinement of their poetic technique.

Greek meters fall into two broad categories, stichic and lyric. Stichic meters, such as dactylic hexameters, elegiac couplets, and iambic trimeters, maintain a variable pattern of long and short syllables that is repeated in every line; they were recited, not sung, although musical accompaniment was common. Traditional lyric poetry was sung, either solo or by a chorus, and the pattern of longs and shorts was fit to the rhythm of an accompanying instrument and performed with melody. The complex meters of lyric were highly variable, and the unit for repeating the pattern of longs and shorts was the stanza (called *strophē*), not the single line. Lyric songs were performed in both public and private settings, as prayers, to praise gods and men, to convey personal emotion, and even for narrative; the songs performed by the choruses of tragedy and comedy were in lyric meters. This lyric system underwent much more extensive changes in the postclassical period than did stichic meters.

The use of the long "six-foot" line of dactylic hexameter for epic of narrative and didactic types continues in the Hellenistic age, as in Apollonius' *Argonautica*, in Callimachus' *Hymns* and his epyllion called *Hecale*, and in Aratus' *Phaenomena*. But Erinna, in writing a woman's lament for the death of another woman, had shown how the hexameter line and even Homeric diction could be used differently, to express emotions traditionally confined to subliterary songs by grieving women. Theocritus' *Idylls* also present innovative use, since many of these poems feature nonheroic characters, such as housewives, herdsmen, and other working men, and part of the pleasing effect of these poems was surely the dissonance between the commonplace sentiments and the Homeric-sounding metrical phrases in which they were expressed. In several *Idylls*, Theocritus also experimented with reproducing the effect of lyric song in hexameters, either by the repetitive use of the refrain (suggesting a chant) or by sound patterns combined with imaginative suggestion. From the early third century, Callimachus and other poets attempted to produce a smoother form of the hexameter by restricting the number of short words and avoiding unusual rhythms. One of the best-known features of this refined versification involves a sense pause after a dactylic fourth foot (consisting of a long and two short syllables); this pattern, which is quite common in Theocritus and so known as a "bucolic diaeresis," may produce a songlike rhythm if used in consecutive lines. Another trend was the spondaic fifth foot, which consisted of two longs and so produced a heavy-sounding line, often involving a four-syllable word at line end. Although Callimachus, Theocritus, and Apollonius made skillful use of such spondaic lines, they are an even more marked mannerism in Antimachus, Aratus, Euphorion (Ch. 4.5), and Eratosthenes (Ch. 4.1).

The elegiac couplet, consisting of a dactylic hexameter followed by a shorter "five-foot" pentameter, underwent a similar development toward refinement in the third century. Traditionally used for a wide variety of topics, including social and political themes and mythical or historical narrative, elegy was the preferred meter for epigrams, whether inscribed or only in books, and was used for narrative mythical catalogues, such as Hermesianax's *Leontion* and Phanocles' *Erotes or Beautiful Boys*, following the model of Antimachus' *Lyde*. The four books of Callimachus' *Aetia* showed how shorter elegies, combining the poet's personal voice with narrative elements, could be strung together, catalogue fashion, to produce a long poem of discontinuous, even autonomous, segments.

Iambic trimeters, with a rhythm very like that of normal speech, continued as the meter used in dialogue sections of tragedy, such as Ezechiel's *Exodus* (Ch. 3.7), and in comedy, including Menander, where a longer line, called trochaic tetrameter, is also used. Comic trimeters were adapted to didactic poetry, normally in dactylic hexameter, in an anonymous work of historical geography called *Circuit of the Earth* (Ch. 4.1). The choliambic line, called the "limping" trimeter (or scazon) because the pattern of short-long reverses abruptly to long-short at line end, was associated with the archaic blame poet Hipponax and was revived for Herodas' *Mimiambi*, Callimachus' *Iambi*, and the *Iambi* by Phoenix of Colophon, all of which have a critical/satirical flavor. Theocritus (*Palatine Anthology* 13.3) used choliambs, rather than the more normal elegiac meter, in writing a fictitious epitaph for Hipponax, apparently to suggest the voice of the dead poet speaking from his grave.

In archaic and classical Greece, lyric songs had an important role in public festivals in honor of deities and in celebration of human achievement, such as athletic victory, while lyric songs conveying more personal sentiments, from the political to the erotic, were passed down through the decades for performance in private symposia. But beginning in late fifth-century Athens, the poets who were composing dithyrambs, a form of choral song performed in public competitions, began to change the nature of their music and its relationship to the words that were sung. The music became more complex in its melodies and harmonies, and the language became filled with colorful compounds that were difficult to understand. As a result, audiences tended to respond emotionally to the sound of these dithyrambic songs rather than intellectually to the words. Plato and other conservative thinkers were dismayed. Professional performers were required for the difficult "new music," and the musically simpler songs of the archaic poets, it seems, ceased to be taught universally in the Greek educational system. These developments had a profound effect on the Hellenistic use of lyric meters. Certainly lyric songs continued to be produced, especially for public festivals celebrating gods or rulers, although many lacked strophic arrangement and their metrical schemes tended toward simplicity. Surviving examples for mortals include the adulatory hymn for Demetrius Poliorcetes performed at Athens (Powell pp. 173–4, see Ch. 1.1), which was composed in a so-called ithyphallic meter, and the conclusion to a paean, in a meter known as dactylo-epitrite, sung by the Chalcidians to honor the Roman commander Titus Flamininus (Powell p. 173).[9] From an inscription at Delphi come two paeans in cretic-paeonic meter, performed for Apollo by a chorus of Athenians (Powell pp. 141–59); the poet of one is identified as Limenius, who also accompanied on the cithara. Musical notation is recorded with the verses so that, for once, the melody can be reconstructed.

By the third century, the lyric compositions of the archaic age were commonly encountered written on papyrus rolls, rather than as performed song, and leading poets of the day began to write poetry in imitation of the lyrics known from book contexts. Lyric meters were now treated as stichic even when stanzaic form was maintained. Examples include Theocritus' *Idylls* 28–31 on themes of love and friendship in the Aeolic meters used by Sappho and Alcaeus, Cercidas' *Meliambi* on philosophical and moral themes (Ch. 3.8), and Philicus' fragmentary *Hymn to Demeter* (676–80 Lloyd-Jones and Parsons) in an innovative long line known as a choliambic hexameter. In one surviving line of Philicus' poem, the "gift of a composition written in a new manner" is offered to "grammarians," as a sign that this sophisticated poem was intended for the educated elite. Papyri have also preserved four fragmentary lyric poems by Callimachus (fr. 226–9). One of these (fr. 228), recounting the apotheosis of Arsinoe II through the eyes of her previously deified sister, might well have been performed at a public commemoration, either sung by a professional singer or recited as pure verse. In *Idyll* 15 Theocritus presents verbatim a lyric hymn (to Aphrodite and Adonis) performed by a gifted artist, but paradoxically set out for the reader in the stichic lines of dactylic hexameter. The use of lyric meters as another form of verse to be read, such as we find in Latin poets like Catullus and Horace, surely had its beginnings in the early Hellenistic period, but the change from song to poetry was gradual and never absolute.

Dialect was another means by which Hellenistic poets demonstrated their art, learning, and versatility. The Homeric epics, because of their long formation through oral composition, had developed an artificial mixture of dialect forms, while some lyric poets of the archaic age composed in literary versions of the dialects spoken in their hometowns. Athenian tragedy and comedy use local Attic, but with a Doric element in the lyric passages, to acknowledge the supposed origins of lyric in Doric lands. By the third century the regional vernaculars were waning, particularly in written speech, in favor of a common or *koinē* form of Greek based on Attic, although local dialects surely remained more current in the spoken language. Koine became the standard for literary prose of the era, as in the histories of Polybius, the Septuagint, and the New Testament. An exception is found in the writings of the Syracusan mathematician Archimedes, whose prose retained elements of his local Doric speech. Hellenistic poets, who signaled their refinement by their relationship to the tradition of earlier Greek poetry, typically chose to compose in one dialect or mixture of dialects, either to recall a specific model or to convey realistically the flavor of contemporary speech. The exact usage of dialect forms is most often impossible to identify, because scribes commonly replaced unfamiliar forms with ones better known to them; nevertheless, the broad picture of dialect usage in poetry can still be assessed.

Apollonius of Rhodes and other epic poets generally reproduced the mixed poetic dialect of Homer, although Aratus innovated with a freer use of Attic forms, occurring only rarely in the *Iliad* and *Odyssey*. Attic was of course the dialect of Athenian writers such as Menander, who used a colloquial form to represent everyday speech. The Attic used by the canonical writers of the fifth and fourth centuries or a mixture of Attic and the related Ionic dialect became the standard that other dialectal uses now varied. So, for instance, Herodas attempted to reproduce the Ionic of old Ephesus, the hometown of his model Hipponax, but some of his Ionic formations seem artificially constructed from Attic. Callimachus, who prided himself on composing in a variety of genres and dialects, included some Doric poems in his book of *Iambi*, which were otherwise in the expected Ionic. Likewise, his six *Hymns* are mixed, the first four in Homeric hexameters with the usual Ionic flavor, and the last two, one in elegiacs and one in hexameters, in Doric. This use of Doric suggests the aural atmosphere of the local festival settings depicted in these two *Hymns*, while also serving to mark Callimachus' self-conscious distance from the older *Homeric Hymns* that were his primary model. Theocritus, who lived much of his life in Doric-speaking areas, first Syracuse and then Cos, also displays great versatility. Some of his hexameter *Idylls*, especially those for the Ptolemies and on mythical themes, are in the epic dialect, chiefly made up of Ionic. But others, including the pastoral poems and his urban mimes, are in Doric. Unfortunately, lack of information about the third-century Doric spoken in Syracuse, Cos, or even the Libyan city of Cyrene (in addition to uncertainty deriving from changes made during manuscript transmission) prevents us from knowing whether Theocritus was reproducing a specific vernacular or reflecting the literary Doric of earlier Syracusan writers of mime and comedy, like Epicharmus or Sophron. His herdsmen utter some specifically Doric words, which become genre markers of "bucolic" speech in the later poetic tradition. Particularly interesting is *Idyll* 15, in which two Syracusan women resident in Alexandria, when criticized for their conservational Doric with its broad vowels, vigorously defend their right as free citizens to "talk Peloponnesian" (15.92). To round out Theocritus' remarkable dialectal versatility, his Aeolic *Idylls* 28–31 imitate the Lesbian dialect in which Sappho and Alcaeus composed, a vernacular form that had, at least in part, vanished by the third century.

In their diction as well, Hellenistic poets demonstrated their erudite knowledge of the poetic tradition. Their language is never, however, simply that of Homer, the lyric poets, or the dramatists; it rather incorporates all that and more, producing a multiplicity and complexity that can only be called Hellenistic. While the hexameter poetry of the age is heavily influenced by Homeric phraseology, emphasis is often on the more unusual words, those that were the subject of scholarly scrutiny and debate. Apollonius of Rhodes, for instance, often uses Homeric words as if to illustrate one of the meanings found in glossographers, who were concerned to interpret rare epic words often no longer fully understood. The poet must have relished the challenge of fleshing out in mythical narrative his own scholarly views on Homeric diction. Other Alexandrian poets as well assert their opinions about a scholarly controversy through poetic usage. An example is provided by the word *kissubion*, which appears in both Callimachus and Theocritus. In the *Odyssey*, *kissubion* designates a kind of drinking cup, used by the Cyclops and by the swineherd Eumaeus. After Homer the word appears only rarely, so that Hellenistic scholars came to hold various opinions about its etymology and meaning.[10] In the *Aetia* (fr. 178) Callimachus explains, or "glosses," the *kissubion* from which a guest drinks wine at a dinner party with *aleison*, a word used by Homer for a fancy cup, sometimes of gold. Theocritus, in contrast, signals his agreement with scholars who considered the *kissubion* a herdsman's cup, made of ivywood (*kissos*). Since ivywood is not in fact suitable for making cups, Theocritus varies the etymological connection. The wooden cup in *Idyll* 1, used by a goatherd for milk, is unbelievably grand, carved with three figured scenes and intricately decorated along the rim with an ivy motif, like ornate silver bowls of the period. The extended play on the "k" sound – in *kissos*, *kissubion*, and the "crocus" color of the ivyberries (1.27–31) – is an excellent example of how the best poets could turn etymology and erudition to pure sensual delight.

Into this vocabulary taken from the canonical poetry of the archaic and classical ages, Hellenistic poets mix local vernacular words, which were likely the subject of learned discussion among scholars or in linguistic treatises, and prosaic words, often taken from technical and scientific literature. Medical terminology from the Hippocratic corpus appears surprisingly often, and curing disease was apparently an interest of the early Ptolemies. In his pastoral poetry, Theocritus displays an extensive knowledge of the technical terminology for plants in the eastern Mediterranean,[11] and Aratus sometimes coins new formations to express astronomical principles within his basically Homeric language. Lycophron's *Alexandra*, spoken by the mad Cassandra, is full of words used in an unusual or etymological sense, to mimic a puzzling oracular style. Even foreign words occasionally occur in some poets. In a self-epitaph (*Palatine Anthology* 7.419) Meleager, from the multiethnic Gadara in Syria, requests that those who pass by his grave give the customary ritual greeting, whether the Syrian *salam*, Phoenician *naidios*, or Greek *chaire*. One of the most successful examples of an everyday Hellenistic word put to poetic effect comes from the *Hecale*, where Callimachus speaks of the "shimmering sky more brilliant than glass" (fr. 238.16). Horace famously imitates the phrase by calling the Bandusian spring on his own farm *splendidior vitro*, "more gleaming than glass" (*Odes* 3.13.1). But the Greek gains its charm from the combination of honed Homeric language with modern novelty. Three of Callimachus' words are found in Homer, though not together: the commonplace *ouranos* for "sky," *ēnops* "shimmering" used in Homer of bronze, and the comparative *phaanteros* "brighter than" to vary the Homeric superlative "brightest." Unknown in Homer's day was *hualos*, "glass," a common Hellenistic item produced abundantly in Egyptian workshops. In addition, ancient glass was normally colored, often blue like the sky. What gives Callimachus' phrase its poetic charm is not just the fresh aptness of the comparison but also the largely vocalic sounds, enhanced by the Homeric ending of the word for "glass": in Greek, *hualoio phaanteros ouranos ēnops* sounds bright and beautiful.

Hellenistic poets also use word plays, puns, and acrostics in meaningful ways, especially to mark their poetic identities and stylistic allegiances. In the prologue to the *Aetia*, when Callimachus rejects the noisy braying of the ass in favor of the shrill song of the cicada, his word for "braying," *ongkēsaito*, plays on *ongkos*, a common term for the weightiness of the grand style. Likewise, in the first *Idyll* when a shepherd's song is, naively, praised as like the taste of a dried fig (*ischada*, 147) from Attica (an oddity for a Syracusan goatherd), Theocritus is clearly alluding, metapoetically, to the plain style (called *ischnos*) and its association with Attic speech patterns. Others pun on their names. Aratus' *Phaenomena* opens as follows: "Let us begin with Zeus, whom we men do not leave unspoken." Here the Greek word *arrēton*, "unspoken," evokes Aratus, so that the poet names himself at the opening of his poem while remaining unnamed (pun intended). In an erotic epigram (*Palatine Anthology* 12.165), Meleager, playing on *Garland* as the title of his anthology, claims that he will plait a wreath made of white-skinned and dark-skinned boys, which puns on one etymology of his name from *melas*, "dark," and *argos*, "white." In imitation (*Palatine Anthology* 5.115), the Epicurean epigrammatist who instructed Vergil claims that his repeated attraction to women named Demo is the fated result of being named Philodemus ("lover of Demo"). Acrostics are a sequence of first letters in consecutive lines of poetry that spell out a word or name. The didactic poet Nicander gives his name acrostically in his *Theriaca* (345–53), as if to place a seal on this poetically styled passage within otherwise rather technical subject matter. Aratus spells out the word *leptē* over five lines (783–7), in a passage that describes the crescent moon as "slender" (*leptē*); this acrostic shows conclusively that Callimachus' praise of Aratus' refined poetic style reflects the didactic poet's own stylistic preference. While acrostics occur also in stone epigrams and in later authors, their appearance in Hellenistic poetry marks the bookish self-consciousness of the age. Puns and word plays can be appreciated in recitation; acrostics must be perceived by a reader looking at a written text.

2.3 Literature as Artefact

In the prologue to the *Aetia*, Callimachus describes how Apollo instructed him in poetry when for the first time he placed a tablet (*deltos*) on his knees (fr. 1.21–2). The poet is here referring to the wooden tablets that were used for literary composition and other nonpermanent writing such as school exercises (figure 2.1). In one form of these, the interiors were hollowed out, and wax was smeared over the surfaces. The sharp end of a stylus was used to impress letters into the wax, while the blunt end was for erasing. In another kind, the surface of the wood was smoothed or coated to receive ink from a pen. Both types could be hinged together so that they closed up like a notebook (figure 2.2). These reusable tablets were excellent for making first drafts, and preliminary versions of poems or prose were also circulated to friends on such tablets.

Papyrus, made from a plant native to Egypt, was the material of choice for most permanent documents, including literature in its finished form. Sheets of papyrus, made from the plant's fibers, were smoothed, cut, and pasted together into rolls. The scribe would rule the papyrus sheets with dots or lines before writing on it in ink. Because of size limitations, these ancient bookrolls did not hold as much text as modern books. In the

Figure 2.1 *Painted terracotta statuette of a girl with a writing tablet on her knees, from Alexandria, 3rd c. Graeco-Roman Museum, Alexandria.*

Hellenistic period a book of poetry would typically run under 2,000 lines, and books of 1,000 lines or less were common. There were even miniature books, which could easily be carried or concealed on one's person.[12] Larger rolls, commonly up to about 45 feet in length (and even longer ones are known), were used for prose texts; for instance, Herodotus' *Histories*, which fill two modern volumes, were divided into nine ancient books, reflecting their original division into nine papyrus rolls. Readers could hold the smaller bookrolls comfortably in the hand, but the fatter ones were likely placed on a table or other support when in use. A tag with author's name and the title, called a *sillybos*, was glued to the back of the rolled papyrus, for ease of finding a text in storage bins or on shelves (figure 2.2). This information was also written at the end of the text, the

Figure 2.2 *Wall painting of a man holding a papyrus bookroll with sillybos, or tag, hanging from the baton, and a woman holding a wooden writing tablet and stylus, from Pompeii. Naples, Museo Nazionale.*

most interior and protected position on the bookroll, and sometimes also at the beginning on the front or back of the first papyrus sheet. The beginning of the roll was the place where damage was most likely to occur, so that information about author and title was often lost, as has happened in the new papyrus collection of epigrams attributed to Posidippus. While earlier Greek poets typically hoped that their compositions would continue to circulate in the mouths of others, Hellenistic poets were acutely aware of the relationship between poetic immortality and the physical preservation of bookrolls. Callimachus (fr. 7.13–14), for instance, asks the Graces to wipe their oiled hands on his elegies to preserve them (a play on their poetic and physical properties), and Posidippus wrote an epigram about a character in Sappho, an Egyptian courtesan Doricha, whose name survives only within the "white columns of Sappho's ode" (122 Austin and Bastianini). Epigrams that purport to be book labels, such as the Asclepiades poems on Erinna and Antimachus, also show the connection regularly made by Hellenistic poets between the physical nature of literature and its aesthetic qualities.

What did an ancient reader typically see when he or she unrolled a papyrus containing a work of literature? The text was copied onto the papyrus roll in columns (*selides*), and the reader would view two or more columns at a time as the papyrus was unrolled with the right hand and rolled up again with the left. For poetry, horizontal column size was determined by the length of the line, but for literary prose a relatively short column of only about two inches was commonly used. The text was written out continuously without word division or distinctive letters at the beginning of sentences or for proper names. Punctuation, when it occurred, consisted of raised dots to indicate pauses, the *paragraphos*, which was a short horizontal line used to indicate a new poem or change of speaker, and the *corōnis*, an elaborate marginal sign or flourish that marked the end of a work. Accents were usually not written by the copying scribe, except, as in lyric poets, for dialects likely unknown to readers. The act of reading involved, then, more active interpretation of the text than is the case with modern books, and papyrus fragments often show reader's marks to indicate proper word division, accentuation, or phrasing, as well as to correct a misspelling or other copyist's error.

Although most Hellenistic literature on papyri comes from copies made in the Roman era, some earlier examples do give evidence of how such texts were formatted in the Ptolemaic period. The third-century copy of Menander's comedy entitled *Sikyonian* (or *Sikyonians*) contains *paragraphoi* to indicate change of speaker, as in a later papyrus preserving Herodas' dramatic mimes.[13] In the Posidippus papyrus of the late third century, the epigrams, written without word division or systematic punctuation, are yet separated by the same mark of punctuation, placed after the last line of each poem in the left margin. This epigram collection also groups the poems into sections with headings that appear on a separate line within the column, and other papyri containing miscellaneous material show that an author's name or an indication of the subject was sometimes written in such a position between poems. A papyrus shows that the aetiological episodes in Callimachus' *Aetia* were separated by a *corōnis*, to mark them as separable poems,[14] and Meleager playfully gives voice to the *corōnis* that ends his anthology since this mark of punctuation speaks his final epigram (*Palatine Anthology* 12.257). Important or difficult texts also eventually acquired scholia, or explanatory notes, written between lines or in margins, and this was true for the *Aetia* within a few decades of its composition.[15] These interlinear notes, often consisting of a simple synonym for a difficult word, illustrate the everyday textual practice that stood behind the scholarly task of collecting glosses and the poetic "glossing" of rare words by learned authors like Callimachus. By the second century AD, some copies of Callimachus' *Iambi* and *Hecale*, as well as his *Aetia*, also had head notes or summaries, called *Diegeseis*.[16] Because Aratus' *Phaenomena* dealt with technical astronomical matters, explanatory scholia began to be added almost immediately, and at least three commentaries were written in the second century, of which that by the astronomer Hipparchus of Nicaea is still extant. Bookrolls concerned with technical or scientific subjects were usually illustrated, and the didactic material in Nicander and Aratus was likely accompanied by drawings already in the Hellenistic period.[17] A recently discovered papyrus fragment of the geographer Artemidorus of Ephesus, active around 100 BC, contains the earliest known map of Spain, marked with rivers running across the peninsula and drawings of buildings and towers.[18] Even if prose treatises made less claim than refined poetry to beauty of sound or language, the images inserted in them, likely drawn by talented artists, would have enhanced the aesthetic experience of reading.

One difficulty for scholars in dealing with smaller fragments of papyri is to distinguish between professionally produced bookrolls, which contain the formatting and arrangement of the author or an editor, and private copies made to suit the inclinations or needs of a single reader. Since all books had to be copied by hand, it was common for individuals to produce their own texts, by personally copying whatever they wanted to own or paying a scribe to do so. A well-known example is an anthology of personal favorites, including selections from Athenian tragedy, New Comedy, and epigrams on Ptolemaic monuments by Posidippus, written out by two brothers who lived at the Serapeum in Egyptian Memphis during the second century.[19]

Long-term preservation of ancient literary works depended upon continuing interest in the text, as well as a certain amount of luck. The sort of book format familiar today came into use in the first century AD, and by the third century had generally replaced the bookroll. This codex, as it is called, was composed of pages made of either papyrus or parchment and bound in a volume. Much more text could be included in a codex than in a papyrus roll, and as a result several bookrolls were typically copied into a single codex, which often contained works by more than one author. Some Hellenistic literature made it into the codex format and was then preserved by recopying in late antiquity, typically in the fifth or sixth centuries AD, and then again in the Byzantine era. Surviving manuscripts containing Hellenistic literature come from the tenth century AD or later, and it was from these Byzantine copies that the first printed editions appeared, usually in Florence or Venice in the late fourteenth or early fifteenth century. Among texts preserved in manuscript are Apollonius'

Argonautica, Callimachus' *Hymns*, Theocritus' *Idylls* and later bucolic poetry, Aratus, Lycophron, Nicander, most Hellenistic epigrams, several books and epitomes of Polybius, works on mathematics and science by Euclid, Archimedes, and others, as well as the Septuagint. Only rarely is some new text found in manuscript form, although we await publication of recently discovered material by Menander, found in the Vatican Library, and scholars are studying for publication a palimpsest (erased and reused manuscript) of Archimedes.

Some of the most important texts of the era (and unknown scads of lesser works) did not survive to the Renaissance, and perhaps not even to late antiquity. This loss was partly due to a preference for canonical literature, which Hellenistic texts were not, for the simple reason that it was the third-century Alexandrians who set up the canons. Contemporary compositions were the "new" stuff, since modernity, then and now, is defined by its complicated relationship to the canon. The loss of so much Callimachus is harder to explain, since hundreds of lines quoted by late authors show that he was read and admired for centuries; yet only his *Hymns* and some epigrams – his minor works – survived in manuscript. A hostile tradition that viewed Callimachus as obscure, dry, and pedantic was, one imagines, partially at fault, though bad luck was surely also a factor.

From the late nineteenth century on, a remarkable number of important and intriguing Hellenistic texts have been discovered on papyrus, mostly from ancient trash dumps in Egypt or from the cartonnage used to encase mummies. The majority of these papyri, preserved by the Egyptian dryness, are frustratingly fragmentary, just scraps, but others, particularly those used as cartonnage, provide continuous text. From papyri have come significant fragments of Callimachus' *Aetia*, his most famous and influential poem, as well as portions of the *Iambi*, *Hecale*, and his lyric poems. Menander, once lost except for quoted lines, has also been resurrected from a series of papyri, since we now have one almost complete play and large portions of several others, and Herodas, whose *Mimiambi* clearly belong to the cultural/literary milieu of third-century Alexandria, was known only as an insignificant name until one crucial papyrus brought him back to life. One of the earliest artefacts containing a literary text is a fourth-century papyrus preserving a dithyramb entitled *Persians* by Timotheus, written out as prose because poetic colometry was still to be invented;[20] it provides our best example of the "new" dithyrambic poetry disliked by Plato. The Lille papyrus preserving the beginning of *Aetia* Book 3, with interlinear scholia, is from the late third century,[21] and the recently discovered book of over one hundred new epigrams by Posidippus also dates to that early period. A group of mostly philosophical treatises, largely Epicurean, and many by Philodemus, has been recovered at Herculaneum in Italy, from a library buried by the volcanic debris produced by the eruption of Mt. Vesuvius in 79 AD. Though the charred papyrus rolls were discovered in the 1750s, multispectral imaging produced by a computer program is now greatly enhancing scholars' ability to read them. Such discoveries provide a fascinating window into the artefactual history of this literature, since we can see, without the murkiness produced by centuries of recopying, the physical appearance – shape, size, color, and format – of Hellenistic books.

3

Authors and Genres

3.1 Menander

New Comedy was a type of situational drama involving a love interest and ending happily in marriage. Menander, a playwright of late fourth-century Athens, was considered the best Greek composer of New Comedy, the ancient forerunner of modern comedy of manners. It has been disputed whether Menander should be classified as a Hellenistic author – because of his early date, because of his direct connection with the tradition of Attic comedy, and because he lacks the scholarly allusiveness character-istic of Alexandrian writers. But he is chronologically within our period since all his plays were composed after the death of Alexander, and his thematic focus on intimate family drama and erotic complications fits with Hellenistic preferences. He also appealed to the Alexandrians, as shown by the famous remark of the Ptolemaic scholar Aristophanes of Byzantium, who ranked him second after Homer in literary greatness: "Oh Menander and life, which of you has imitated the other?" In making this paradoxical reference to imitation, a standard ancient literary concept, Aristophanes was likely alluding not to Menander's plots, which are typically implausible in the comic fashion, but to his subtle and believable characterizations and to the settings of his plays among ordinary people of the contemporary Greek world. Menander's plays became in the second century primary models for Plautus and Terence, who reworked Greek New Comedy for the Roman stage, and it was through these Roman adaptations that later writers of comedy like Shakespeare, Molière, and

Shaw knew the Greek sources of their genre. Despite an immense popularity through the end of antiquity, Menander's plays were not transmitted in the manuscripts of the Byzantine era and remained known only by reputation and in brief quotation until the extensive papyrological discoveries of the twentieth century.

Biographical information about ancient authors is always scanty, and usually some of the information we have is considered unreliable because it appears based on the texts themselves. We do, however, have a bit more information about Menander than most other Hellenistic authors. He was born in 344/3 or 342/1 to a wealthy Athenian family, and the names of his father and mother, Diopeithes and Hegestrate, seem genuine. His youth and adulthood corresponded with the period of Macedonian domination and limiting of democratic freedoms under foreign-supported oligarchic governments, and his choice of subject matter is clearly connected to the politically restrictive atmosphere of early Hellenistic Athens. He was supposedly handsome, though squint-eyed, sharp-witted, and mad about women. While his cleverness and erotic propensity are likely projections of his personality based on his plays, it is less clear whether ancient representations of him with regular features, thick, wavy hair, and even a squint in one late mosaic descend from some realistic portrait made during his own lifetime or are imaginative projections of his character based on his literary biography. Though it seems odd today, physical good looks and attractiveness to women were culturally constructed in antiquity as a sign of effeminacy, and one source reports that he wore perfume, flowing garments, and had a slow, mincing gait.[1] Since he belonged to the highest echelons of Athenian society, he surely knew the leading intellectuals and political figures of the day. There is nothing implausible in the report that he did his youthful military service at the same time as the philosopher Epicurus, a Samian who lived in Athens as a young man, and that he was a student of the Peripatetic Theophrastus, a claim that may reflect intellectual influence. He may also have learned much from the prolific comic poet Alexis, though a reported familial relationship of uncle and nephew is perhaps fictionalized biography. Because of a friendship with Demetrius of Phalerum, the Macedonian regent in Athens from 317 to 307, he was subjected to a lawsuit and nearly became a victim of the purge that took place after Demetrius' expulsion. The connection with Demetrius, who ended up in Alexandria, makes all the more likely the story that he and his rival Philemon were invited by Ptolemy Soter to Egypt. We know of this invitation only through two fictional letters by the imperial writer Alciphron (4.18–19), in which Menander refuses Ptolemy's offer because he cannot bear to part from his mistress Glycera. Though a liaison with a woman of the hetaira (or courtesan) class is altogether plausible for an upper-class Athenian man, the reliability of the story has to be weighed against the fact that Glycera appears as a character's name in more than one of his plays. His death occurred in 293/2 or 292/1, when he was about fifty, and although the story that he died while swimming near the Athenian port of Piraeus seems suspiciously dramatic, its historicity becomes more likely because it was known already to Callimachus. His statue was set up soon afterwards in the Theater of Dionysus with an inscribed base that survives, and his tomb was still visible in the second century AD on the road from Athens to the Piraeus.

Menander composed over one hundred comedies, with at least ninety titles now known. Attic comedies were performed in competition at the dramatic festivals of the Lenaea and the Greater Dionysia, but the large number of his plays indicates that he must have written also for festivals elsewhere. His earliest play called *Anger* (*Orgē*), now lost, was produced in 323/2 or 321/0 when he was quite a young man. He won his first prize in 316 with the *Grouch* (*Dyskolos*), the one essentially complete surviving play, but otherwise he was victorious in Athens only seven other times during a career lasting about thirty years. Whatever the reason for these relatively few victories, later audiences and readers adored Menander. He is surpassed only by Homer and Euripides in number of papyri found, and scenes from his comedies were represented in mosaics and paintings throughout the Greco-Roman world. Mosaics of eleven plays, found in a third-century AD house in Mitylene on Lesbos,[2] indicate that his plays were still being performed almost six centuries after his death. Only as a result of the papyrological discoveries of the past century have scholars begun to understand what endeared Menander to his ancient audience. While most papyri provide mutilated textual fragments, a few large-scale finds have given us major sections of plays. In 1905 an archaeologist discovered the fifth-century AD Cairo codex, which contains major sections of the *Men at Arbitration* (*Epitrepontes*), the *Girl with Cut Hair* (*Perikeiromenē*), and the *Samian Woman* (*Samia*). After World War II publication of the Bodmer codex gave us the *Grouch* essentially complete, additional sections of the *Samian Woman*, and about one-third of the *Shield* (*Aspis*). Since 1960 fragments of *Sikyonian* (or *Sikyonians*) have been recovered from a papyrus of the third century reused as mummy cartonnage, and a papyrus from Oxyrhynchus has provided a section of *Twice Deceiving* (*Dis Exapaton*), which was adapted for the Roman theater in Plautus' *Bacchic Sisters*. The recent announcement of some two hundred lines of an unknown play, found in palimpsest (under erasure) in a Vatican manuscript, makes it clear that the recovery of Menander will continue, even from unexpected sources.

Menander's plots derive from a combination of earlier tragic and comic form. Old Comedy, as practiced by Aristophanes, involved the social and political issues important to fifth-century democratic Athens, and prominent Athenians, not just politicians but intellectuals like Socrates and literary figures like Euripides, often appeared as characters to be mocked in these plays. During the fourth century the political aspects of comedy, as well as its ribald obscenity, lessened in favor of more developed plots, often involving the domestic problems of ordinary Athenians. The plays of this period, called Middle Comedy, are known in a great many fragments, but the plot lines are lost to us. By the era of Menander, New Comedy had emerged, peopled by stock characters identifiable by the type of mask they wore; the list of these includes the father figure, the young man, the soldier, the matron, the young girl, the clever slave, the hetaira, and the cook. While scenes involving low-status characters like slaves and cooks are generally played for laughs, the plot itself with its love interest has a more serious aspect concerned with the formation or continuance of a family unit. These more involved situations derive, in part, from tragic plots, especially from fifth-century tragedies that have happy endings, typical of late Euripides. Menander has also taken over from the tragedians, especially again Euripides, the use of the prologue, in which a deity or personification reveals the background for the situation at hand and may hint at the outcome. The coalescence of comic and tragic plots is not as improbable as it may at first seem, since already in the fifth century the reciprocal relationship between the two dramatic forms was recognized and explored. A number of Aristophanes' plays parody tragedy, mostly the plays of Euripides, who appears as a character in the *Acharnians* and the *Thesmophorizusae*, and Euripides in turn introduces comic elements in a number of his tragedies. In the *Helen*, for instance, the heroic Menelaus appears on stage incongruously dressed in the tattered remains of a sail, and the recognition of his lost Helen and their reconciliation as a couple foreshadow the moment of familial recognition that turns the plot in many New Comedies. A character in Menander's *Men at Arbitration* even cites the example of tragic heroes abandoned at birth to point out how the tokens left with an exposed baby may someday help the child to find his true parents, and in numerous places in the plays a character quotes a tragic line to better define the comic moment.

With the gradual recovery of sustained portions of some plays, scholars have come to recognize that Menander was a master of plot construction. Aristotle identified the typical or most desirable pattern for tragedy as a turn from good fortune to bad for a noble character whose downfall results from an error (*hamartia*), and error here means a mistake or misjudgment rather than a moral failing. In Menander's comic reversal of the pattern, the turn is from bad fortune to good when some impediment to a young man's desire to win a girl is removed through a stratagem or the revelation of a hidden truth. The complications in New Comic plots usually involve Athenian laws about citizenship, legitimacy of children, inheritance, or other culturally specific circumstances, but the complex and subtle inter-action between character motivation and happenstance is what holds the audience's attention. Menander's known plots show that he had perfected the division of the action over five acts, while the choral songs of earlier tragedy and comedy have disappeared in favor of interludes of playful singing and dancing that are simply marked "chorus" in our manuscripts. Early on in the play, and often through the guidance of the god or personified figure delivering the prologue, the audience's sympathies are engaged with some helpless, innocent, or naively pious individual, such as an endangered child or a young woman who has been abused, raped, or denied the opportunity to marry. In the dramatic complication, the audi-ence's sympathies are then aligned against a character who obstructs a young couple's happiness, and this blocking figure is typically a mature male represented as selfish, greedy, socially inept, or perhaps just misin-formed. The impediment to the desired union is resolved in the fourth act, usually through some recognition of true blood relationships and perhaps Athenian citizenship. This description is of course overly schematic, and Menander often leads the audience to expect a standard development of the plot only to move the action forward in a different way. For instance, in the (largely reconstructed) fourth and fifth acts of the *Shield*, a clever slave's stratagem of faking a death to trick the greedy Smicrines, who wants to marry his niece for her money, is rendered unnecessary when her brother, thought dead, returns to give the girl to the youth who loves her. Even more interesting is Menander's use of the fifth act, which ends with marriage. While the external impediments to the generational renewal of the household normally resolve in the fourth act, the last scene is typically devoted to final reintegration of the family, accomplished, in Menander, not just through the wedding but also through a strengthening of emo-tional bonds among other family members.

Menander is famous as well for his subtle characterizations. The stock character types of New Comedy were often used in contrasting pairs, such as clever and stupid slave, opposing father figure and helpful one, love-maddened youth and more rational friend, and their masks marked the contrast with some visual difference, such as hair color. Menander had an uncanny ability to individualize within type so that his characters seem incredibly real in terms of consistency and complexity. Although all speak a colloquial form of Attic, some have personal speech patterns. This is true in the *Samian Woman* of Demeas and Niceratus, who are friends, neighbors, and also fathers of the youth and the girl who will marry, but Demeas is kind-hearted and slow to anger while Niceratus is explosive and hard-headed. The unmarried girls of Menandrian comedy often have little stage time since their real Athenian counterparts lived sheltered lives, but other female figures tend to acquire audience sympathy through chancy acts or assertions of independence. Menander's women are often the true heroes of his plays, though their goodness may render their characters less complex because less fallible. Chrysis, the Samian woman living with Demeas, risks the security of her domestic relationship to help the raped girl next door by falsely claiming to be the mother of her baby. Pamphile, the young wife in the *Men at Arbitration* who believes her husband has fallen in love with a hetaira, nevertheless nobly refuses her father's urgings to desert him.

Other characters are given psychological depth by being constructed against type. The soldier Thrasonides in the *Hated Man*, an example of the arrogant soldier who was usually the butt of fun in comedy, becomes sympathetic because he is so crushed by the refusal of the woman he lives with to welcome his love. Audience reaction to his character is set up at the play's beginning by a (fragmentary) monologue he delivers to the goddess Night as he walks up and down in front of his house (A1–13):

> Oh Night – since of all the gods you are closest to Aphrodite,
> and in you . . . . discourse about these matters
> . . . . and erotic cogitation –
> by Apollo, have you ever seen a more wretched person?
> Or anyone more unfortunately in love?
> I'm now standing in front of my own door
> . . . . I'm walking up and down,
> . . . . as you, Night, are just about in the midst of your course,
> while I could be sleeping and holding my beloved girl.
> For she's within, inside my house, and I have the opportunity
> and I want this as much as anyone who's absolutely madly in love,
> but I don't do it. I've chosen this pacing up and down out here
> under the open sky.

Thrasonides is particularly ridiculous, and pitiable, because he plays the traditional role of the "excluded lover," but, ironically, before his own house where his beloved is ensconced. His restraint, contrary to a soldier's stock characterization, is the clearest sign of his true passion. Explanation of motivation for action is one means by which Menander provides vividness to his characterizations. For instance, audience dislike of the misanthropic Cnemon in the *Grouch* is tempered when he eventually explains his considered belief in self-sufficiency; though an extreme case, his personality takes on a degree of plausibility if he is viewed as an old-fashioned Attic farmer, devoted to the land and opposed to the bustle and perceived corruption of city life. We might in fact not fully comprehend the system of stock characters used in New Comedy if it had been Menander's nuanced plays that survived in manuscript rather than the adaptations of Plautus, who plays his clever slaves and strict fathers for broader laughs.

The *Grouch* (*Dyskolos*), staged when Menander was in his mid-twenties, lacks the subtlety of characterization and dramatic entanglement evident in certain of his later comedies. The plot is set in force by the rural god Pan, who, as he tells the audience in the prologue, wishes to help Cnemon's pious daughter by arranging for her marriage to the wealthy young Sostratus. Once Sostratus has seen the girl and fallen in love with her, his desire to ask for her as wife is blocked when the crotchety Cnemon reacts violently to any attempt to make contact, even a knock at the door. Allying himself with the noble Gorgias, the girl's half-brother and Cnemon's estranged stepson, Sostratus plans to win the old man's attention and respect by working in the fields. But in typical Menandrian fashion, this stratagem fails to accomplish its designed goal, although it does prove the resolve of the pampered Sostratus as he suffers from the hard labor of farming. The happy resolution comes from an unexpected turn of events. When Cnemon falls down a well, he is rescued by his stepson Gorgias and, because of the young man's willingness to help someone who had treated him ill, the grouch recognizes the error of his ways. In a speech in which he turns his property over to Gorgias and agrees to marry his daughter to Sostratus, Cnemon admits his long-standing mistake in assuming that life can be lived apart from the society of others. Menander seems to be struggling in this early play to avoid the clichéd conclusion that marriage into a rich family equates with happiness. When Sostratus proposes to unite further the two families by marrying his sister to Gorgias, the young hero-farmer initially resists on the basis that he wants to earn his own just rewards. Although Menander appeals here to the Athenian popular view that the simple, hard-working farmer is the model for the democratic citizen, practicalities quickly set in and Gorgias yields to his good fortune. The most unsettling event occurs in the fifth act when the cook and a slave, previously rebuffed by Cnemon in the matter of borrowing a pot, rather cruelly rag the old man and force him to join the marriage celebration. Cnemon's injuries and admission of a serious error in judgment problematize the audience's ability to join fully in the comic merriment of this abusive tease. The viability of the happy ending as a celebration encompassing the audience is saved by its stylization, through music and a different meter.

A number of Menander's plays reflect the military realities of the post-Alexander era. The complication in the *Shield* (*Aspis*) results from the supposed death of Cleostratus, who has gone to fight as a mercenary in Lycia in order to obtain a dowry for his sister. The opening scene, in which his faithful slave Daos returns with the baggage and abundant booty to report his master's death in war, presents a marvelous combination of comic and tragic models. While scenes of slaves bearing burdens provided a standard source of laughs in Old Comedy, as in the opening of Aristophanes' *Frogs*, here the tone is somber, and Daos' vivid description of the night raid in which his master's death (supposedly) occurred derives from the messenger speeches of tragedy. The *Shield* is also the most metatheatrical of known Menandrian dramas, and as such an important forerunner of Plautus' even more involved play with playwriting. Cleostratus' miserly uncle Smicrines asserts his right under Athenian law to marry his niece, in order to get his hands on her new-found wealth from the Lycian booty. But the girl is happily betrothed to the stepson of her younger uncle Chaerestratus, and Daos proposes to prevent the misfortune that would result from Smicrines' villainy by means of a play within a play. In addition, by granting the prologue to personified Fortune (Tyche), Menander encourages the audience to understand that this play dramatizes the mechanics of a comic plot with its reversal in fortune. Those in on the stratagem pretend that Chaerestratus has been struck by a sudden illness, and a "doctor," costumed in disguise and sporting a fake Doric accent, declares his imminent death. The point of tricking Smicrines with this feigned "tragedy," as Daos calls it, is to induce him to give up his claim to Cleostratus' sister through expectation of marrying the even wealthier daughter of Chaerestratus. Although most of the second half of the play is lost, we do know that Cleostratus returns to save his sister from Smicrines and that the fifth act ends with a double marriage, as Cleostratus weds Chaerestratus' daughter and his sister marries her betrothed. Whether Smicrines, Menander's most villainous character, was reformed in some way or punished, perhaps just with his own self-isolation, is unknown because of the loss of the play's conclusion.

The presentation of erotic anguish, for which Menander was famous in later antiquity, appears most clearly in his plays about soldiers. The comic stereotype was of the braggart soldier (as in Plautus' *Miles Gloriosus*), who offended with exaggerated claims of his military exploits but was conquered and humiliated by his love for some girl. Menander brilliantly manipulates the audience's sympathies with the tension between their loathing of the soldier's abusive behavior and the tender feelings that drive his actions. In the *Girl with Cut Hair* (*Perikeiromenē*) Glycera dramatically appears at the play's opening with shorn tresses, the result of a

jealous rage on the part of her lover, the soldier Polemon. A personification of Misconception (Agnoia) then explains in the prologue that
Polemon has misinterpreted Glycera's embrace of Moschion, the brother
from whom she was separated at birth. The plot involves an attempt to
win Glycera back by assault on the neighboring house where she has taken
refuge, but despite this heavy-handed approach Polemon's tender description of his mistress and the finery he has given her reveal a genuine love
for the girl. The happy ending involves not only Glycera's discovery of her
father but also the emotional reconciliation of the couple as she forgives
Polemon for his abusive action and he promises to give up the violent life
of a soldier. In the opening scene of the *Hated Man* (*Misoumenos*), where
the soldier Thrasonides appears at night outside of his house to lament
that his mistress Crateia now refuses a sexual relationship with him, it is,
again, the incongruity of the soldier's tender feelings for the girl and his
violent tendencies that drives the emotional aspects of the plot. Crateia,
we learn, has rejected her lover because she believes he killed her brother
in battle. In the end, of course, she is reunited with both her father and her
brother, found still alive, but the marriage with Thrasonides is settled only
after Crateia freely agrees that it pleases her.

The *Men at Arbitration* (*Epitrepontes*), containing one of Menander's most
intricately constructed plots, involves a young couple whose marriage is
endangered when the wife Pamphile gives birth to a child only five
months after the wedding. Charisius, who loves his wife, attempts to
deal with his distress over the pregnancy by partying with a hetaira
Habrotonon. Pamphile's father Smicrines plays the role of the blocking
figure by attempting to get his daughter to end the marriage, but only
because he does not understand what is motivating Charisius' behavior.
He is unaware of the pregnancy, since it was kept secret and the child
exposed. In understanding why his ignorance was plausible to an ancient
audience, we should keep in mind the seclusion of Athenian citizen
women. The men who require arbitration are a shepherd and charcoal
burner, who are involved in the baby's rescue and argue over possession of
the tokens left with it. Ironically, Smicrines, the child's grandfather, serves
as arbitrator of the dispute, but without ever recognizing the identity of the
infant. Since one of these tokens is a ring that Pamphile acquired when she
was raped during a nighttime festival, it is finally revealed, with the help of
Habrotonon, that the rapist was in fact Charisius, then a stranger. So by
this improbable but plausible series of events Pamphile, Charisius, and
their child are united as a family bound together by both blood and law.
How to reestablish the bond of trust and love between the couple is the
more difficult question, and it is here that Menander excels. He creates a
scene in which Charisius overhears Pamphile refuse to abandon their

marriage even though she believes that he, her husband, has fallen in love with Habrotonon; as a result, Charisius recognizes his wife's nobility of character, her willingness to forgive his misbehavior, in contrast to his own resentment at her giving birth to a child seemingly fathered by another man. By admitting to Pamphile his own character flaw and recognizing that moral behavior involves acceptance of imperfection as well as one's own right action, Charisius manages to reestablish his marriage on a steady course.

The *Samia* is, arguably, the best of Menander's known plays. As in the *Men at Arbitration*, none of the main characters is villainous; rather, the complications of the plot result from misunderstandings and typical emotional reactions. Consequently, the characters all transcend their comic types to appear fully human. Once again a young man, Moschion, has impregnated a girl during a rape at a festival, but he loves her and intends to marry her. The problem is that the wedding cannot be arranged until his adoptive father Demeas and the girl's father Niceratus return from a long business trip. In the meantime the girl has given birth. To avoid scandal, Demeas' concubine Chrysis, who cannot produce legitimate heirs for Demeas because she is a Samian of the hetaira class and not a marriageable citizen of Athens, is pretending that the baby is her own. When Demeas returns, he is unhappy that Chrysis has not exposed the child that he assumes is their illegitimate offspring, but since he is a good-natured sort, he seems likely to forgive her – until he overhears a slave speaking of Moschion as the father and jumps to the conclusion that Chrysis and his son are the baby's parents. Deeply hurt because of the assumed betrayal, and now inwardly seething with rage, he expels Chrysis, whom he clearly loves, from his house. In a beautifully constructed scene involving Demeas, Moschion, and Niceratus, Moschion gradually recognizes his father's mistake and so admits the truth about his rape of Niceratus' daughter. Demeas is quick to support his son, and once he soothes his more irascible friend Niceratus, the marriage is arranged. As usual, there remains a complication: Moschion now decides to punish his father for suspecting him of an affair with Chrysis by pretending to join a mercenary expedition. It is perhaps the finest final act in extant Menander, as Demeas gently reminds his son that not holding grudges but accepting human fallibility is what it means to be a family. In this play in which Demeas' household is constructed not through blood ties but through adoption and an irregular romantic liaison, Menander shows us that the true basis for happy family life is an active choice to love, understand, and forgive.

Menander's plays have a clear relationship to the political and intellectual climate of his era. Although the biting political/social satire of earlier comedy had been in decline throughout the fourth century, the control exerted by external powers over early Hellenistic Athens pushed its citizens toward a focus on the personal problems of individuals and families rather than larger issues addressed in fifth-century drama. At the same time, philosophy had turned away from the transcendent idealism of Plato to a concern with the perceivable world around us; as a result, ethical behavior was a topic of particular importance for the intellectuals of the age. For Aristotle in his *Nicomachean Ethics* and *Eudemian Ethics*, the question of absolute right or wrong was less compelling than asking what was fair or equitable under a given set of circumstances; he also argues that the degree of relationship between individuals was an important factor in determining how they should treat each other. A work called *Characters* written by Aristotle's follower Theophrastus describes, entertainingly, the human traits that accompany individuals of certain personality types. Menander was not simply dramatizing Aristotelian ethical views, nor did his stock comic types match Theophrastus' characterizations. Nevertheless, it is clear that he shares with these philosophical thinkers a certain view of human action and relationships. For Menander, as for Aristotle, a central human problem is how to deal with the messiness of life, given our tendency toward misconception and our susceptibility to emotional forces, and for both of them the answer involves basic human decency and a willingness to cement personal relationships through bonds of affection. While for Aristotle philosophical understanding is the key to such a right way of living, Menander's comedies suggest that the goal is achievable for anyone, rich and poor, male and female, slave and free. It is this that made his plays so appealing to ancient audiences and ultimately, though indirectly, spawned the long tradition of comedy of manners.

3.2   Callimachus

With the force of his remarkable intellect, Callimachus reinvented Greek poetry for the Hellenistic age by devising a personal style that came, through its manifestations in Roman poetry, to influence the entire tradition of modern literature. In the amazing range of his writings, he eludes classification. He prided himself on his *polyeideia,* or ability to compose in various poetic genres and dialects, while the subject matter of his poetry often intersects with the topics he discussed in his over eight hundred prose works as well as in his prodigious activity as a bibliographer. Controversy always followed him, and the reason was apparently both his poetic originality and his personal contentiousness. His aesthetic focus on the small, detailed, precise, and refined instead of the grand and weighty sparked criticism from those with more eclectic tastes; in turn, he viewed contemporary poets, from his position at the center of Alexandrian intellectual life, with either strong distaste (a group including Asclepiades and Posidippus, less certainly Apollonius) or strong admiration (certainly Aratus, probably Theocritus). The continuance of disagreement about Callimachus' aesthetics long after his death demonstrates his lasting importance. Several Alexandrian scholars of the next generation carried on his approach to literary criticism, and as late as the first century AD their descendants, grammarians who picked apart poetry for minor inaccuracies, were satirized as "bitter and dry dogs of Callimachus" (*Palatine Anthology* 11.322). These ancient assessments of Callimachean scholarship have, misleadingly, supported a modern view of the master as a sterile and erudite poet, more interested in word games than in emotional appeal. But in fact the poetry of Callimachus, more than that of any other Greek figure, animated the personal tone and complex allusiveness of Latin poetry in the late Republican and Augustan ages. The prologue to the *Aetia*, with its dense concentration of poetic metaphors (see Ch. 2.1), was the single most imitated passage in Latin poetry. Ovid's reference to Callimachus as "strong in art though not in genius" (*Amores* 1.15.14), often cited as a judgment on the Alexandrian's poetic limitations, was in fact offered as an explanation of his poetic immortality. Ovid's words succinctly summarize Callimachus' central belief that knowledge and technical skill, not simply talent, make the poet.

Although most of Callimachus' poetry cannot be precisely dated, we do know that he was writing, for the Ptolemaic court at Alexandria, from about 280 to after the ascension of Berenice II in 246/5. He was a native of Cyrene, an old Greek colony just to the east of Egypt, which was under Ptolemaic control during the earlier and later years of Callimachus' life. He came from a leading Cyrenaean family, and according to one source served as "youth at court," an official position held by aristocratic young men from cities allied with the Ptolemies. It is hard to reconcile this account with the more colorful story from the *Suda* (a tenth-century AD Byzantine compilation) that he came to the notice of Ptolemy Philadelphus when he was teaching school in the Alexandrian suburb of Eleusis, although his own claims to poverty in some of his epigrams may support the anecdote. The report in the *Suda* biography that his parents were named Battus and Mesatma and that he married the daughter of one Euphrates of Syracuse has more the ring of authenticity. In two sepulchral epigrams (*Palatine Anthology* 7.415, 7.525), written as self-epitaphs, he declares himself the grandson of another Callimachus, who was a Cyrenaean general, and calls himself Battiades, "son of Battus."

Again, though, his poetry may have led to mistakes in his biography. Battus was the legendary founder of Cyrene, whose name meant "stammerer" or "weak-voiced" (*ischnophōnus*),[3] and it is just possible that Callimachus is giving himself this nickname to insinuate both his noble Cyrenaean ancestry and his own stylistic manner of "dry" or "slender" (*ischnos*) speech. Despite his prolific output in both prose and poetry, there survive in manuscript, in addition to several hundred short fragments, only his six *Hymns* and about sixty epigrams. His most famous works, the *Aetia* and the *Hecale*, as well as his *Iambi* and a few lyric poems, became known during the twentieth century from a series of papyrological finds. As a result, the assessment of Callimachus and his influence, from knowledge of what he actually wrote, is still an ongoing process.

Although Callimachus never held the official position of librarian in Alexandria, his work with the Ptolemaic book collection was of utmost importance. He produced, in 120 bookrolls, a sort of catalogue entitled *Lists of those Distinguished in Every Branch of Learning and their Writings*. These *Lists* (*Pinaces*) were organized by literary genre and included authors' names in alphabetical arrangement, biographical data, the titles of their works, and probably the opening words of each work and the number of lines in it. Callimachus' cataloguing work was the basis for the later bibliographies of antiquity, and it involved much more than just listing. The cataloguer had to identify the correct genre, distinguish between authors with similar names, assemble biographical data, and decide about the authenticity of possibly spurious works. Although Callimachus surely had assistants for this enormous task of sifting through the thousands of bookrolls collected by the Ptolemies, he likely made the trickier decisions personally. From the same desire to collect and organize information, much in the Peripatetic tradition, came his prose works, which have such titles as *Foundations of Islands and Cities and their Names*, *On the Rivers of Europe*, *On Wonders and Miracles in the Peloponnesus and Italy*, *On the Names of Fish*, *On Winds*, and *On Birds*. While earlier Greek writers tended to focus on the traditions of their own *polis* and a few Panhellenic stories of the mythical past, Callimachus, from his position within the vast collection of material in the Ptolemaic library, looked at the Hellenic world more holistically, in terms of how its various components, both natural and institutional, could be organized and understood.

Callimachus' most influential and original poetic work was the *Aetia*, published in four books. This long poem in elegiac couplets consisted of a series of disconnected aetiologies, or explanations for the origin of some current circumstance, such as an unusual ritual, a monument, a constellation, anything with roots in the past, yet still to be seen. In addition to book fragments, the *Aetia* is known to us from a good number of papyri,

He wrote one book long after the others.

most containing lines of poetry and one preserving the *Diegeseis*, ancient summaries of the episodes. The date of the poem is problematic. Some of the episodes seem to belong to the earlier part of Callimachus' career, but others come from a later period of activity, these being the prologue in which the poet speaks of himself as an old man and the episodes that begin Book 3 and end Book 4 concerning Berenice II, who became queen in 246/5. The most common scholarly explanation is that the first two books were composed when Callimachus was still a relatively young man and the last two much later when the aetiologies concerning Berenice, who was from Callimachus' native Cyrene, were of current interest; the epilogue was clearly added at the time of this final organization, and perhaps the prologue as well.

The poet uses a different method of linking the episodes in the two halves of his work. Just after the prologue Callimachus reports that as a young man he dreamed of being transported to Mt. Helicon in Boeotia. He here alludes to the famous scene of poetic inspiration in the *Theogony*, where Hesiod tells how, when he was pasturing his sheep on Mt. Helicon, the Muses appeared to grant him poetic skill. Callimachus' encounter with these goddesses is quite different. Instead of their breathing into him some mysterious poetic power or knowledge, they rather satisfy his curiosity about the origins of unusual customs by answering his questions; this Q&A is then reported in the poem as a series of aetiologies. It is not clear, however, how far Callimachus' fantasy of directly accessing the knowledge of the Muses was carried through the entire four books of the *Aetia*. In an episode that may have begun the second book (frs. 178–85), the poet attends an Alexandrian dinner party, where the Attic festival of the Anthesteria was being celebrated, and he asks the man reclining next to him, a stranger from the island of Icos, to explain why the Icians grant cult honors to the Thessalian Peleus, Achilles' father. Here the questioning of the Muses is replaced by a scene representing what was likely a common source of Callimachus' information, conversations with the many Greek visitors to Alexandria. When Callimachus characterizes himself and his dining companion as water drinkers who prefer sober talk to the drunken partying of those celebrating the Dionysian Anthesteria in the more normal fashion, he is clearly substituting rational, often systematic acquisition of knowledge for the heady inspiration of the Muses.

In Books 3 and 4 the Muses are no longer in evidence, and the aetiologies are presented directly by the poet-narrator, who acknowledges his own researches and observations as the source for his poetic subject matter. At the conclusion of the Acontius and Cydippe episode from Book 3 (frs. 67–75), Callimachus reports that this story "flowed down to his Calliope" (one of the Muses) from the prose accounts of Xenomedes of Ceos, a fifth-century chronicler. In contrast to this footnote-like ending, the episode itself is one of the most charming in the *Aetia* and often echoed in Roman erotic poetry. It concerns the desire of Acontius, an aristocratic youth from Ceos, to marry Cydippe, an equally elite young woman from the island of Naxos. His strategy, taught him by Eros, was to roll toward her an apple inscribed with an oath to marry him. It happened that Artemis was present at the moment Cydippe picked up the apple and read aloud the oath, so that the girl became bound by it. After three failed attempts to wed her to another, her father discovered through an oracle her unwitting commitment to Acontius, and so the young man happily obtained his bride. While Callimachus' scholarly researches into obscure customs would seem to make him an unlikely erotic poet, a few key passages, such as the Acontius and Cydippe story and the final "Lock of Berenice" (as well as his erotic epigrams), won him a reputation as the principal model, together with Philitas, for the later Roman love elegists.

The innovative quality of the *Aetia* needs to be assessed against the background of earlier narrative elegy. We now know that narratives in elegiac couplets existed already in the archaic age, alongside epic poetry. Although our evidence is meager, it seems likely that longer elegies were typically used for local myths, recounting city foundings and cataloguing legendary ancestors of elite families: the lost *Smyrneis* of the seventh-century poet Mimnermus, to which Callimachus may allude in his prologue, was likely of this type. Whether Mimnermus framed his legendary accounts of his hometown Smyrna, on the coast of Asia Minor, with personal references is unclear, although some scholars have identified the *Smyrneis* with his *Nanno*, the name of a mistress. A later poet from the same district, Antimachus of Colophon, whose elegiac *Lyde* belongs to the early fourth century, gave as an excuse for telling a series of mythical stories the need to console himself for the death of his beloved Lyde. The stylistic quality of Antimachus' episodic elegy, in at least two books, became a lightning rod for critical discussion of poetics in the early Hellenistic period (see Ch. 2.1), with Callimachus taking a critical view of the *Lyde* as "fat," or not refined. Quite possibly more to his liking was another poet from Colophon, Hermesianax, a friend of Philitas and so active in the early third century. He composed an elegiac work called *Leontion* in three books, a work that, like the *Lyde* and Mimnermus' *Nanno*, was inspired by a courtesan he loved. The first two books of the *Leontion*, lost but for one line, included a number of erotic stories, including the Cyclops' love for the sea nymph Galatea (later the subject of Theocritus' *Idyll* 11; fr. 1 Powell, p. 96) and the passion of Daphnis, a bucolic hero in Theocritus, for another herdsman Menalcas (fr. 2 Powell). About Book 3 we know more, since there survives from it a catalogue, in nearly one hundred lines (fr. 7 Powell, pp. 98–100),[4] concerning the women loved by famous poets and philosophers. The chronological list of poets begins with Orpheus, who tried to rescue his dead wife (called Eurydice in later accounts, but here Agriope) from Hades, and ends with Philitas, whose love is named Bittis (or Battis?). Of philosophers he mentions the geometer Pythagoras, Socrates, and the hedonist Aristippus. But the list of loves of Hermesianax's catalogue is exceedingly odd, since, for instance, Homer loves Penelope, the lyric poet Alcaeus loves his compatriot Sappho, and Socrates loves Aspasia, the intellectual companion of Pericles. What becomes clear is that Hermesianax is playing with the tradition of elegiac narrative catalogues, to make the point that great intellectuals are driven by passions, either for certain subjects (Penelope) or certain models (Sappho, Aspasia). The wife of Orpheus, the earliest Greek singer/poet, surely represents the natural song of uncivilized people, since Agriope means "wild-voiced" (cf. the Muse Calliope, "beautiful-voiced"), and Philitas' Bittis/Battis seems to represent his passion for studying odd words. The importance of the *Leontion* for Callimachus was that Hermesianax apparently pointed the way to a more playful, idiosyncratic, subjective style of elegy, in which stories are not told in a linear fashion, but shaped by the narrator's personal patterns of thought.

Indeed, one of the most influential features of the *Aetia* was the insertion of the poet's own voice into the narrative. One example of this innovatively intrusive narrator comes from the Acontius and Cydippe story. Toward the end of that episode, the poet describes Acontius' joy in consummating his marriage with Cydippe as follows (fr. 75.44–9):

> Not do I think, Acontius, that in place of that night
>> When you touched her maiden's girdle
> You would have chosen Iphicles' swiftness to run upon
>> Cornstalks nor the wealth of Midas of Celaenae,
> And all those who have experienced the difficult god
>> Would witness to the correctness of my opinion.

No spicy details of the wedding night are given us, through which we might spy on the happy couple or vicariously enjoy their lovemaking, as somehow like our own experiences. Rather, the poet presents his personal sense of what his passion must have been like, that is, better than possessing the swiftness of foot that would bring athletic victory or the boundless wealth of a king. These are choices that, in the poet's own opinion ("I think," he says), Acontius would not have preferred, and he is so certain of his understanding of the young lover that he even addresses him here, a hint that Acontius has existence – as the imagined subject of Callimachus' tale. The poet's personality comes out in another way as well, through his allusive and learned style. The reader is expected to activate prior knowledge in order to understand that Iphicles was a mythical runner so swift he sailed over the tops of grain, to remember that King Midas' golden touch assured his fabulous wealth, and to identify the difficult god as Eros. Reminiscent of Hermesianax is not only the learnedness of the style and the general objectivity of the narrative, here derived from an acknowledged prose source, but also the sympathetic linkage between poet and his subject as Callimachus conveys the depth of Acontius' happiness in winning his beloved. Since Callimachus begins the episode with the statement that Eros helped the clueless, lovelorn Acontius by teaching him "art" (*technē*, fr. 67.3), we might read here Acontius' desire for Cydippe – on the model of Hermesianax's lovers of poetic mistresses – as an emblem of the poet's own creative desires, likewise fulfilled through the exercise of art.

Callimachus' strongly marked personality reveals itself in other ways as well, such as through deflection of the grand to the mundane. An example occurs in the so-called "Victory of Berenice," a celebration of the queen's chariot victory in the Panhellenic games at Nemea (frs. 254–68 Lloyd-Jones and Parsons). This first episode in Book 3 was patterned on the epinician odes of Pindar, in which an athletic victor's triumph was mirrored in, and so aggrandized by, a story from the mythical past. In a similar way, Callimachus punctuates the celebration of the victory with an aetiological story, that of Heracles' founding of the Nemean games by killing a lion. But his manner of telling the well-known myth, the first of Heracles' twelve labors, is to focus on a nonheroic and otherwise unknown subsidiary event, his visit to the hut of a poor peasant named Molorchus. The Molorchus story contains (in Chinese box fashion) yet another aetiology, as the poet explains how the good peasant had dealt with a threat to his personal wellbeing – a plague of mice – by inventing the mousetrap. In Callimachus' oblique narrative style, Molorchus' triumph over his pesky tormentors replaces the famed story of Heracles killing the Nemean lion, the mundane mirroring the heroic, mirroring in turn the contemporary achievement of Callimachus' own queen. The poet must have known, from personal familiarity, that Cyrenaean Berenice shared his taste for wit and irony, since this playful form of praise is vastly different from the earlier epinician poetry of Pindar or known instances of Hellenistic sycophancy, such as the Athenian hymn for Demetrius Poliorcetes (see Ch. 1.1).

The final *aition*, the "Lock of Berenice" (fr. 110), also provides a quirky and specifically Callimachean perspective on contemporary Ptolemaic events. The episode was long known in only a few Greek quotations and more fully through a Latin translation in Catullus 66, which provided the model for Pope's "Rape of the Lock." But, again, from papyrus discoveries of the early twentieth century, more substantial portions of the Greek text have become known. The poem was written to commemorate, and apparently to shape, public understanding of a specific event associated with the political marriage of Ptolemy III Euergetes to Berenice of Cyrene. When Ptolemy marched off to a war in Syria and left behind his new bride, the queen dedicated a lock of her hair in the temple of Aphrodite with a prayer for his safe return. When the goddess transported the lock to the sky, the astronomer Conon of Samos spotted it there as a new constellation, the one still known today by its Latin name of Coma Berenices. All of this must have been engineered by the court as a kind of foundational story for the third generation of the Ptolemaic dynasty. Callimachus' contribution to the effort (after Conon had done his part) was to give the events a pleasing and memorable poetic form. He chose to deal with the difficulty of telling this implausible story by impersonating, tongue in cheek, the lock itself, and this lock, though recognizing the great honor of its catasterism, nevertheless laments its separation from the adored queen. Once again, Callimachus deals with an erotic story by deflection, as the lock's longing for Berenice is amply explored, in substitution for direct exploration of the queen's longing for her bridegroom. It was one of the most successful solutions to the problem of writing light and refined poetry that yet promotes the political agenda of monarchs who were on the road to divinity.

In the epilogue to the *Aetia*, Callimachus declares that he will now pass on to the "pedestrian field of the Muses" (fr. 112.9). This phrase (translated by *pedestris Musa* in Horace *Satires* 2.6.17) refers to his book of thirteen *Iambi*, which, written mostly in limping choliambs, revive the critical, satirical tone of the archaic iambographers. The poems themselves remain quite fragmentary, but the prose summaries, or *Diegeseis*, preserve the sequence and main topics. The *Iambi* allow Callimachus to adopt a moralistic tone in order to comment on the issues of interest to him, which mostly involve personal relationships and aesthetics, not politics or ethics. In the first *Iambus* the sixth-century iambographer Hipponax of Ephesus returns from the dead to harangue the scholars in Alexandria about their quarrelsomeness. Other *Iambi* draw upon the fables of Aesop, which circulated in a subliterary fashion as stories with variable wording, though Demetrius of Phalerum, and perhaps others before him, produced a fixed text. In the second *Iambus* the story of how Zeus once transferred the power of speech from animals to humans illustrates what is wrong with various types of literature: writers have inherited the loquacious speech that once characterized different types of animals. In *Iambus* 4 a debate between a laurel and an olive exemplifies the alternative positions of arrogant self-assertion or pretended modesty that could be adopted in contemporary literary debates. Other *Iambi* again involve aetiologies, while Callimachus' interest in aesthetic issues seems to underlie the three that concern statues – the great cult statue of Zeus at Olympia by Phidias (*Iambus* 6), a wooden statue of Hermes in Thrace carved by Epeius, who made the Trojan horse (*Iambus* 7), and a statue of Hermes with erect phallus addressed by a lover of boys in a wrestling ground (*Iambus* 9). This theme of the parallel between poetry and art culminates in *Iambus* 12, our earliest extant birthday poem (for a little girl), where Callimachus makes explicit the superiority of poetry to crafted objects by claiming that Apollo's gift of song for the little goddess Hebe was better than the golden toys brought by other gods. In the last *Iambus* the poet defends himself against those who criticize him for composing in various genres, meters, and dialects (his *polyeideia*), by pointing out that no one complains about a carpenter who crafts many different objects. Overall, Callimachus' revival of the abusive tone of archaic iambography suited his polemical nature; his thirteen *Iambi*, carefully arranged in a poetry book with opening and closing poems that set out his poetic agenda, became a primary model for the later Roman satires of Lucilius and Horace.

In the sequence of *Diegeseis*, four lyric poems follow the *Iambi*, although it is not clear that they constituted a separate poetry book. Horace's seventeen *Epodes*, an unusual number for a book of poems, suggest that he read the thirteen *Iambi* and the four melic poems as a single unit. But given the finalizing nature of *Iambus* 13, it is not likely Callimachus intended the lyric pieces to be a continuation of his iambic book. Of the fragmentary lyric poems the best preserved is the "Apotheosis of Arsinoe." Surely written shortly after the queen's death in 270 or 268, the poem describes how she was snatched away by the Dioscuri, Castor and Polydeuces, and taken to assume her new life as a goddess. Callimachus charmingly and pathetically describes her sister Philotera, who had predeceased Arsinoe and was already divinized, noticing from the island of Lemnos the smoke of the funeral pyre and sending Hephaestus' wife Charis to the peak of Mt. Athos to discover what was happening in her beloved Egypt (fr. 228).

Following the lyric poems in the *Diegeseis* comes the *Hecale*, Callimachus' one attempt to write a mythological narrative in dactylic hexameter. Because this poem was probably only about 1,000–1,200 lines long, short enough to fit on one bookroll, it has come to be called an "epyllion" in the sense of "little epic," although the term was not so used in Callimachus' day. A scholium (on *Hymn* 2.106) reports that Callimachus was compelled to write the *Hecale* by those who mocked him for not being able to compose a poem of sustained length. Apparently, then, this epyllion represented Callimachus' view of what Hellenistic mythological narrative should look like. Its structure is surprisingly similar to that of the first episode in Book 3 of the *Aetia*, the Heracles and Molorchus story. Ostensibly, it recounts an exploit of the young Athenian hero Theseus, who rid the district about Marathon of a destructive wild bull. In fact, the poem was primarily concerned with the old woman Hecale, who gave Theseus a night's shelter from a storm as he was on his way to Marathon. Callimachus described in detail the humble fare offered by Hecale as an evening meal and the equally humble furnishings supplied for the young man's bed. The point was clearly the contrast between the elderly woman's poverty and her good-heartedness, a theme that reappears as well in the Baucis and Philemon episode in Ovid's *Metamorphoses* (8.617–724). Only snippets of their after-dinner conversation remain, but it appears that Hecale revealed her former life as an upper-class woman and how she had lost her sons, one of whom had been killed by a brigand who terrorized the Isthmus between Corinth and Attica. Since Theseus had rid the Isthmus of its murderous villains, we can imagine that a strong bond was forged between the heroic youth and the sad but kind old woman. Much of the charm of the poem lay in the details of their conversation, as, for instance, when Hecale describes meeting a handsome man, perhaps her future husband (fr. 253.10–12 Pfeiffer = fr. 42.4–6 Hollis): "I remember his lovely . . . cloak held with golden brooches, the work of spiders." In typical Callimachean fashion, the narration of the bull's capture on the following day was passed over in favor of an indirect report of peripheral events, presented as a conversation between two birds. One, a crow, describes to the other the heroic welcome given Theseus when he returned from his exploit and then recounts how crows were once turned from white to black for revealing bad news to Athena. The point of this bird aetiology seems to be a warning to the listening bird, of unknown species, not to bring to Theseus the bad news of Hecale's death. The epyllion ended with Theseus establishing an annual festival, called Hecale's Dinner, in honor of his hostess, as well as founding a sanctuary for Zeus Hecaleius and naming an Attic deme, or district, after her. The poem is thus another of Callimachus' aetiologies, a version of a heroic exploit updated to focus on remembrance of an old woman's kindness. The poem's celebration of humble nobility of spirit is well conveyed by a fragment preserving words of farewell to Hecale (fr. 263 Pfeiffer = fr. 80 Hollis):

> Go, gentle woman,
> On that road not traveled by griefs that pain the heart.
> Often, good mother, we will remember the hospitality
> Of your hut, for it was a common sanctuary for everyone.

The *Aetia*, *Iambi*, and *Hecale*, all substantially recovered now from papyri, were much more influential in antiquity than Callimachus' *Hymns*, which happened to be preserved in manuscript. But the six *Hymns* – to Zeus, Apollo, Artemis, the island of Delos (as the birthplace of Apollo), Athena, and Demeter – are nonetheless fascinating examples of Callimachus' literary response to the new world order being constructed in Ptolemaic Alexandria. Callimachus modeled his hymns, all but one in dactylic hexameters, not only on the archaic *Homeric Hymns*, composed in epic meter, but also on lyric hymns, such as those by Pindar, that were originally sung. The task of praising the Olympian deities was vastly complicated by the now common practice of identifying monarchs, overtly when dead and more subtly while alive, with divine beings. This was happening in varying degrees in all the Hellenistic kingdoms, but in Egypt the process was influenced by the native tradition of viewing the pharaoh and his sister-wife as gods incarnate. The deities celebrated in Callimachus' *Hymns* preserve their traditional Greek attributes and character, but they also reflect, usually indirectly, his Ptolemaic patrons.

The arrangement of the first four *Hymns* to focus on the triad of Zeus and his twin children by Leto is particularly telling. From the time of Ptolemy I, the Greek kings of Egypt presented themselves as earthly instantiations of Zeus, and from the time of his successors, the Philadelphoi, brother–sister pairs were the desired pattern for dynastic marriage. The Greek divine model for brother–sister marriage was clearly Zeus and Hera, but the twin siblings Apollo and Artemis provided another mythical lens through which to view the cooperative activities of Ptolemy Philadelphus and his sister Arsinoe. In addition, through his support for the arts, Ptolemy II was naturally associated with Apollo, the chosen patron god of Callimachus' poetry. The god himself draws the parallel in the fourth *Hymn*, when, prophesying from the womb, he urges his mother Leto to avoid Cos, where the second Ptolemy is destined to be born, and instead to seek out Delos (another Ptolemaic protectorate) as his own birthplace. While the *Hymns*, or some of them, may have originated as occasional poems composed for festivals, probably in Alexandria, they nonetheless bear the stamp of Callimachus' personality and aesthetic preferences and, whatever their original function, whether for performance or as book poetry, they should be analyzed as sophisticated literary works.

Three of the *Hymns*, those for Zeus, Artemis, and Delos, appear to be spoken in the voice of the composer. In this respect, they follow the model of the *Homeric Hymns*. But Callimachus' narrative emphases give these poems a flavor that is characteristically his own. He imaginatively conceives the stable geography of the world he knew as the result of past actions of the gods, who move with ease across the landscape as if in a different dimension of space. In the "Hymn to Zeus," for instance, the rivers of Arcadia came into being when Rhea, needing to wash after giving birth to Zeus, struck a mountain and loosed their waters. The Plain of the Navel in Crete acquired its name as the place where Zeus' umbilical cord fell off as a nymph was carrying him from Arcadia to Mt. Dicte on Crete. The story of how Rhea hid her youngest son from his father Cronus, who was swallowing his children as they were born, was told in Hesiod's *Theogony*. Callimachus simply assumes that his audience is familiar with the ancient story and focuses instead on how these events helped to shape the world as it existed in his own day. The central story of the "Hymn to Delos" also concerns geography, as Leto searches throughout the Mediterranean basin for a place to give birth to Apollo. The islands, mountains, and rivers, conceived both as actual places and as deities resident in the landscape, flee when she approaches fearing the anger of Hera. Only the small and pure Asteria, later Delos, though then a floating island, is brave enough to give her shelter, and for her service she is rewarded with a fixed place in the Aegean and honors from Apollo. In the "Hymn to Artemis" Callimachus describes how the goddess's attributes and cult associations resulted from her assertion of her character as a maiden huntress when she was but a child. When Artemis sits on the lap of her father Zeus to ask for gifts – perpetual maidenhood, as many epithets as her brother Apollo, a small tunic for hunting, choruses of nymphs all nine years old, and the mountains, all of them, but no cities – Callimachus creates for us not only the tone of a spoiled little girl but, perhaps as well, some hint of the behavior of imperious Ptolemaic princesses, demanding from an indulgent father the most extravagant of gifts.

The voice heard in the other three *Hymns* is that of ritual participants present at the very moment of the ceremony, although the poet's own interested self intrudes in various ways to complicate the illusion of dramatic representation. The "Hymn to Apollo," representing the celebration of the Carneia in Callimachus' hometown of Cyrene, begins with the announcement of the god's epiphany at the temple and a call for the chorus of young men to sing and dance. As in the other two mimetic hymns (5 and 6), it seems best to take this opening voice as that of a person in charge of the festival, probably a priest of Apollo, but the lack of any narrative frame also invites the reader to hear the poet's own voice. The choral song then proceeds, although the use of epic hexameters rather than the lyric meters marks it as a mimetic representation of such a song. At the end of the chorus' praise for Apollo, which includes his role in the foundation of Cyrene, there appears a final passage, often called a coda, in

which Apollo rejects the jealous criticism of Callimachus' detractors and
validates his poetic technique (*Hymn* 2.105–12):

> Envy spoke secretly in the ear of Apollo:
> "I don't admire the poet whose song is not as extensive as the sea."
> Apollo kicked Envy with his foot and said this:
> "The Assyrian river has mighty flow, but it carries
> in its water much filth and much trash from the land.
> The Bees do not bring water from everywhere to Deo,
> But only that which flows forth pure and undefiled from
> A holy spring, just a small trickle, the very best of waters."

Here we find the familiar terms in which Callimachus characterizes his
poetic style and manner: the large, polluted river (the Euphrates) emblem-
atizes the grand style that seeks solemnity through excess verbosity, while the
pure droplet from a sacred spring (brought to Demeter by bees, or by
priestesses called Melissae or "Bees") represents Callimachus' preference
for the select and refined. What is not so clear is the source of the voice,
whether it is now the poet marking the poem with his "seal" (*sphragis*), the
person supervising the choral performance, or, less likely, even the chorus
itself. The final effect is to blur the distinction between this very public
celebration of the god and Callimachus' personal claim to Apollo's support.

The fifth and sixth *Hymns* clearly constitute a pair, although the "Bath
of Pallas" is written in elegiac couplets while the "Hymn to Demeter"
returns to hexameters. Both are spoken by a ritual participant, presumably
a priestess, who addresses a chorus of maidens in the first poem and
women celebrants in the second. In each the priestess relates a mythical
story that provides a warning about disrespectful behavior toward the
deity. In the "Bath of Pallas," set at the annual washing of Athena's cult
statue in Argos, the myth concerns Tiresias, the son of one of Athena's
companions; while hunting, he happened to see the goddess nude when
she was bathing at a spring in the mountains. For this offense, she blinded
him but gave in compensation, because of her friendship with his mother
Chariclo, the gift of second sight or seership. The priestess offers this story
to ward off the prying eyes of men who might offend the goddess by seeing
her nude statue during the washing ritual.

The "Hymn to Demeter" is set at a celebration of the Thesmophoria, a
festival conducted by women in many Greek communities, from which
men were, again, excluded (as comically depicted in Aristophanes' *Thes-
mophoriazusae*). The dramatized setting for this Thesmophoria is the second day of the festival when the women participants fasted. The priestess's
narrative concerns a young man named Erysichthon who was punished by

Demeter for arrogantly chopping down her sacred grove to build a gigantic banqueting hall. His punishment was insatiable hunger (which the participants must have been feeling), and the description of his plight has a comic tone as he eats up all the goods of his parents' household, including the pet mongoose. Although both these hymns are spoken in the voice of a ritual agent and involve human transgression against a deity with its resulting punishment, it is far from clear that Callimachus intends for his reader to derive any serious moral or religious lesson. Athena's act of blinding an innocent youth in the very presence of his mother seems cruel by any human standard, and Demeter's punishment of the hubristic Erysichthon, though more justified, is ultimately undercut by Callimachus' comic tone, as his parents struggle in vain to avoid the social embarrassment of having a ravenous son. One wonders whether he may have modeled these goddesses, with their absolute power to punish both the morally innocent and the naïvely guilty, on Ptolemaic queens, such as the powerful Arsinoe II. While the male deities in the *Hymns*, Zeus and Apollo, are celebrated as sources of benefit, all the female deities, including Artemis who shoots her bow first at trees, then at wild beasts, and lastly at cities of unjust men, arouse anxiety as sources of vengeful harm. Quite obviously, these hymns were not suitable for performance at the religious ceremonies they depict. They are rather the representation of such a local ceremony (the hymnal equivalent of a Callimachean *aition*) for the enjoyment of a distanced audience, perhaps an audience at a Ptolemaic festival, but ultimately a literary audience of the *Hymns* in book format.

Callimachus' epigrams, of which about sixty survive, are best discussed in the section on the epigrammatic genre (Ch. 3.6). Suffice it to say here that his *Epigrammata* was the most admired single-authored epigram collection of antiquity. Schoolboys studied it, and in the late first century AD Pliny praised its qualities of humanity, charm, and wit (*Epistles* 4.3.3–4). The speaking voice of these poems shows a preference for young males over women as love objects, tells about suffering a period of relative poverty, and identifies certain close personal friends. One of the most famous and admired pieces in his poetic oeuvre is this epigram on the death of an old friend and fellow poet (*Palatine Anthology* 7.80):

> Someone told me of your fate, Heraclitus, and it brought
>   A tear to my eye. I remembered how often the two of us
> Sank the sun with our talk. But you, Halicarnassian friend,
>   Have perhaps been ash for a long, long time.
> Yet your nightingales live on, untouched by the hand
>   Of Hades, the snatcher of all.

Even in this touchingly original commemoration of a lost friendship, Callimachus reveals that his bond with Heraclitus had at its base a common belief in aesthetic principles: Heraclitus' nightingales, as Callimachus calls his supposedly immortal poems, echo the sweet-voiced nightingales that in the prologue to the *Aetia* outdo the migrating cranes and the long shot of bowmen. Ironically, only one of Heraclitus' poems survives, a tender epitaph for a woman who leaves behind one child and takes its twin with her to the grave (*Palatine Anthology* 7.465).

3.3 Apollonius of Rhodes

Among the major poets of third-century Alexandria, only Apollonius chose to write an epic poem. As the one surviving epic composed between the time of Homer's *Iliad* and *Odyssey* and Vergil's *Aeneid*, his *Argonautica*, in 5,835 lines over four books, has considerable importance. Belonging to the familiar category of "quest" narratives, it tells the story of how Jason and the Argonauts journeyed from Greece to Colchis, a land at the furthest ends of the Black Sea, to retrieve the golden fleece. Apollonius modernized this traditional tale for Alexandrian tastes by emphasizing, through aetiology, the lasting effects of the Argonauts' journey, along the Black Sea and then on the return journey through other parts of the world, including North Africa, and by introducing Jason's romance with Medea as the source of the Argonauts' success. Because of the influence of this romantic element on ancient novel and later epic (such as, prominently, Vergil's Dido story), the story pattern of the *Argonautica* came to have a profound effect on narrative patterns in western literature, and even modern adventure film. The long-standing difficulty in interpreting Apollonius involves his relationship to Callimachean aesthetics. While an older strand of scholarship viewed his epic as oppositional to Callimachus' concern with brevity and nonheroic topics, contemporary scholars tend to view the *Argonautica* as a bold attempt to adapt the Alexandrian literary style to the one poetic genre least compatible with it. In support of this view is an emerging understanding that the *Argonautica*, through its reflection of the present in the past, provided a mythical foundation story for the new Ptolemaic kingdom, with its mixture of Greek and Egyptian culture.

Unlike most Ptolemaic poets, who were immigrants, Apollonius was born in Alexandria. Said to be a student of Callimachus, he held the post of librarian for a number of years under Ptolemy Philadelphus, until 245 when the new king appointed Eratosthenes to the position. Two biographies attached to the Apollonian scholia report the colorful story that his first reading of the *Argonautica* in Alexandria was so disastrous he departed for

Rhodes. There he revised the poem, which later received critical acclaim. This story, while explaining why he is called Rhodian, is difficult to synchronize with the more secure information about his appointment as librarian. The old chestnut of Hellenistic scholarship that Callimachus and Apollonius engaged in a bitter quarrel has been almost completely banished from current assessments. Scholars in recent years have emphasized that the sources for this quarrel are late[5] and that Apollonius is missing from a list of Callimachus' critics, satirized as Telchines, in the Florentine scholia to the *Aetia* Prologue. The *Argonautica* contains many verbal parallels to the poetry of Callimachus, and two episodes present material – Heracles' loss of his boy companion Hylas and Polydeuces' boxing contest with the Bebrycian king Amycus – also found in Theocritus (*Idylls* 13 and 22, respectively). These similarities in wording and subject matter probably indicate a close social and intellectual association rather than poetic rivalry. In addition, Apollonius' reuse of Homeric language, to be expected in a mythological epic, follows the practice of his contemporary Alexandrians in glossing difficult words, varying formulaic language, and making meaningful allusions.

It seems most likely, then, that Apollonius was a member of the poetic circle around Callimachus during the heyday of Ptolemaic literary experimentation. His specialty was *ktisis*, or "foundation," poetry, which narrated mythical stories about the founding of cities; he wrote poems of this type, lost except for a few fragments (frs. 4–12 Powell, pp. 5–8), for Alexandria itself, Caunus and Cnidus in Caria, Naucratis, the first Greek settlement in Egypt, and Rhodes, his adopted home. If the longest of these fragments, by the "poet of the founding of Lesbos" according to Parthenius (21) (see Ch. 4.5), is indeed by Apollonius, then the romantic theme of a woman's betrayal of her fatherland, so prominent in the *Argonautica*, also appeared in his other foundation poetry. Another lost poem, *Canobus* (frs. 1–3 Powell, pp. 4–5), which concerned the death of Menelaus' helmsman on the shore of Egypt at the future site of Alexandria (also in Nicander, *Theriaca* 309–19, quoted in Ch. 3.5), fits with his interest in delineating mythical origins for Ptolemaic cities. The *Argonautica*, as his masterpiece, apparently builds on these simpler and presumably shorter narratives.

Structurally, the four books of the *Argonautica* fall into two halves, organized around the motif of the journey. The first two books report the adventures of the Argonauts from the time they leave Thessaly until they reach Colchis. The narrative for this first half is crisp and episodic, divided by references to setting sail at dawn or putting in at night. Among the more memorable events are these: an interlude spent with the women of Lemnos, who have slaughtered all the male inhabitants of the island,

during which time Jason forms a romantic liaison with their queen
Hypsipyle; Heracles' loss of his boy companion Hylas, who is snatched
by water nymphs, an event that ends with the hero's departure from the
expedition; the Argonauts' rescue of the blind seer Phineus from the
Harpies, who torture him by stealing and fouling his food; their safe
passage through the clashing rocks called Symplegades, when they are
aided by the advice of Phineus and the unseen hand of Athena. In Book 3,
which is the most famous section of the work, the pace slows and narrative
tension builds. There the poet tells of the challenge given Jason by the
Colchian king Aeetes (plowing a field with fire-breathing bulls and killing
the armed men who sprout from sown dragons' teeth) and of the developing romance between Jason and Medea, Aeetes' daughter, who helps
the hero accomplish his task through magic. Book 4 returns to a faster-
paced, almost impressionistic style for the return journey, which involves
the Argonauts' escape from the pursuing Colchians by means of murdering Medea's brother Apsyrtus, the expiation of their resulting blood guilt
by Circe, the marriage of Jason and Medea on the island of the Phae-
acians, and finally a period of near disastrous wandering in the shoals off
North Africa before a rapid return to Thessalian Pagasae.

The epic does not, therefore, focus on a single episode from a mythical
cycle, as the *Iliad* focuses on Achilles' anger over the death of Patroclus,
nor does it have the *in medias res* ("in the middle of the events") structure
of the *Odyssey* and the *Aeneid*, both of which partially relate their hero's
adventures through flashback narrative. The linear, chronological progression of the *Argonautica,* though organized around the journey to and from
Colchis, lacks a certain unifying cohesiveness, because of its emphasis on
episodic narrative (cf. Callimachus' dislike of the "one continuous narrative about kings and heroes," fr. 1.3–5). Part of the reason for this sense of
narrative discontinuity is that the narrator leaves many blanks to be filled
in by the reader, from often contradictory information given in the epic or
from external sources. For instance, the reader is offered multiple, partial,
and sometimes conflicting reports about the reason for the quest for the
fleece. These include Hera's anger at Pelias for neglecting her sacrifice,
Apollo's warning that Pelias should beware a man wearing one sandal,
Pelias' own wicked desire to retain his kingship, and somewhat cryptic
reports of Zeus' anger at the Minyans that could be expiated only by the
retrieval of the fleece. In addition, the adventure ends abruptly, without a
narrative account of their return to Thessaly. The last events that the
narrator describes in any detail concern a ritual to Apollo that the Argonauts established on the Aegean island of Anaphe and a dream by one of
the heroes, Euphemus, concerning a clod of earth that gave birth to a
woman with whom he then slept. The reader clearly needs to have some

external knowledge in order to understand why these events are important enough to usurp the expected homecoming. The story behind the ritual on Anaphe was one of the first aetiologies told in Callimachus' *Aetia*, Book 1 (frs. 7–21), where the return voyage of the Argonauts is briefly related, and it seems likely that the Ptolemies had taken an interest in the cult of Apollo there. Pindar's fourth *Pythian* ode, a victory celebration for the fifth-century Cyrenaean king Arcesilaus, provides crucial background information about the mysterious clod in Euphemus' dream. There the clod is connected with the island of Thera, where Euphemus' descendants (born from the Lemnian women) are destined to live before they migrate to Africa to found the city of Cyrene. The essential conclusion to the Argonautic adventure, then, is not the heroes' return to the Greek mainland but a foreshadowing of the future migration of Greeks to Libya (considered part of Egypt by the Greeks since Herodotus), and the final episode on Anaphe links back to the heroes' first adventure on Lemnos in a kind of a "ring composition." The *Argonautica* is ultimately a foundation story, in which the Argonauts' connection to Africa becomes a mythical precedent for the new Ptolemaic kingdom.

The task of obtaining the golden fleece, from a magical ram that had saved a relative of Jason named Phrixus by carrying him to Colchis, fell to Jason because of his lineage, not his heroic abilities. At the death of his father Aeson, his uncle Pelias had unjustly assumed the throne of Thessaly. When Jason grew to manhood and appeared to Pelias wearing only one sandal (because the other was lost when he rescued Hera, disguised as an old woman, from a river), Pelias devised the quest to recover the fleece as a ploy to get rid of Jason. This background history, well known to ancient readers, is mentioned only elliptically in the introductory lines, and the narrative proper begins with a catalogue of the fifty heroes who joined Jason to sail in the Argo, a special ship constructed with the help of Athena. These Argonauts, who belonged to the Minyan clan, are all sons or grandsons of gods, and many have superhuman powers. Jason, on the other hand, has no special talent, no unusual expertise as a warrior, and no razor-sharp intelligence. One problem in reading the *Argonautica* is to understand what makes Jason a hero. When he first addresses the assembled Argonauts, he asks them to select "the best man" as their leader, and he defines leadership as the ability to deal with the "quarrels and alliances" that will arise as they encounter strange peoples on their journey (1.338–40). The heroes immediately look to Heracles, the mightiest among them, but he declines and indicates that the job should go to that man who assembled them. As the scene suggests, Apollonius appears to be offering a new definition of heroism, for which physical might is of secondary importance. When the Argonauts do become involved in a number of "quarrels," scenes of fighting are briefly described; the events reported in more detail tend rather to involve "alliances," and it is through these that the Argonauts are ultimately successful.

When Jason first speaks in the *Argonautica*, it is to soothe his mother's anxiety as he prepares to set sail. He advises her not to act as a bad omen for the expedition but to put her faith in the favorable oracles of Athena and Apollo and the aid of the heroes who will accompany him. Although a certain callousness typical of the young sounds in Jason's words, the speech also exemplifies the qualities that will eventually carry him through – a pious and trusting attitude toward the gods, faith in his company of heroes, and a manner of speaking that calms and persuades. His ability to put the best face on any situation and to win over the support of others – what we might call his managerial style – proves crucial throughout the adventure. So, for instance, when the Argonauts meet the sons of Phrixus in flight from Aeetes, the king of Colchis who is their grandfather (since his older daughter Chalciope married Phrixus), Jason provides a version of their common family history that convinces them to return to Colchis and help the Argonauts persuade the king to hand over the fleece. Later, in the face of Aeetes' paranoid anger and violent threats, Jason responds with calm reasoning and an offer to compensate for the fleece with mercenary service. The narrator aptly characterizes Jason's demeanor as "fawning with a gentle voice" (3.396). Related is his capacity to forgive and forget, as he does when Telamon accuses him of deliberately abandoning Heracles in Mysia. Much has been made of the fact that the narrator at times reveals Jason's inner state to be one of uncertainty, with feelings of "helplessness" (*amechaniē*) bordering on despair, and in the company of his fellow adventurers he sometimes shows himself overwhelmed by the task at hand. For instance, as soon as the Argonauts have passed safely through the Symplegades (their last trial before reaching Colchis), Jason has a kind of "meltdown," as he expresses regret for exposing the Argonauts to the dangers of the expedition. While such a reaction to release from extreme tension is relatively normal human behavior, it is not typical of heroes. What saves the reader's sympathy for Jason here is awareness that he is reacting to his sense of responsibility for the lives of his companions, not personal fear.

Jason is, then, a new kind of hero for a new kind of world. Gone are the days when a single champion might turn the tide of battle through sheer might (a cultural change symbolized by the loss of Heracles from the journey). Jason's talent lies in his ability to assemble a good team, to win over necessary allies, and to carry the task through to the end. His romance with Medea, the central narrative episode occupying most of Book 3, is the one task for which he is best suited, though also, from the perspective of ethical behavior, his most problematic alliance. While Medea has been driven by Eros into mad love for Jason, his motivation in meeting secretly with her is based on the need to elicit her magic for the task of taming Aeetes' bulls. The narrator reports in detail their private conversation, complete with shy glances and ever bolder promises, but fails to give us full interpretive clues to Jason's emotional state. It is unclear whether he is attracted to Medea or merely doing his job well. The story he tells in order to convince Medea to betray her father Aeetes and her countryland – how Ariadne fell in love with Theseus and helped him to kill the Minotaur – seriously misrepresents this well-known myth; he also omits altogether Theseus' abandonment of Ariadne after their departure from Crete. From this point forward, Jason's moral behavior becomes increasingly problematic. It is his idea to lure Medea's brother Apsyrtus to a secret meeting away from the band of Colchians he leads and then to murder him. While this treachery allows the Argonauts to escape the Colchians, it entails blood guilt (since Medea has murdered a close relative) and brings upon the Argonauts a period of wandering. Unlike Achilles in the *Iliad*, whose undoing stems from his insistence on personal honor at great cost to his fellow warriors, Jason's adaptation of his persuasive powers to the point of murderous deceit and sacrilege is not motivated by personal honor or gain; it is rather in the service of his quest and the safety of his band. Is Apollonius painting a morally complex world in which deceit and wrongdoing may be necessary (and so forgiven) to achieve larger goals? The ancient reader may have found Jason's problematic moral choices to reflect those of contemporary monarchs, whose marriages were usually in support of dynastic alliances and whose family members were all too often expendable in the interest of maintaining sovereignty.

Apollonius assumed that his readers were familiar with certain earlier literary works, most especially Euripides' *Medea*. That play, set in Corinth several years after their marriage, dramatizes Jason's decision to take a new wife and Medea's decision to punish him by slaughtering their children. Apollonius does not directly allude to these later events, but his characterization of the young Medea is clearly constructed as a kind of "prequel" for Euripides' play. The split personality that scholars have so often noticed – part naïve girl infatuated with a handsome stranger, part powerful witch capable of betraying her father and country – is designed to explain her later behavior, how she can make the horrendous choice to murder her beloved children. The narrator's portrait of the young Medea in love is the fullest psychological rendering of erotic desire in Hellenistic poetry, and one of the few presented through an objective narrator rather than subjectively through a lover's own voice. The cause of her sudden,

intense emotional response to the sight of Jason in her father's hall is a tiny
Eros, who enters the hall unseen, crouches beneath Jason's feet, draws his
bow, and shoots Medea in the heart. For the Greeks, desire, like other
emotions, was conceived as a physical reaction to a stimulus, and Apollonius so represents it (3.284–98):

> He shot at Medea, and speechlessness took hold of her soul....
> The shaft burned beneath the girl's heart, like a flame.
> She kept glancing at Jason with sparkling eyes, her breath
> came in panting gasps in her distress, she could think
> of nothing else, and her heart melted with sweet pain.
> As when a poor woman piles twigs around a blazing brand,
> A woman who makes her living by weaving, so that she
> May kindle a fire beneath her roof in the dark when she
> Wakes before dawn, that flame then grows wondrously
> From the small brand and consumes all the kindling,
> Just so destructive Eros curling beneath her heart
> Blazed secretly. Her delicate cheeks kept changing color,
> From pale white to red, because of her mind's distress.

The elaborate simile of the poor woman building a fire is much in the
Homeric manner; yet here the simile is in the service of a quintessentially
Hellenistic subject, a girl's erotic awakening. The now trite image of Eros'
bow as the source of love was in Apollonius' day relatively new, providing
a perfect visual image for the concept of desire as a painful wound in the
internal organs, inflicted suddenly by invisible external forces.

Even so, reason remains as a possible counterforce to the impulse
of desire, and Apollonius gave to Medea the one important scene of
decision-making in the epic. In doing this, he may be alluding to a famous
monologue in Euripides' *Medea* in which the central character debates
whether to murder her children, as she alternates between desire for
revenge against Jason and love for the two boys. Apollonius creates a
similar debate at an earlier point in her life, but represented mostly
through objective narration. As Medea remains alone in her room the
night before she is to meet Jason, her agony gives way to a deep sleep
during which she has a "deceptive dream." In her dream-world construction of reality, Jason has undertaken the trial by bulls simply in order to
carry her home as his wife, and it is she who contends with the bulls and
accomplishes the task. When a quarrel arises between her father and the
strangers about the legitimacy of the contest, Medea is given the responsibility of deciding, and she of course chooses Jason. The dream is
partially misleading wish fulfillment, since Jason is in truth not motivated
by love for Medea. But partially it signals what is true, since Jason's

success is entirely dependent on a choice that belongs to Medea, a choice she will ultimately make on the basis of her emotions, not reason. Awake throughout the rest of the night, Medea agonizes as she is torn between her desire for the stranger and her sense of shame, the emotion that traditionally bound young Greek women to the dictates of their fathers. In the end she decides that her only way out of an impossible choice is suicide, and she is on the point of swallowing poison when dawn breaks and she suddenly recalls the joys of life. This scene is perhaps the most psychologically realistic moment in the epic, as the success of the expedition is decided on the basis of a young girl's natural response to the sweet sight of the morning sun. In addition, Apollonius' portrait of Medea indicates a very real change in attitudes toward women. While in earlier Greek culture powerful female figures were typically an object of fear and often demonized (sometimes literally represented as demons), Medea's psychological bifurcation as a sorceress, who will tame the dragon guarding the fleece and then treacherously kill her own brother (as well as later Pelias and her own children), and as a naïve teenager, driven by the forces of first love, suggests a cultural audience coming to terms with women's power and privilege. Again, we may be reminded of the new roles being played by Hellenistic queens, especially those in Egypt.

The influence of the gods upon human events is a standard part of epic narrative. In Apollonius' account, though the gods do set in motion and look after the Argonautic expedition, their actions are often only partially explained by the narrator or presented from the limited point of view of the characters. As a result, Apollonius' narrator seems at times to lack the omniscient perspective typical of traditional epic. For instance, he offers readers multiple divine explanations for the action, explanations that do not so much complement each other as provide a confusing, overdetermined causality. For instance, at the opening of Book 1 we are told of Hera's anger at Pelias for neglecting her during a sacrifice, but this simply explains why she will help the Argonauts, not what sets the adventure in motion. Only much later, toward the end of Book 2, do we learn, from Jason, that the primary reason for the expedition is to expiate the anger of Zeus against the Aeolian race by completing the "sacrifice of Phrixus" (2.1194), an ambiguous phrase that might mean either a sacrifice attempted by Phrixus or the original sin of expelling him from Greece. Later, one of the sons of Phrixus offers Aeetes a fuller, but still not entirely clear, account, in which he states that Zeus will give up his wrath and remove the "unbearable pollution and retribution of Phrixus" (3.338) only when the fleece has been returned to Greece. The characters thus have knowledge of divine causality that the reader must struggle to construct, without certainty of result. Apollo, addressed by the narrator in the opening lines, also plays an important, if not fully explicated, role. His prophecy that Pelias is to perish because of a man wearing one sandal motivates the king to send Jason, after he appears with one sandal, on the seemingly hopeless task. During their journey the Argonauts twice glimpse the god, once on their way to Colchis when he passes by at dawn and then near the journey's end when they are lost in a deadly darkness off Crete. In this later scene Apollo appears bringing the dawn in answer to Jason's prayer and saves the troop by revealing the nearness of the island Anaphe. In terms of the structure of the epic, then, Apollo's actions are given a singular importance, although his motivations remain unrevealed, shadowy like his epiphanies before the heroes. In Book 2 the seer Phineus explains to the Argonauts that Zeus blinded him for revealing to men the knowledge of the future given him by the gods; as a result, he continues, he will furnish them only partial information about their coming journey, by revealing the outward route to Colchis but not the return path. Phineus has been read as an internal model for the narrator of the *Argonautica*, who likewise provides the reader with partial knowledge, just what pertains at any given point in the narrative.

The one exception occurs at the opening of Book 3, when the narrator calls upon Erato, the Muse of erotic poetry, to help him with the story of Medea's passion for Jason. Immediately following this request occurs the famous scene on Olympus, in which the gods are shown rather comically interacting with each other. Hera and Athena discuss how to help the Argonauts, who have just reached Colchis, but Athena, the goddess of wisdom, can, surprisingly, think of no plan and meekly agrees to ask Aphrodite for help. They then visit the goddess of love, who is grooming her long tresses, to request that she convince her son Eros to inflame Medea with love for Jason. In an attempt to refuse, Aphrodite explains how willful her son is, how exasperating his insolence. Hera and Athena smile at each other, with the amusement typically directed at parents of difficult children. While even in Homer the gods were depicted as subject to human frailty and sometimes comically amusing, the new Hellenistic element in Apollonius' divine scene is the reduction of the god's behavior to familiar, even bourgeois social interactions and parental difficulties. Finally agreeing to help, Aphrodite finds Eros playing dice with Ganymede – and cheating. After a mild reprimand, she bribes him with a magical ball that was once the toy of Zeus, and he sets off to wound Medea with his blazing arrow. The scene is one of the most charming in the epic. But as the earliest dramatization of the god Eros in fully anthropomorphic form, it is also laden with erotic symbolism – love's force as a difficult child, indifferent to others' pain and willing to gamble for his own pleasure with the very soul of the one who loves. In addition, the magical ball, which blazes "like a star" (3.141) when tossed in the air, seems to emblematize the earth's sphere, shown here as once the plaything of Zeus, now the prized possession of the childishly cruel Eros.

Mythological epics, like Apollonius' *Argonautica*, were apparently quite rare in the Hellenistic age. Rejection of epic as a suitable poetic medium (who could compete with the invincible Homer?) was supported by the anecdotes concerning Choerilus of Iasus, who traveled with Alexander and wrote of his exploits. Choerilus was such a bad poet that Alexander reportedly said he would prefer to be Homer's Thersites (an ugly, cowardly Greek soldier shamed by Odysseus) than Choerilus' Achilles.[6] The tradition about Choerilus suggests that from the time of Alexander, whose tastes were apparently carried forward by his senior commanders into the coming age, epic poetry written in the traditional manner of Homer, especially if it concerned contemporary affairs, was considered a risky business. Poets, like Callimachus and Theocritus, found other ways of praising their royal patrons. The most prolific third-century writer of epic poetry was Rhianus of Crete, who was also an editor of Homer. Since he was active in the second half of the third century, he would have been writing in the aftermath of Apollonius' eventual success. His *Heracleia*, probably in four books, was surely mythological, but his other known epics were ethnographical, concerning various regions of the Greek mainland. For instance, his *Messeniaca* presented the historical legends concerning the Second Messenian War (with Sparta) promulgated after the Messenians shed Spartan overlordship in the fourth century. From Pausanias' summary of Rhianus, it is clear that the epic had as its hero Aristomenes, who led the Messenian resistance of the early fifth century; he was as prominent in the epic, Pausanias says (4.6.3), as Achilles in the *Iliad*. The fragments of Rhianus, unfortunately, do not reveal conclusively whether he composed in the style of old-fashioned epic or with the economy of narrative and the romantic elements that are featured in Apollonius. Since Rhianus also wrote epigrams that imitate Callimachus, the more modern approach is quite likely.

In recent years, scholars have come to a better understanding of Apollonius' achievement in composing the *Argonautica*. As a large-scale mythological epic, it had always seemed to fail in comparison with the *Iliad* and the *Odyssey*, which were surely Apollonius' principal models. As the central hero, Jason lacks the superhuman strength and confidence of an Achilles, or sharp wit of an Odysseus, and the plot is constructed without the expected tragic turning point, in which the hero confronts his own inadequacy in terms of human relationships. In contrast, Apollonius' epic presents a more nuanced and realistic approach to ethical behavior, in which right and wrong are not always easy to distinguish, even in consequence. It has long been clear that Vergil constructed the *Aeneid* on the Homeric model, but we now recognize more fully how the older epics are refracted through the lens of the *Argonautica*. Vergil's great accomplishment of mirroring imperial Rome in the mythical story of Augustus' ancestor Aeneas was in fact modeled upon Apollonius' innovative use of mythological epic to foreshadow, in various imperfect ways, the Egyptian kingdom of the Ptolemies. The journey to Colchis, a city founded, according to Herodotus, by a legendary Egyptian king, and the return voyage in the company of Aeetes' daughter constitute a mythical prototype for the amalgamation of Greek and barbarian in Ptolemaic society, just as the final episode in Book 4 foreshadows the eventual migration of Argonautic descendants to found a Greek city in North Africa. As is so often the case, an innovative Hellenistic exemplar set the course for this poetic genre throughout later antiquity.

3.4   Theocritus and the Other Bucolic Poets

Theocritus is the most accessible and best loved among Hellenistic poets. As part of that Alexandrian group who sought to renew the tradition of Greek poetry by turning to genres of small scale and personal reference, he wrote short poems in dactylic hexameters in a variety of types. These *idylls*, as they are called, include mimelike dialogues with both rural and urban settings, hymns, mythical narratives, pederastic love poems, and encomia for monarchs. From the perspective of literary history, Theocritus is important as the first practitioner of pastoral poetry, one of the major poetic genres of the western tradition. Pastoral, in its basic form, is poetry about herdsmen, usually in dialogue, often involving erotic love, and commonly incorporating songs, such as singing contests between herdsmen, love serenades, or laments for the dead. Although other Hellenistic poets wrote on rustic themes, Vergil sealed Theocritus' claim to be the first pastoralist by modeling his *Eclogues* on those poems of his Greek predecessor that featured herdsmen. Theocritus' seven pastoral poems thus form his most lasting contribution, and yet from the perspective of the period in which they were written, they should be assessed as only one strand among the diverse poetic types constituting his hexametric *Idylls*.

Theocritus came from the Sicilian city of Syracuse, and the names of his parents, Praxagoras and Philinna, are preserved in an epigram that apparently opened an early collection of his works (*Palatine Anthology* 9.434). Syracuse, originally a colony of Doric-speaking Corinth, was the largest and most cultured city in Sicily, and certainly no literary backwater. Wealthy Syracusan tyrants of the fifth century had attracted the services of such poets as Aeschylus, Simonides, and Pindar, and Plato later lived there for a while in an attempt to establish an ideal state. Syracuse had also exported to other parts of the Hellenic world its native literary tradition, formed by the comic works of Epicharmus and the mimes of Sophron. Another Sicilian, Timaeus (ca. 350–ca. 260) of Tauromenium, was the most important ancient historian of the West; he lived in exile in Athens during the period of Theocritus' youth. If Theocritus grew up in Syracuse in the first quarter of the third century, as seems most likely, he would have experienced the turbulent period of foreign wars and civil conflict leading up to the tyranny of Hiero II, which began in the 270s. The only firm chronological pegs in his biography are provided by *Idyll* 16, which was written shortly after Hiero came to power, and *Idylls* 15 and 17, both composed not much later, during the reign of Ptolemy II Philadelphus and his sister Arsinoe II. At some point Theocritus spent time on the Aegean island of Cos, where he apparently received literary patronage from members of the landed aristocracy; it was perhaps there that he struck up a friendship with Nicias, a physician from Miletus who may have studied at the famed Coan school of medicine. Shortly afterwards, as it seems, Theocritus was writing poetry for the Ptolemies in Alexandria, where he surely knew Callimachus and Apollonius of Rhodes. His poetic allegiance to this Alexandrian group is made explicit in the seventh *Idyll* where a character named Simichidas, often identified with the poet, states his admiration for Philitas of Cos and Asclepiades of Samos, both forerunners of Callimachean poetics. Since datable references within Theocritus' poetry are confined to the 270s, his productive period may have been short, and the publication of his collected oeuvre was perhaps posthumous.

The manuscript tradition for Theocritus' poetry is unusually complex and uncertain. In all likelihood, his corpus was gathered for publication within the third century BC in an edition entitled *Idylls* (or *Eidullia*). Our association of the word *idyll* with pastoral poetry developed only much later, and etymology suggests that *eidullia*, a plural form and a diminutive of *eidos* ("type," "genre"), initially meant "little types." Following early Hellenistic practice, the editor, whether Theocritus or another, apparently gave the collection a title that emphasized both diversity of generic type and slenderness in length and style. By the second century, however, Theocritus had become known primarily as a composer of "bucolic poetry," or *bukolika*, an adjectival form meaning "pertaining to a cowherd"; the term *pastoral* derives from the Latin *pastoralia*, "pertaining to a shepherd." Within a few decades of Theocritus' death, his *Idylls* about herdsmen had apparently been separated out and published in editions that included certain spurious bucolic poems, such as *Idylls* 8 and 9.

Theocritus' *Idylls* on herding themes thus became the model for a new genre of poetry called bucolic, of which the only other known practitioners were Moschus of Syracuse, apparently of the second century, and Bion of Smyrna, who probably flourished about 100. In the first half of the first century, the corpus of bucolic poetry was gathered by the scholar Artemidorus of Tarsus into an edition headed by the following epigram: "The bucolic Muses, once scattered, are now all gathered into one fold, into one flock" (*Palatine Anthology* 9.205). Here we find the metaphor of poems as herd animals, tended by the poet/cowherd, that underlies the development of the bucolic concept in the later Hellenistic age. Artemidorus' collection was likely known to Vergil, perhaps even the one on which the *Eclogues* were based. Although the Byzantine families of manuscripts display no authoritative order for the *Idylls*, the herding poems stand first in all strands of the tradition, indicating that already in the Hellenistic age Theocritus had come to be conceived primarily as a composer of bucolic.

The poems attributed to Theocritus in the manuscripts number thirty, although bits of a thirty-first, known from a papyrus, and a few book references, including lines from a poem entitled *Berenice* (fr. 3), show that there were once more. Of these only twenty-four (*Idylls* 1–7, 10–18, 22–4, 26, 28–31) are commonly accepted as genuine. Except for *Idylls* 28–31, written in the lyric meters of the Sapphic type, all are in dactylic hexameters. While the lyric poems use Aeolic dialect, the hexametric *Idylls* display either the usual epic dialect mixture or, especially for the pastorals, contain Doric forms meant to suggest colloquial, even rustic, speech. Theocritus' poems are commonly grouped into such categories as pastorals, urban mimes, mythical poems, court poetry, and erotic monologues. More and more, however, scholars are recognizing an underlying uniformity in theme and style, which may signal the poet's own conception of what the *Idylls* were meant to be.

As a group, the *Idylls* are consistently focused away from traditional poetic topics associated with the heroic or the aristocratic, and toward the humble, the personal, or the ordinary. Theocritus' herdsmen, who sing of their loves, country deities, and flocks, form a counterpart to his urban characters, ordinary men and women who in a similar manner are concerned with romantic relationships, religious festivals, and everyday occupations. His mythical characters are commonly presented as young, vulnerable, or erotically inclined. In fact, the speakers in almost all his poetic types, whether these be praise poems for patrons or monologues by frustrated lovers, tend to express personal rather than communal concerns. A good example is *Idyll* 11 (the main model for Vergil's second *Eclogue*), in which Theocritus begins by explaining to his physician friend Nicias, as a lesson for their own erotic longings, how the Cyclops

Polyphemus, when he sang of his love for the sea nymph Galatea, demonstrates that no medicine exists for love other than poetry. The poet then quotes a highly comical song that the lovelorn Polyphemus sang in a fruitless attempt to win Galatea. It begins as follows:

> White Galatea, why do you reject the one who loves you,
> You who are whiter than cream cheese to see, more tender than a lamb,
> More skittish than a calf, brighter than an unripe grape?

While the effect is humorous and charming, the reader's appreciation of the poem is enhanced by recognition of allusions to Homer's story of Polyphemus being blinded by Odysseus. Of course in Homer the Cyclops is a brutish monster, who devours Odysseus' men; in contrast, Theocritus presents him in the throes of his first erotic passion, and highly self-conscious about his looks, especially that one long shaggy eyebrow that "extends from ear to ear" (11.32) with one eye beneath and a wide nose upon his lip. Despite the comic distancing from this bizarre lover, Theocritus makes a point of emphasizing the universality of his erotic experience – how the mythical Sicilian monster offers a pertinent model for the poet and his friend.

Ancient commentators, who are excerpted in the bucolic scholia, found part of the novelty of Theocritus' poetry in its mixture of dramatic and narrative styles. As often in Hellenistic poetry, Homeric epic provides both the general shape of scenes and much of the diction, although Theocritus commonly subverts the epic precedent by adding elements drawn from other genres. The elaborate universalizing scenes that decorate Achilles' shield in the *Iliad* are, for instance, converted in the first *Idyll* to the simpler figures that adorn a herdsman's wooden bowl – young lovers, an old fisherman, and a boy weaving a cricket cage, emblems of the stages of a single human life rather than society at large. The "Little Heracles" (*Idyll* 24) reworks a scene from Pindar's *Nemean* 1, in which the baby Heracles strangles a pair of snakes sent by Hera to destroy him, into a more domestic scene of parental concern. The scholiasts report that both the "Sorceress" (*Idyll* 2) and the "Women Who Attend the Adonis Festival" (*Idyll* 15) had models in dramatic skits by Sophron. It is unfortunate that we have only fragments from this late fifth-century writer of prose mimes, who impressed Plato and may have contributed to the development of his philosophical dialogues. Clearly Theocritus, too, was influenced in his dramatic technique and character choice by his famous countryman.

A sense of verbal consistency among the *Idylls* results from the poet's persistent mixture of stylistic registers within individual poems.

Theocritus' use of various dialectal forms and levels of diction – for instance, juxtaposing humble Doric vocabulary with Homeric phraseology – results in an unsettling mixture of the elevated and the colloquial built into the very fabric of the poetry. In addition, many of the *Idylls* have embedded within them an orally performed song adapted to epic-style verse. Examples include herding songs (*Idylls* 1, 5–7), incantations (*Idyll* 2), erotic serenades (*Idylls* 3, 11), a harvesting song (*Idyll* 10), a ritual lament (*Idyll* 15), a marriage song (*Idyll* 18), and a lullaby (*Idyll* 24). His fondness for mimicking popular song may be related to another of his stylistic devices, symmetry between clauses and symmetrical repetition of words. Examples occur in the refrain to a shepherd's song in the first *Idyll*,

"Begin the bucolic song, dear Muses, begin the song,"

followed by

"Cease the bucolic song, Muses, come cease the song,"

and in a mother's lullaby sung to the baby Heracles and his twin brother (*Idyll* 24.7–9):

Sleep, my babies, a sweet and waking sleep;
sleep safely, twin brothers, my children, my very soul;
happily may you rest and happily seek the dawn.

While this adaptation of song to hexameter poetry is characteristic of Theocritus' *Idylls* as a group, the herdsmen's songs, both those performed in competition and those sung by a single individual, became the model for a new generic type. The label *bucolic* given to these songs by Theocritus was perhaps the term by which the rustic ditties performed in the Sicilian countryside were known, but in addition to its basic meaning of "herding" or "cowherding," the Greek adjective *boukolikos* also shaded connotatively to "soothing," "beguiling," or "deceiving." Its transformation into a genre term, designating first Theocritus' herding *Idylls* and then later poetry modeled on them, was facilitated by a semantic range suggesting the effect of soothing enchantment and poetic illusion typically produced by pastoral.

As the first poem in all ancient and Byzantine editions of Theocritus, *Idyll* 1 became the source for many of the conventions associated with later pastoral poetry. The shepherd Thyrsis and an unnamed goatherd spend the hour of noon in a shady grove, exchanging conversation and song. The famous opening of the poem – "Sweetly sings the whispering of that pine by the spring, goatherd, and sweetly do you pipe" – illustrates how Theocritus' use of verbal repetition and parallel structure contributes to the idealized pastoral vision of oneness between man and nature. While Thyrsis asks his companion to pipe, the goatherd induces Thyrsis to sing by offering a goat to milk and a carved cup. The goatherd's loving description of the decorations on the cup – plant motifs surrounding three vignettes with human figures – functions as a verbal counterpart for the song performed by Thyrsis. The shepherd's song dramatizes the death of Daphnis, a mythical cowherd of the Sicilian countryside. The closeness of Daphnis to the land and its deities is revealed by the list of those who visit him in his dying hour: wild and domestic animals, Hermes, various herdsmen, Priapus, and finally Aphrodite herself. Although the precise reason for Daphnis' death remains unclear, his demise seems associated with resistance to love. Aphrodite's presence finally provokes him to speak, vowing his defiance of the goddess even as he breathes his last. At the close of the poem, the goatherd compliments Thyrsis on his song as he turns his attention back to his flock. The *Idyll* is remarkable for its air of dreamy irreality, enhanced by mellifluous assonance, abundant parallelism of phrase, and the balanced structure of cup versus song. Daphnis' death suggests the loss of a happier age, partially recoverable through the charming exchange between shepherd and goatherd.

The other pastoral *Idylls* range from the realistic and earthy to the mythical and idealizing. The youthful Cyclops in *Idyll* 11 illustrates the Alexandrian trick of dramatizing a point in time preceding the one made famous in earlier epic, and in *Idyll* 6 a romance between Galatea and her monstrous suitor becomes the subject of songs exchanged by two young cowherds named Daphnis and Damoetas, who show their affection for each other by a kiss and mutual gift giving. In *Idyll* 3 an absurdly senti-mental goatherd threatens suicide as he sings before a cave in which resides Amaryllis, the girl he loves. As in the first *Idyll*, these poems are set in a mythical terrain or an unspecified locale where past and present, human and divine, are scarcely to be distinguished. Two other *Idylls*, however, located specifically in southern Italy, portray contentious con-versations between herdsmen and offer a more realistic portrait of rustic existence. In *Idyll* 4 Battus and Corydon spar about the detrimental effect produced for the cattle by the absence of the cowherd, who has gone off to compete in athletic contests. In *Idyll* 5 Comatas and Lacon rehearse a number of old grudges, including thefts and a sexual encounter; their quarrel culminates in a singing contest, judged by a passing shepherd and won by the triumphant Comatas. Both ancient sources and modern parallels indicate that singing contests of this sort were a genuine feature of herding life in rural Greece; through Theocritus' adaptation to epic-style verse they became a standard feature of the pastoral genre throughout its long history.

Of special importance to the later history of pastoral is the *Thalysia* (*Idyll* 7), featuring a noontime encounter between the urban poet Simichidas and a mysterious goatherd Lycidas in the Coan countryside. Since the poem is narrated in the first person by Simichidas and makes clear allusion to the poetic investiture of the shepherd Hesiod by the Muses in the *Theogony*, it has been often interpreted as Theocritus' dramatization of his own induction into bucolic poetry. But whether Theocritus had fully developed the concept of bucolic poetry is uncertain, and as a result another reading of the poem finds an exploration of the complex inter-relationship between sophisticated poet and rustic singer, perhaps both versions of Theocritus himself. Simichidas narrates the events that took place as he journeyed through the countryside to the Thalysia, a harvest festival held on the estate of two Coan aristocrats. Traveling along the road, he meets Lycidas, known to him as a famed piper and singer of bucolic song. Theocritus plays on the ancient paradigm of mysterious noon encounters with disguised deities, and scholars have offered a number of possible divine identifications for Lycidas, including Apollo, Pan, and a satyr; however, Simichidas describes him as a goatherd with typically smelly attire, and Theocritus' ploy may be to substitute the talented herdsman for the expected deity. After some verbal sparring, the two agree to exchange songs and Lycidas explains his poetic preferences, couched in concrete imagery but reminiscent of refined Callimachean aesthetics: "I hate greatly the builder who seeks to raise his house as high as the peak of Mt. Oromedon (a mountain on Cos), and I hate those cocks of the Muses who toil in vain by crowing against the bard of Chios (Homer)" (7.45–8). Both house-building and the song of birds are commonplace analogies for poetry in the literary criticism of the Hellenistic era. The songs then sung by the two travelers offer a contrast between Lycidas' depiction of rustic romance and Simichidas' vision of urban love affairs. At their conclusion, Lycidas, laughing, signals his approval by giving Simichidas a staff as a guest gift from the Muses, and the poem ends with a description of the sensual delights experienced by Simichidas at the Thalysia, including the smiling approval of the goddess Demeter. This lavishly described *locus amoenus*, "pleasant place," on the rural estate of Simichidas' wealthy friends has seemed to many readers to emblematize the rich sources of inspiration gathered from Theocritus' personal experience of the Coan countryside, resulting in an abundant harvest of poetry.

From as early as the Hellenistic period, Theocritus' pastoral *Idylls* have been interpreted either mimetically, as direct representations of rustic reality, or in a symbolic or allegorical manner, as statements about the poet's own world disguised under the veil of rustic manners ("the bucolic masquerade"). The symbolic interpretations were fostered by the earlier uses of the herdsman figure in Greek culture to stand for either the good king or the wise poet (cf. "the Lord is my shepherd" in the Hebrew tradition). It was natural, then, that in later Greek bucolic the poet identified himself metaphorically with a cowherd and his poetry with the animals he tended. While the herding *Idylls* display many similarities of structure and style with the other *Idylls*, their mysteriously suggestive quality, the appearance they can give of referring to something beyond their own limited world, led historically to the development of their separate conceptualization as pastoral. While Theocritus is rightly credited with the invention of pastoral, attributing to him a fully developed concept of a new genre is made difficult by the many similarities between his herding poems and other *Idylls*, as, for instance, *Idyll* 10, where a conversation between two reapers culminates in an exchange of songs, one an escape into an erotic fantasy and one on the necessity of hard work. This poem's liminal position on the borders of pastoral – its characters are rustics but not shepherds – problematizes the easy assumption that Theocritus' aim was to create a new genre of bucolic poetry.

The urban mimes are in many ways counterparts to the pastoral *Idylls*. The setting shifts from the country to the city, and the voices of men heard in the rustic poems are now balanced by the voices of women. In the "Sorceress" (*Idyll* 2), Simaetha, a young woman who lives independently with only an old servant, practices magic in an attempt to win back the handsome Delphis, who has seduced and abandoned her. Her internal turmoil is revealed first by the dramatization of her magic spells and then by a monologue in which she recalls the details of her brief love affair. Much of the poem's appeal lies in the tension between Simaetha's turbulent emotional state and the quiet nocturnal setting, tense with the practice of black magic; Theocritus thus creates an uncertain balance between the girl's helplessness and her power. *Idyll* 14 dramatizes a male character's erotic disappointment, as Aeschinas describes to his friend Thyonichus how his girlfriend abandoned him for another lover in the midst of a dinner party. Thyonichus in turn advises his friend to overcome his sorrow by joining the army of Ptolemy Philadelphus, an excuse for Theocritus to offer a laudatory description of that monarch. Both *Idylls* 2 and 14 display a thematic pattern found also in pastoral poems (*Idylls* 3, 11), the revelation of a failed love affair concluding with the possibility that the lover will find a remedy, or *pharmakon*, for love's pain. This goal of finding a therapy to counteract the harmful effects of desire for what one does not possess was common to the various schools of Hellenistic philosophy, in their quest for *eudaimonia*, "wellbeing," and may, in its Theocritean form, most closely resemble Epicurean thought and practice.

Praise of the Ptolemies suggests that, like *Idyll* 14, "Women Who Attend the Adonis Festival" (*Idyll* 15) was written in an Alexandrian context. The two main characters are housewives, natives of Syracuse now resident in Alexandria, who set out, with servants in tow, to view the celebration of the Adoneia, lavishly presented in the palace of Arsinoe II. This charmingly realistic skit provides an invaluable mirror onto the lives of ordinary individuals within Ptolemaic society (cf. fig. 1.5). From it we gain knowledge of friendships among women, relationships between masters and slaves, tensions between Greeks of various origins, aesthetic appreciation of art by ordinary individuals, and the influence of court propaganda on the citizenry. Artistically, the poem is unified by the contrast between the stressful, sometimes contentious marriages of Gorgo and Praxinoa and the romantic vision of love offered by Aphrodite and her young lover Adonis, represented in the palace both in three-dimensional figures and in hymnal song.

Theocritus' *Idylls* on mythical topics were also influenced by Ptolemaic ideology. Heracles, the principal subject in *Idylls* 13 and 24, was claimed as the ancestor of Alexander the Great and his Ptolemaic successors in Egypt; in *Idyll* 17 Ptolemy Soter, the father of Philadelphus, is depicted enthroned on Olympus beside his reputed forbears, Alexander and Heracles. The image-making in these mythical *Idylls* involves associating the monarchs with the heroic and divine while humanizing the deified heroes with whom they were associated. In *Idyll* 13 Heracles' love for the boy Hylas, who was stolen by water nymphs as the pair traveled with the Argonauts, illustrates for Nicias the ubiquity of erotic passion among both mortals and immortals. *Idyll* 24 celebrates Heracles' youthful life by focusing largely on his mother Alcmene: her nurturing of her twin sons, her reaction to the threat posed by the serpents who attempt to strangle them, her consultation of the seer Tiresias, and her devotion to the young hero's education. *Idyll* 22 is a hymn to the Dioscuri, Castor and Polydeuces, who, like Ptolemy Philadelphus and Arsinoe II, were heralded as the "saviors" of sailors. After an opening celebration of the protections they provide on the sea, Theocritus presents two main episodes that, in typical fashion, balance each other by contrast. In one Polydeuces bests the brutish Amycus in a boxing match (a story found also in the *Argonautica*), and in the other Castor slays his cousin Lynceus, who with his brother is contesting the theft of their promised brides by the Dioscuri. While the first episode seems to celebrate the civilizing influence of the deified twins, the second more bluntly suggests the power of gods who walk in mortal guise. Written under the influence of the Ptolemies *domesticating the gods.*

who, like the Dioscuri, anticipate deification after death, the poem is decidedly ambivalent in tone. *Idyll* 26, about the dismemberment of Pentheus by the daughters of Cadmus at the instigation of Dionysus, even more disturbingly reveals the gods' awesome power to destroy those who offend them. All these poems, whether charming or unsettling in their effect, are characterized by the remaking of earlier heroic ideals in a more human scale.

Idylls 16 and 17 illustrate the changed relationships between poets and patrons in the Hellenistic era. In "Charites" or "Hiero" (*Idyll* 16), Theocritus' personification of his poems as Charites, or "Graces," cleverly signifies both the poetic charm of his verse and the reciprocity of favor between poet and patron; when the Charites, both maidens and poems, return to the poet's house after an unsuccessful journey in search of patronage, they reprove him and bow on cold knees in an empty coffer. The remarkable symbolism of this image introduces Theocritus' complaint that men of power and wealth no longer care to support the poets who will bring them undying fame, as did Simonides for the monarchs of old. Theocritus pins his own hope for patronage on Hiero of Syracuse, and we know that, under the right circumstances, Hiero was willing to reward poets generously. A poet named Archimelus composed an epigram of eighteen lines (202 Lloyd-Jones and Parsons) to celebrate an enormous ship, the *Syracusia*, constructed for the tyrant, and was rewarded with 1,500 bushels of wheat. According to a certain Moschion who wrote a description of this ship, it was appointed with every luxury, including a gymnasium, promenades, gardens, a library, rows of paintings and statues, and mosaics illustrating the story of the *Iliad*.[7] Appealing to this taste for grandeur, Theocritus provides Hiero a foretaste of the praise that could be lavished upon his coming expedition against the Carthaginians. But his emphasis on the aftermath of war, an idyllic picture of a peaceful Sicilian landscape and its rustic inhabitants, suggests that he hopes to persuade Hiero to support this new poetry, in place of more traditional epic descriptions of military exploits. Although *Idyll* 16 recalls throughout the victory odes of Pindar and Simonides, the tone of praise found in earlier epinician poetry is here replaced by the concerns of the poet himself, who feels socially and culturally estranged from those in positions of power.

In "Encomium to Ptolemy" (*Idyll* 17), the poet less hesitantly negotiates the difficulties of constructing praise for monarchs who anticipate their imminent deification. Beginning with a comparison between Zeus and Ptolemy Philadelphus, Theocritus maintains the distinction between the king of the gods and the mortal king while subtly suggesting parallels between them. After a celebration of the monarch's deified parents, Soter

(now enshrined in heaven with Alexander and Heracles) and Berenice I
(now assimilated in cult to Aphrodite), Theocritus compares Ptolemy II's
birth on Cos to Apollo's birth on Delos, a passage paralleled in Callimachus' "Hymn to Delos." Here the composer's personal voice is largely
absent, though praise of the monarch's generosity concludes with his
benefactions to poets. Though a valuable historical source for Ptolemaic
ideology, the *Idyll* has more in common with the Pergamum altar, where
the Attalids implied an identification of their victory over the Gauls with
the defeat of the Giants by the Olympian gods, than with the more
personal tone of Callimachus' playful praise in "Victory of Berenice" or
"Lock of Berenice." Since Theocritus' own *Idyll* 15 offers indirect praise
of Arsinoe II through a dialogue between two Syracusan women, we may
wonder whether it was the queens who were more tolerant of innovative
and indirect modes of encomium.

Love poems for young males, known as *paidika*, form a small group:
two in hexameters (*Idylls* 12 and 23) and two in lyric meters (*Idylls* 29–30,
although the fragmentary 31 suggests there were once more). Each consists of a monologue by a lover who analyzes the circumstance of his
desire for a boy. In *Idyll* 12 the speaker has successfully won the lad, and in
Idyll 23 the lover commits suicide upon the boy's doorstep. The poems
display similarities to Hellenistic erotic epigram and may follow the model
of Asclepiades' lost love lyrics. They also anticipate the genre of erotic
elegy later developed by Roman poets like Catullus, Propertius, Tibullus,
and Ovid. One other Aeolic poem, *Idyll* 28, was composed to accompany
a gift for Nicias' wife, a distaff for spinning, upon the occasion of Theocritus' visit to their home in Miletus. It is likely that the poem marks
Theocritus as one of the admirers of Erinna, whose *Distaff* enunciated
through epic verse a young woman's passionate attachment to her lost
friend Baucis. But apart from any literary allusion, Theocritus' poem on
the distaff offers striking confirmation that in this age of civic rootlessness
and social mobility one of the strongest bonds of affection was that among
friends.

In addition to the *Idylls*, the bucolic manuscripts preserve twenty-two
epigrams, in elegiac couplets and other meters, ascribed to Theocritus
(*Epigrams* 1–22 Gow [1952a, b]), and the manuscripts of the *Greek Anthology* offer two more (23–4 Gow [1952a, b]). Although some may be
spurious, as a group they give evidence for Theocritus' participation in
this popular literary form. The arrangement of the epigrams in the bucolic
manuscripts indicates that they were edited in antiquity to form a poetry
book. The preserved collection is divided into a section of six bucolic
epigrams, a mixed section of epitaphs and dedications, and a third section
of poems in various meters primarily on literary greats. The bucolic

epigrams are the most likely to be spurious because of the tendency to attribute poems on pastoral topics to the founder of the genre. Among those probably genuine are a dedication by Nicias to a god of healing (8), a dedication to Aphrodite Ourania (a favorite goddess of Arsinoe II) made by a loyal wife (13), and an inscription for a bronze statue of Epicharmus, the comic poet of Syracuse (18). While dedications and epitaphs were standard epigrammatic forms for Hellenistic poets, Theocritus' epigrams on literary figures, all inscriptional in type, suggest a special interest in maintaining connection to the Greek poetic tradition through the physical form of burial sites and statues.

Theocritus' *Idylls* appeal to readers because of their dramatic power, their suggestive combination of fantasy and realism, their humanization of heroic and divine figures, and their sympathetic portraits of commonplace characters. Human emotion, most particularly erotic longing, lies at the center of his poetry. In his most complex *Idylls* a tension set up by parallels and contrasts, often between the frame and insets, suggestively entices the reader to seek universal implications in the apparently simple portraits presented. For reasons that have to do with the traditional uses of the herdsman figure to stand for kings or poets and with Theocritus' closeness to local Sicilian culture, the *Idylls* about herdsmen most effectively create this impression of broad meaningfulness. As a result, the herding poems were generically distinguished from the others and set at the head of a long tradition of pastoral poetry, which thrived until the age of romanticism and lives on, as William Empson has shown in *Some Versions of Pastoral* (1935), in numerous transmuted modes. The experience of the urban sophisticate who feels superior to those living a simpler life in a natural world and yet appreciates the wisdom derived from that existence has become associated with a poetic genre of which Theocritus is rightly considered the founder.

The bucolic manuscripts contain a surprisingly large number of spurious poems, and apparently there developed a late Hellenistic mania to "be" Theocritus. The earliest examples of post-Theocritean bucolic poetry are probably *Idylls* 8 and 9, which were added to the end of a collection of Theocritus' herding poems, made in the later third or earlier second century BC. Both of these concern a singing contest between the mythical herdsmen Daphnis and Menalcas and are filled with mannered allusions to Theocritus' poetry. At the end of *Idyll* 9 the narrator offers to the "Bucolic Muses" a version of the song he sang in the company of those mythical singers, and this insertion of the poet himself into the bucolic world becomes our first instance of the metaphorical identification of the poet with the herdsman, known as the "bucolic metaphor." It is therefore our earliest certain evidence for the existence of the concept of bucolic poetry. Other bucolic poems by unknown poets also became attached to the Theocritean corpus in antiquity. The longest of these, *Idyll* 25, which adopts the Theocritean manner of reworking heroic myth in a bucolic mode, can be classed as an epyllion. The well-known story of Heracles' enormous labor of cleaning the stables of Augeias is here told in three dramatized vignettes focusing on the magnificence of the king's herds of cattle, an account of Heracles' struggle with an extraordinary bull, and finally the hero's narrative of his first labor, his defeat of the Nemean lion. While likely not by Theocritus himself, the poem brings the heroic into confrontation with the pastoral in a way closely reminiscent of the Syracusan master. Other apparently spurious *Idylls* contain an attempted seduction of a maiden by a cowherd, who in one instance is named Daphnis (*Idylls* 20 and 27), a brief scene in which the boy Eros, stung by a bee, is derided by his mother Aphrodite because he too has a sting (*Idyll* 19), and a conversation between two wretchedly poor fishermen about the value of hard work versus dreams of golden fish (*Idyll* 21). All these post-Theocritean poems were apparently considered "bucolic," a concept that by the end of the Hellenistic era had passed beyond simple herding themes to encompass a wider range of pleasures and delusions, typical of Theocritus' original "bucolic" world.

A few short poems and fragments attributed to the only other known bucolic poets, Moschus and Bion, have been preserved in manuscript sources, especially by the Byzantine compiler Stobaeus. While rustic characters and country motifs still appear in their poetry, they sentimentalize the bucolic genre by turning it toward light-hearted erotic topics and playful mythical themes. Examples include Aphrodite's charming description of her runaway son Eros (Moschus I) and a bird-catcher's warning to a boy that he should avoid trying to trap the winged Eros who flits in the trees (Bion fr. 13). Bion, in particular, reveals his awareness of generic shifts: in one short poem the speaker/poet, identified metaphorically as a cowherd, describes how Aphrodite appeared in a dream to demand that he instruct Eros in bucolic music and how instead Eros taught him about the loves of the gods and mortals (fr. 10). A few longer bucolic poems have been preserved. Moschus' bucolic epyllion *Europa*, about the seduction of a young girl by Zeus in the form of a bull, narrates a mythical story while also cultivating the sweet, mellifluous sound patterns and the romantic atmosphere characteristic of the later bucolic genre. While the poem is full of charm, Moschus also adapts the light humor that runs through much of ancient bucolic, as in these lines on Europa's attraction to the bull (95–8):

> She touched him all about and gently with her hands wiped
> much foam from his mouth and then kissed the bull.

He in turn lowed sweetly. You would say that you heard
the sweet sound of the Mygdonian flute being played.

The *Lament for Adonis*, probably by Bion, contains the same kind of
generic mixture. Modeled on Thyrsis' lament for Daphnis in *Idyll* 1, it
represents a ritual song, punctuated by a refrain simulating cries of mourning, such as sung by (usually female) worshippers at the Adoneia. This
poem, in turn, became the model for the anonymous *Lament for Bion*
(falsely attributed to Moschus), in which all of nature and bucolic characters like Pan and Galatea mourn the poet-cowherd. The unknown poet
makes clear the sense of a poetic tradition that has developed within the
bucolic concept, as he positions himself as the poetic heir of Bion, who
was in turn a follower of Syracusan Theocritus. A fragmentary papyrus
lacking the author's name offers an example of the type of mythical
narrative that may have characterized much of later bucolic poetry.[8] In
one of its two fragments, Silenus teasingly reproaches Pan for coming to a
contest without his syrinx, while in the other his construction of such a
panpipe from beeswax is described. Though it is not possible to piece
together the sequence of events here narrated, allusions to Theocritus'
poetry and his characters, such as Daphnis, Lycidas, and Thyrsis, are
present throughout. This tantalizing fragment reveals how little we
know of the tradition of later Greek bucolic poetry.

3.5 Didactic Poetry

The most important composer of didactic poetry between Hesiod and
Lucretius was Aratus of Soli. His *Phaenomena* (*Visible Signs*), a poem of
1,154 lines on astronomy and weather signs, demonstrated how traditional wisdom literature composed in hexameter verse could be adapted
to the rationalistic, scientific knowledge of the Hellenistic age. Aratus'
poem at once became admired and extensively read, both as an authoritative source of knowledge about the natural world and as a remarkable
example of the new poetic style. By the end of the second century, the
Phaenomena had acquired at least two commentaries on astronomical
matters, one by Attalus of Rhodes (lost) and another by Hipparchus of
Nicaea (extant), and yet another commentary by Boethius of Sidon (lost)
that may have dealt with the literary or philosophical aspects of the work.
The epigram in which Callimachus admires Aratus' refined imitation of
Hesiod (quoted in Ch 2.1) is only one example of praise by Hellenistic
writers. Another third-century epigrammatist, Leonidas of Tarentum, also
celebrated his "refined (*leptēi*) intellect" (*Palatine Anthology* 9.25), and one

of the Ptolemaic kings, perhaps Philadelphus, wrote an epigram awarding Aratus pride of place among astronomical poets by granting him the "scepter of refined description (*leptologou*)" (Page, pp. 84–5). The central interpretive problem in scholarship on Aratus has always been to reconcile his enormous ancient popularity with the modern reaction, which is often tedium. Much of the reason for this difference is that we, as modern readers, no longer need to study the rising and setting of the stars to tell time and scientific methods have all but eliminated reliance on observations of celestial phenomena and animal behavior for weather predictions. But even so, it has struck many as odd that this catalogue of constellations and weather signs was considered the pinnacle of Hellenistic *leptotēs*.

Aratus' hometown of Soli was in Cilicia, a district in Asia Minor. The *vitae*, or biographical sketches, in the manuscripts of the *Phaenomena* preserve the names of his parents, Athenodorus and Letophila, and three brothers. Aratus studied with the Stoic philosopher Zeno in Athens, and a letter purportedly written by him to Zeno was extant in antiquity. He associated with other intellectuals, including Zeno's student Persaeus, the Skeptic poet Timon, and Menedemus, who developed his own philosophical circle at Eretria. His short poetry was collected under the title *Kata Lepton*, which was later applied as well to the poetic works attributed to the young Vergil (*Catalepton*). Known titles of his other works in the field of scientific or didactic literature included *Medicinal Substances* and *Canon*, which concerned the musical movement of the planets. One of the defining events in Aratus' life was the invitation to join the circle of philosophers and poets who gathered at the court of Antigonus Gonatas in Macedonia, where he attended Antigonus' marriage to Phila, daughter of Seleucus I. The date of this marriage, about 276, is the only certain chronological point in his biography. Shortly after establishing himself at the Macedonian court, Aratus composed a *Hymn to Pan*, a deity who was apparently of special significance to Antigonus since he appears on Macedonian coinage and the king later established a festival at Delos for him. It was on Antigonus' instructions that Aratus composed his most famous work, the *Phaenomena*. The king reportedly gave him a copy of a prose treatise on celestial phenomena written by the mathematician Eudoxus of Cnidus and asked him to put it into verse. He added that in versifying this treatise Aratus would make "Eudoxus more Eudoxus," a play on words that may be translated to make "Illustrious more Illustrious." Later Antiochus I called Aratus to Syria to work on Homer, and he produced early scholarly editions of both the *Iliad* and the *Odyssey*.

Didactic poetry, usually written in hexameter verse, had the purpose of instructing the reader in a subject of a philosophical, scientific, or technical nature. The earliest Greek didactic poet was Hesiod, who was likely following a long tradition of wisdom literature inherited from the civilizations of the East. His *Theogony* concerns the generations of the gods, and the *Works and Days* contains advice about how workers, particularly farmers, should live a good life. Two other Hesiodic poems that are now lost but were known in the Hellenistic age, *Ornithomanteia* on bird signs (once attached to the end of the *Works and Days*) and *Astronomy* on the movements of the stars, mirror more closely Aratus' subject matter. In the fifth century Parmenides and Empedocles produced didactic poems arguing about the nature of the universe from a philosophical perspective. In the Hellenistic age, perhaps partly in reaction to Plato's critique of poets as repositories of wisdom (as in the *Ion* or the *Republic*), didactic poetry underwent a fundamental change. The poet no longer represented himself as the source of knowledge about the subject at hand, but his role was more limited to providing poetic expertise, that is, the ability to express the material well in verse. In the first part of the *Phaenomena*, Aratus versified the astronomical knowledge of Eudoxus (ca. 390–ca. 340), who made advances in geometry as well as describing the constellations and their calendrical uses, while the latter part on weather signs is related to material preserved in *On Signs* attributed to Theophrastus. The accuracy of his descriptions of the heavens, which made the *Phaenomena* useful for centuries to come, indicates that he had a good understanding of the technical material in his source. It was the combination of his skill as a poet with his learnedness as a scholar of astronomy, rather than as a practicing scientist or theoretical mathematician, that earned him the admiration of his contemporaries. The commentator Hipparchus, whose interest was solely in elucidating and critiquing the astronomical content, lists his poetic virtues as simplicity, conciseness, and clarity.[9] The adjectives *leptos* and *leptologos* that Hellenistic writers used to characterize Aratus' refinement as a poet may refer to his exact expression of precise details as a way of creating vividness or accuracy, and it seems that this focus on the small and particular within the representation of something more universal was an essential part of the Callimachean concept of *leptotēs*.

The *Phaenomena* falls into three major parts: a description of how to locate key stars within clusters and what constellations they form (19–461); a description of the star belts that cross the night sky and what sequences of constellations appear within them (462–757); and a catalogue of celestial phenomena, animal behavior, and other natural occurrences that portend certain types of weather (758–1141). Although Aratus used at least two different prose sources, his poem has an underlying thematic unity. What ties together the three main sections is his purpose to describe how things perceptible to human senses (*phaenomena*) function as signs (*sēmata*) of what is true but not perceptible. The first task for the reader/observer is to sort the stars mentally into artificial groupings, conceived as animal or human shapes that are then associated with a mythical narrative. Once knowledge of the constellations has been acquired, the next task is to identify the star belts on which they move – the tropics of Cancer and of Capricorn, the equator, and the ecliptic – for the purposes of telling time, either to mark the periods of the night (especially useful when sailing) or to follow seasonal progression (so that farmers know just when to perform various tasks in the agricultural year). The ecliptic, on which lies the sun's path, is the most important of these star cycles and contains the twelve signs of the Zodiac. A transitional section on how to keep track of the days of the month by observing the phases of the moon leads to the section on weather signs, first those connected with heavenly bodies and then those observable on the earth. While this information was extraordinarily useful in third-century Greece when the main time-telling instruments, sundials, could be used only during the day and calendars were not well synchronized with seasons, the details of Aratus' poem also served to convey the more universal message that the visible world, despite its apparent randomness, has a purposeful arrangement beneficial to humans if only they know how to use their powers of intellect to read its perceptible signs.

This larger purpose is made evident in the short introduction, or proem (1–18), which praises Zeus and invokes the Muses. While the form of this proem derives from Aratus' Hesiodic models, the content reflects contemporary Stoic thought. Zeus is here presented as the force of reason that pervades the entire universe; it is through his kindness that the stars have been organized into signs useful to men. In content, Aratus' proem resembles a *Hymn to Zeus* (fr. 1 Powell, pp. 227–8)[10] composed by Cleanthes (331–232), who headed the Stoic school after Zeno (Ch. 3.8). Cleanthes, like other early Stoics, believed that poetry and myth were useful means of illustrating difficult philosophical concepts. Zeus appears with some frequency throughout the *Phaenomena*, in his capacity as the traditional weather god, as the mythological deity in his relationships with the figures of the constellations, and simply as a personification of the sky. While these familiar functions of the god help to situate Aratus' poem within the Greek literary tradition, they also recall the opening hymn in which Zeus is the god of Stoic cosmology. In the brief invocation of the Muses, again a traditional poetic element, Aratus asks the goddesses to reveal to him "as a sign" "all the poem" that he is about to sing (18). In this way, the words that follow become, like the constellations being described, a divinely given indicator of the invisible truth, made visible.

The Greek word for the constellations was simply "signs" (*sēmata*) because the stars when conceived as groups stood for some figure known only through report or myth. The unique poetic texture of the astronomical section of the *Phaenomena* derives from Aratus' need to describe both the physical appearance and location of the stars forming the constellations and the imagined characteristics of the mythical beings they represent. To do so, he had to employ what the ancients considered two different literary techniques: *mimēsis*, or imitation, which involved the accurate description of perceptible objects or events, and *phantasia*, or imagination, by which the poet invites the reader to form a mental picture of something that does not physically exist. An example of his fusion of *mimēsis* and *phantasia* is the description of Cassiepeia, an Ethiopian queen whose daughter Andromeda was almost sacrificed to a sea monster (188–91, 195–6):

> Before him [Draco] revolves the unfortunate Cassiepeia,
> not very large but visible even during a full moon.
> Only a few zigzagging stars make her shine,
> as they delineate her with a distinct shape....
> She stretches forth her arms just above her small shoulders,
> so that you would say she is grieving for her daughter.

The phrase "you would say" evokes the language of ecphrases, or passages concerning works of art. But here Cassiepeia is not a lifelike statue or painting, rather a small cluster of stars that can be transformed into a representational figure only by the observer's powers of imagination. Surely this tension between what the constellations can be seen to be and how they are to be imagined plays a significant role in Aratus' poeticizing of Eudoxus' astronomical work.

In other cases, Aratus enlivens his description by briefly narrating the origin of a constellation. Aetiologies, as such stories of origin are called, are common in Hellenistic poetry as a way of defining through the past what exists in the present. The most extended example (96–136) involves the constellation called the Maiden, who, as Aratus says, may be the daughter of Astraeus, the father of the stars, or, according to another report, may be immortal Dike or Justice. Aratus' account of Dike is another Hesiodic element, since it combines Hesiod's story of the ages of man (*Works and Days* 109–201) with his description of how Justice brings the wrath of her father Zeus on men who abuse her (256–62). In Aratus' account, the Maiden dwelt in human society during the Golden Age, when she taught men how to live justly and provided the simple necessities of life. In the Silver Age she withdrew to the mountains and would appear only briefly to harangue the people about their wicked ways and to predict impending evils. In the even more criminal Bronze Age (the last to be mentioned in Aratus, although Hesiod has also the Age of Heroes and the Iron Age), she flew up to her heavenly abode, where she remains visible as a star cluster. The point of this extended account of the Maiden is to provide Aratus' Stoic cosmology an ethical element: Zeus' kindness to men in creating signs to guide everyday activities extends as well to a visible reminder of the central concept of justice, how to live harmoniously with other human beings. In this way Aratus expands his specific didactic purpose – to convey knowledge of a technical kind – to a broader range of instruction, so that the constellations, as star signs from Zeus, point to the interconnectedness between the physical universe and human ethical behavior.

The transitional passage about the phases of the moon contains the famous *leptē* acrostic (783–7), which Callimachus interpreted as a refer- ence to the poetic style he preferred (see Ch. 2.2). In context, however, it literally concerns the "slender" or crescent moon under discussion. It is followed a few lines later (803–6) by another acrostic spelling out *pasa*, "total" or "whole," in a discussion of the full moon, and then *mesē*, "middle of," spelled out as *me-sē* over the first and second letters of the next two lines (807–8), which concern the mid-month moon. While these acrostics marking the three main stages in the moon's cycle may seem only an erudite game, they are given thematic relevance by a preceding passage that again points to Zeus as the source of all signification (768–74):

> We men do not yet know everything (*panta*) from Zeus, but still many things are hidden, of which Zeus will soon give us signs if he wishes. For certainly by that means he benefits the human race, as he shows himself on all sides (*pantothen*) and everywhere (*pantē*) reveals signs (*sēmata phainōn*). Some things the moon will perhaps tell you when in half form on either side of full or just then when full. . . .

The acrostics thus serve as a poetic example of the many signs waiting to be discovered by the astute observer, so as to indicate that the linguistic fabric of his poetry is part of the signifying fabric of the universe. Just as early Stoics like Cleanthes and Chrysippus believed that poetry, if correctly interpreted, could convey truth more effectively than prose, so Aratus constructs his own poetic signs that guide the reader in interpreting the visible signs offered by heavenly bodies.

The weather signs section is in many ways the most charming part of the poem. It illustrates the Hellenistic interest in animals, the landscape in which they dwell, and those ordinary individuals, especially sailors, farmers, and herdsmen, who benefit most from predictions about wind, storm, and fair weather. In many instances, Aratus goes beyond the bare necessity of describing behavior that portends a certain kind of weather to provide details that linger in the reader's poetic memory: swallows striking a lake's surface with their bellies (944–5), "domestic birds," those born from the cock, picking off lice and cackling loudly with a sound like raindrops drumming in succession (960–2), cows looking up to the sky and sniffing the air (954–5), mice squeaking and skipping around like dancers (1132–3). It is also in this final section that Aratus displays most effectively his poetic artistry, as the sounds made by nature, whether it be the cry of an animal or the howling of wind on the headland, are reproduced in the pattern of vowels and consonants in his lines. In the earlier section on the constellations, the steady, predictable progression of the stars across the sky was conveyed by fairly repetitious and somewhat spare vocabulary. But in the weather signs segment the diction is more colorful and varied, and the images more striking. The "old age" of thistle is its white fluffy down (921), clouds have the look of fleeces (939), and the "fathers of tadpoles" are a boon for watersnakes (946–7). Sometimes the behavior has a sympathetic connection to the weather it portends, as when ravens imitate the sound of raindrops when a storm approaches (966–7). Spots like millet seeds collecting in a circle around a lamp's wick signal snow, and naturally so since the word used for "spots" is *sēmata* (1040). Through this linguistic play, Aratus makes it evident that Zeus' beneficence in providing humans with signs of what cannot be seen does indeed pervade all, including the patterns made from the ashes of a wick.

By combining scholarly knowledge of technical matter with a high level of poetic artistry, Aratus demonstrated how Hesiodic didactic poetry could be retooled for a new age. As contemporary Hellenistic poets acknowledged the importance of Aratus' achievement, so too Latin writers expressed their admiration through translation and imitation. Surviving are translations by the young Cicero, Germanicus, and Avienus. Portions of the weather signs were adapted by Vergil in the *Georgics*, a work that followed Aratus' new approach to didacticism, and Ovid in his *Fasti* was also concerned with the connections between astral signs and human endeavors. As in other genres of poetry, the Latin poets who came to write didactic poems in the Greek manner approached their archaic models through the modernizations initiated by a key Hellenistic poet.

The amount of didactic poetry composed in the Hellenistic age was extensive, but most of these works are lost, the main exceptions being two poems by Nicander on poisonous animals and plants. In both *Theriaca* (*On Harmful Animals*) and *Alexipharmaca* (*On Antidotes for Poisons*), Nicander names his hometown as Clarus, the site of an oracle to Apollo near Colophon on the coast of Asia Minor. Beyond this fact, the biographical tradition concerning Nicander is hopelessly confused. While in one fragment (fr. 110 Gow and Scholfield) the poet names his father as Damaeus, an inscription from Delphi concerns a Nicander of Colophon, an epic poet, who was the son of one Anaxagoras,[11] and a biography in the *Suda* calls his father Xenophanes. In addition, the transmitted biographies allot him three different dates, making him a contemporary of Aratus in the first half of the third century, setting him at the end of that century in the reign of Ptolemy V Epiphanes, or later yet during the reign of Attalus III (138–133). Since it was a common Greek practice to name a child after a grandfather or uncle, there may have been two literary Nicanders from Colophon who were relatives of different generations. Of the three dates, the least likely is the early one, since synchronization with Aratus may have arisen from a desire to connect the two didactic poets. The most likely date is the latest one. A fragment addressed to an Attalus (fr. 104 Gow and Scholfield) is said to concern the last Pergamene king, and it is tempting to associate the didactic poems on poisonous animals and plants with this ruler, who cultivated and studied medicinal and poisonous plants.

Nicander's didactic poems are probably much more typical of the genre than the *Phaenomena*. Again, there were prose sources. The serious study of zoology and botany takes its beginning from fourth-century work in the Lyceum, where a heavy emphasis was placed on classification or taxonomy. Still extant to illustrate the attempted scientific nature of these studies, which, however, relied heavily on report rather than observation, are several works on animals by Aristotle and Theophrastus' *Inquiry into Plants* and *Plant Explanations*. Nicander likely knew these influential Peripatetic works, but his main source, identified from remarks in the scholiasts, was apparently one Apollodorus, who wrote a treatise entitled *On Harmful Animals* as well as a medical study of plant poisons, probably in the early third century. The *Theriaca* contains information about how to ward off noxious creatures when outdoors and then a catalogue of harmful snakes, spiders, scorpions, lizards, and fish, followed by information on remedies for their bite or sting. The *Alexipharmaca* lists substances that are deadly to humans, each followed by the antidotes that may be employed; the substances include poisonous plants and other consumables, a few animals such as leeches, salamanders, and toads, and even harmful minerals. Nicander's poems clearly found interested readers, since fragments of commentaries of the *Theriaca* survive in two papyri of the first century AD; the scholia surviving in the manuscripts of both poems descend from treatises of this sort.[12] In addition, Tertullian, a

Christian writer of the late second to early third century AD, reports that the illustrations of scorpions in his copy of the *Theriaca* descended from Nicander himself, and it is entirely credible that painted drawings originally accompanied the poetic text, since prose treatises of the period were often illustrated.

Another characteristic that connects Nicander's didactic poetry with the technical treatises of the era is his use of addressees (see Ch. 3.10), including King Attalus in a fragment of an unknown work. In the proem to *Theriaca*, addressed to his kinsman Hermesianax (apparently not the poet of the *Leontion*, though perhaps a relative or descendant), Nicander sets out the fictional purpose for which Hellenistic didactic poetry was composed: Hermesianax, he promises, will be respected for his knowledge of cures by any plowman, cowherd, or woodcutter harmed by a poisonous creature. While Hesiod's poetry was seemingly written for the direct benefit of his audience, the didactic poet of the Hellenistic age presents specialized knowledge to a class of educated readers, standing at a significant remove from the working folk who might actually benefit from the information. By introducing an addressee through whom his material will supposedly be filtered to those who might benefit from it, Nicander acknowledges the problematic relationship between the poet, his intended audience, and the fictionalized audience of sailors and herdsmen found in Aratus. The proem continues with an acknowledgment of his two primary models by citing the myth about the scorpion and the hunter Orion. If Hesiod told true stories, he says, harmful insects and reptiles are born from the Titans' blood, and Leto, a Titan's daughter, sent a scorpion to sting Orion when he attacked Artemis. In ending with a reference to Orion's catasterism, Nicander directly recalls Aratus' account of the constellations of the Scorpion and Hunter, although he fails to name expressly his Hellenistic model.

From time to time Nicander attempts to relieve the gloomy description of deadly creatures and plants with a digression into a mythical aetiology, although opportunity for this kind of embellishment is more limited than in the *Phaenomena*. An example is the story of how Helen struck and injured permanently the snake known as the bloodletter (*Theriaca* 309–19):

If true, Destructive Helen, coming from Troy, became angry at this species,
When they beached their ship by the much-whirling Nile
In flight from the destructive blast of the north wind,
And at that time she spied her helmsman Canobus
Expiring on the sands of Thonis; for a female bloodletter
Had struck him in the neck when he pressed on it in his sleep
And injected strong poison into him; it thus made him an evil bed.

Helen crushed the middle of its body and broke the connecting bonds
Of its back along the spine, so that the backbone protruded from its body.
From that time forward bloodletters and crooked-moving horned vipers
Alone of snakes move as if limping, burdened with the injury.

The better-known aetiology involved the mythical origin of the Canopic mouth of the Nile from the helmsman's death there (as told by Apollonius), and the early Ptolemies were keen to promote stories about Helen in Egypt as a way of making mythical precedent for their own Greek rule in that ancient kingdom. But here Nicander focuses on a lesser-known aspect of the Canobus story in order to make the aetiological connection to his rather dry subject matter, which was possibly enlivened with illustrations like those found in some manuscripts. The poet marks another aetiological passage, explaining why the bite of the *dipsas*, a kind of viper, produces extreme thirst in its victim, with an acrostic of his name (*Theriaca* 345–53). Again, he follows the example set by Aratus, but with a much more conventional use of the acrostic.

Some of the *vitae* explain Nicander's specialized knowledge of poisons by supposing him trained as a physician, but he wrote didactic poems on farming and mythology as well. More likely, he was working within a tradition of Colophonian catalogue poetry, exemplified by Antimachus' *Lyde* and Hermesianax's *Leontion* (Ch. 2.1, 3.2). A charming fragment on garland flowers from the second book of his *Georgica* (fr. 74 Gow and Scholfield) has quite a different atmosphere from the depressing works on poisons and harmful animals. Vergil may have been influenced by Nicander's *Georgics* in his work of the same name, but the fragments on how to prepare garden vegetables suggest that the Greek poem presented different subject matter; it certainly did not have Vergil's universalizing perspective. A number of the stories told in Nicander's *Heteroeumena*, a poem on mythical transformations apparently in five books, are preserved in a prose version in Antoninus Liberalis (probably second century AD). This work seems to have provided a model for Ovid's *Metamorphoses*, and we know that the Colophonian was one source for the Alcyone and Ceyx story in Ovid's *Metamorphoses*, a tender account of marital love and devotion transcending death itself.

3.6   Epigrams

Etymologically, the word *epigram* refers to any "writing" placed "upon" an object, but the term is generally used of inscriptions in verse. These are among the earliest forms of Greek poetry. From the late Geometric age, shortly after the time of Homer, verses began to be inscribed upon grave monuments, to name and commemorate the dead, and upon dedicated objects, to document the deity, the donor, and sometimes the reason for the gift. While the first metrical inscriptions consist of only one or two hexameters, by the late archaic and classical ages elegiac couplets had become the standard form (although lyric and iambic-trochaic meters were sometimes used as well). Epigrammatic verses continued to be engraved on monuments throughout antiquity, but in the hands of the professional poets of the Hellenistic age they took on a literary quality and acquired the status of aesthetic objects. Although the range of topics found in epigrams was extended over time, brevity remained an essential marker of the genre.

Verse inscriptions traditionally lacked any indication of author's name, and this anonymity at the inscriptional site clearly reflects a subliterary status. A few epigrams preserved in manuscripts are ascribed to important lyric poets of the pre-Hellenistic age, such as Simonides and Anacreon, and likely they did compose inscriptions of the sort. Yet some of the poems ascribed to them are clearly later forgeries, and the authorship of others cannot be verified. By the classical age, epitaphs for legendary figures, such as epic heroes and early poets, were circulating apart from any tomb. An example is the epitaph for the Phrygian king Midas, quoted by Plato (*Phaedrus* 264d):

> I am a bronze maiden and I stand on Midas' tomb.
> For as long as water flows and tall trees bloom,
> Remaining right here on his much-lamented tomb,
> I will announce to passersby that Midas is buried in this place.

The epitaph's oral character is shown by the interchangeable order of the lines, on which Socrates remarks in the dialogue, and later authors liked to comment on the mistaken claim that it marked the tomb of Midas for all time to come, since no tomb with such an inscription was known. The circulation of such epigrams independent from an inscriptional site likely influenced the development of Hellenistic literary epigrams.

As the only poetic genre originally written to be read, rather than orally performed, epigram anticipated the bookish practices of the Hellenistic age. In addition, the brevity, conciseness, and personal tone of the form appealed to the new literary tastes sweeping the Greek world, and as a result, the epigram genre came to be practiced by all the major poets of the period. They continued to write traditional sepulchral and dedicatory epigrams, though these were expanded into modified types, such as ecphrastic epigrams on objects of art or poems to celebrate a victory or to accompany a gift. Another type of epigram, mostly erotic and sympotic in subject, seems to have developed from the oral recitation of poetry at drinking parties called symposia. Importantly, the new literary character of Hellenistic epigrams is closely tied to the emergence of the first author-edited poetry books, a phenomenon of the third century. Inscriptional and occasional epigrams, when gathered by a poet into an ordered arrangement on a papyrus roll, were naturally viewed by readers from the distanced perspective that constitutes an aesthetic reading rather than simply as sources of information about real persons and events. Although it is often impossible to know whether surviving epigrams were originally occasional or inscriptional, some, especially those that introduce or close a poetry book, appear to have been composed specifically for the collection.

Most Hellenistic epigrams have been preserved in the *Greek Anthology*, a large compilation that also contains imperial and Byzantine epigrams. Editors, from ancient to modern, have always felt free to select and reorder epigrams found in earlier collections, and our *Greek Anthology* has a complicated history leading back through layers of earlier compilations to original publication contexts. The *Anthology* is based on a single manuscript derived from a tenth-century AD epigram collection assembled by Cephalas in Constantinople, supplemented with additional epigrams from a later, partially overlapping manuscript by Planudes. Cephalas made his compilation from ancient anthologies, including Meleager's *Garland*, which contained Hellenistic epigrams written before about 100, and Philip's *Garland*, which contained epigrams of the late Republican and Julio-Claudian periods. Meleager's anthology was organized into four major categories of sepulchral, dedicatory, erotic/sympotic, and (what came to be called) epideictic ("display") epigrams, while Philip's anthology was organized alphabetically. Behind these multi-authored *Garlands* were earlier, now lost, poetry books containing epigrams by a single poet. Although certain extracts from Meleager and Philip have been preserved by Cephalas in their original order, the earlier single-authored sources were dismembered by the ancient anthologists and their principles of ordering are no longer known. The one exception is the recently discovered Milan papyrus of the late third century,[13] which contains over a hundred previously unknown epigrams, arranged in at least ten thematic sections. This important new find, containing the poetry of Posidippus, a native of Macedonian Pella, gives us a unique example of a collection compiled close to the life of the epigrammatist. Since the epigram book was evidently not used by Meleager, it suggests that the types of epigrams collected in the *Garland* may reflect Meleager's personal preferences rather than the range of subjects produced in the Hellenistic age.

Sepulchral inscriptions are an integral part of the monument on which they are engraved. The passerby is enticed to pause, to contemplate the memorial and grave, and to learn from the inscription the name of the deceased and of the parties who set up the grave marker. The interest of the passerby in the unknown deceased might be simply a momentary sense of their common humanity, acknowledged by the ritual greeting *chaire* (meaning both "hail" and "farewell"). But when sepulchral epigrams are encountered in a more literary context, such as a bookroll, then the reader's interest tends to shift from curiosity about the deceased as a historical person to an assessment of the verses as a poetic object. Some Hellenistic poets, like Posidippus who was honored in an inscription of 263/2 as a "composer of epigrams,"[14] may have collected all or most of their commissioned epigrams into bookrolls, but the process of anthologizing into collections of poems by multiple authors surely tended to winnow out those of lesser poetic interest. At their most basic, epitaphs recorded the deceased's name, father's name, and homeland, as in this starkly beautiful couplet by Callimachus (*Palatine Anthology* 7.523):

> You who pass by the tomb of Cimon from Elis,
> > know that you are passing by Hippaeus' son.

The double reference to the transitory moment of passing by increases the pathos of the reminder that someone's child lies here, dead. In the epitaphic section of the Milan papyrus, Posidippus shows a preference for more extended descriptions focusing on key details of the life lost (55 Austin and Bastianini):

> All Nicomache's favorite things, her trinkets and her Sapphic
> > conversations with other girls beside the shuttle at dawn,
> fate took away prematurely. The city of the Argives
> > cried aloud in lament for that poor maiden,
> a young shoot reared in Hera's arms. Cold, alas, remain
> > the beds of the youths who courted her.

We do not know whether this epitaph for Nicomache was inscribed on her stone, or was perhaps written just to comfort her family, or was even a purely imaginative creation of the poet, but it does convey through specific detail what the loss of such a young woman means. An example of an epitaph that is more certainly literary, not inscribed, is this poem in which Callimachus dramatizes the reaction of a passerby who recognizes a deceased as someone he knew (*Palatine Anthology* 7.522):

> "Timonoe." Who are you? By god, I wouldn't have known you
>   if your father's name, Timotheus, and your city, Methymna,
> hadn't been on your tomb. I say, your husband Euthymenes
>   must be in great grief since he's bereft of you.

This is not a genuine inscription, but a passerby's reaction to one, made known through his quotation of the name he reads on the stone and by his paraphrase of the remaining words, consisting of the name of Timonoe's father and her homeland. The passerby adds what he knows from his personal acquaintance with the family, the husband's name and the surety of his grief, while the reader's reaction, disinterested in Timonoe herself, has to do with the aesthetic pleasure of reading an epigram that itself represents the reading of an inscription.

Other epitaphs from the *Anthology* betray their literary nature in a variety of ways. Anyte of Tegea in Arcadia, who is perhaps among the earliest Hellenistic epigrammatists, seems to have had a special interest in women (for whom she wrote epitaphs), children, animals, and nature. She is particularly famous for her tender laments for animals. While her epigrams for a war horse and a hunting hound were just possibly commissioned by the proud owners of these animals,[15] it is difficult to believe in an original inscriptional context for her epitaphs for a cock killed by a predator, a beached dolphin, or these two insects (*Palatine Anthology* 7.190):

> For her grasshopper, the nightingale of the fields, and her cicada,
>   dweller in the oak, Myro made a common tomb,
> A girl shedding a maiden's tear. For Hades, hard to dissuade,
>   took away both her playthings.

Since grasshoppers and cicadas were symbols of tuneful poetry, this epigram may have been intended as a tribute to another woman poet, or even a projection of Anyte's own earlier self, a girl entranced by a childish version of mellifluous sound.

Another poet from the first half of the third century, Leonidas of Tarentum, a composer of inscriptions and dedications, became the most imitated of the early epigrammatists. It is unfortunate that we know little of his life, except that he lived in exile from his native city, which was one of the most important Greek colonies in southern Italy. Perhaps if we knew more about his biography it would be evident why he focuses on a class of people not usually represented in the inscriptional record. His epigrams detail the professional lives of many ordinary individuals, particularly the working poor such as carpenters, fishermen, and weavers; at the same time, the language he uses to commemorate these commonplace people is some of the most complex and sophisticated known from the Hellenistic period. The dissonance between the ordinary subject matter and the erudite diction in which it is expressed strongly indicates that Leonidas' epigrams were composed for the book rather than the stone. Where, for instance, would this epitaph for a merchant lost at sea have been inscribed (*Palatine Anthology* 7.654)?

> The Cretans have always been thieves, pirates, and criminals.
>   Who has ever known justice from Cretans?
> As I was sailing along with only a modest cargo, men from Crete
>   threw me, wretched Timolytus, into the sea.
> The gulls who live at sea lamented me, the real me,
>   and not under my tomb is there Timolytus.

Cenotaphs, inscriptions placed on empty tombs, constitute a subcategory of sepulchral epigram, generally concerning the shipwrecked. Literary epigrammatists were fond of inverting the inscriptional motif of a tomb lacking a body to voice the sentiments of the body lacking a tomb. Here Timolytus, pathetically mourned by gulls, claims that his true identity belongs properly, not to an empty grave, but to his lost body. Whether or not the drowned Timolytus is historical or fictional, the epigram likely formed part of a section in an epigram book that was devoted to shipwrecked individuals; such a section, with the heading *nauagika*, "on the shipwrecked," is now known from the Posidippus collection.

Epitaphs for poets, often long dead, form another type of literary epigram. Early poets who had crossed over into the realm of heroes and received cult worship, like Homer and Hesiod, were commemorated with fictitious epitaphs already in the classical era. Hellenistic poets extended this practice to a wide range of poets, sometimes to mark their sense of separation from the great figures of their poetic heritage and sometimes to spotlight a contemporary poet for praise or blame. One of their favorite subjects was the lyric poet Anacreon, whose reputation as a drunken lout with a hankering for boys appealed to the Hellenistic focus on personal longings and pleasures. Anacreon was also conceived as a predecessor for the epigrammatic genre, since the *Anthology* preserves a series of, at least partially spurious, epigrams attributed to him. The epigrammatist Dioscorides, who probably dates to the late third century, wrote several epitaphs for dramatic poets – Thespis (the inventor of tragedy), Aeschylus, Sophocles, Sositheus (a Hellenistic writer of satyr plays), and Machon (a Hellenistic comic poet; see Ch. 3.8).[16] Since the satyr who adorns Sositheus' grave seems to refer to the Sophocles epitaph, it seems likely that this set of dramatic epitaphs descends from an epigram book in which they were juxtaposed. Hellenistic epigrammatists sometimes wrote their own self-epitaphs, probably to end their collected epigrams or sections within those books. Leonidas laments dying in exile far from Tarentum (*Palatine Anthology* 7.715), Callimachus seeks to shape his poetic reputation both in an epitaph for his father (7.525) and in his own epitaph (7.415), and Meleager rounds off the *Garland* section on dead poets with no fewer than four self-epitaphs (7.417–19, 7.421). Although tombs did sometimes bear more than one sepulchral poem, this set of interrelated epigrams was composed as book poetry, designed to identify the poet with his art in a key position in his anthology.

Dedicatory verses, composed to provide basic information about a gift to a deity, are the other major type of inscribed epigram. The most talented of Hellenistic poets knew how to rework the familiar form with crisp, often elegant wit. This example (in iambic meter), in which a Cretan mercenary dedicates his weapons to Sarapis after a victory in Libya, is by Callimachus (*Palatine Anthology* 13.7):

> Menoetas of Lyctus
> dedicated this bow,
> saying: "Here, Sarapis,
> I give you my bow
> and quiver. The arrows
> the men of Hesperis have."

The epigram may commemorate a genuine dedication, erected by some soldier who served the Ptolemies in one of several known conflicts in western Libya. But what makes the poem worth preserving is its linguistic construct, the clever explanation why Sarapis is not presented with Menoetas' arrows as well as his bow and quiver, namely, that the arrows remain in their enemy target. In another poem, Callimachus reworks the obligatory information of dedications into a staccato exchange of questions and answers between the presented object and the recipient god Heracles (*Palatine Anthology* 6.351):

> To you, lion-strangling, boar-killing lord, I, an oak club, have been given
>   by –
>   Who? –
>   Archinus –
>   From where? –
>   Crete –
>   I accept.

Although "speaking objects" are found in even the earliest inscriptions, this couplet, ostensibly inscribed on a wooden club like the one used by Heracles, may be a purely literary epigram. Much of the wit of the poem lies in the contrast between the voice of the club, with his sycophantic compound epithets for Heracles, and the laconic reply of the god, who shows his no-nonsense character through his one-word questions. But wit was only one aspect of Hellenistic epigrammatic artistry. Leonidas' dedicatory epigrams often encourage the reader to appreciate the beauty of tools used by the working people who dedicate them. In one example, three sisters who have supported themselves as weavers offer their equipment to Athena upon retirement (*Palatine Anthology* 6.289):

> Autonoma, Meliteia, Boiscion, the three Cretan daughters
>   of Philolaides and Nico, have set up in this temple,
> stranger, as a gift for Athena of the Spool, on the occasion
>   of their retirement from the labors of Athena:
> from the first, an ever-whirling spindle that works the thread,
>   from the second, a basket that tends the wool at night,
> and from the third, her shuttle, that skillfully working maker
>   of fine garments, the guardian of Penelope's bed.

The elegant descriptive phrases, coupled with reference to the famed story of Penelope's faithful weaving, give an almost heroic dignity to the long labors of these commonplace weaving women.

The category of dedicatory epigram overlaps with what we today call ecphrastic epigrams, poems on works of art. Nossis, a woman poet from Epizephyrian Locris in southern Italy, composed a series of epigrams on women's dedications of their own portraits and other artistic objects in a temple of Aphrodite. These poems anticipate purely ecphrastic epigrams because the poet imagines that she and her acquaintances are actually viewing the paintings and reacting to the realistic qualities of the depictions. Callo's charm can be seen to blossom, Melinna has a gentle face and peers out softly, Samytha's dedicated headband is finely worked and smells sweetly of nectar (*Palatine Anthology* 9.605, 6.353, 6.275). Another set of early ecphrastic epigrams is found in the Posidippus papyrus in the section on bronze statues by famous sculptors. Here in fragmentary form is the earliest epigram on the *Cow* sculpted by the fifth-century artist Myron; remarkably, this *Cow* became the most popular subject in the *Anthology* and epigrams celebrating its naturalness were composed through late antiquity. Antipater of Sidon, who worked in the second half of the second century, wrote six couplets on the subject, of which this is one (*Palatine Anthology* 9.720):

> If Myron had not fixed my feet to this stone, I, a heifer,
>   would be pasturing with the other cows.

The epigram on Hecataeus' realistic statue of Philitas (63 Austin and
Bastianini, quoted in Ch. 2.1), in which the artist's precision in sculpting
is set in parallel with the scholar-poet's precision in thought, also occurs in
the statue section of the Milan papyrus. Here we find the dedicatory aspect
as well, since king Ptolemy has set up this statue of his old tutor "for the
sake of the Muses."

Dedicatory epigrams overlap with yet other subcategories, as again
shown by the Posidippus papyrus. Epinician epigrams, commemorating
athletic victories, are well attested in the inscriptional record; they often
accompanied a statue of an athlete or of a victorious racehorse dedicated
in a sacred precinct. The Milan papyrus offers a whole section of these,
focusing on the victories of the Ptolemaic royal family at Panhellenic
occasions such as the Olympic and Nemean games. Surprisingly, the
emphasis is on victories won by queens, who of course were not riders
or charioteers, but owners of racehorses. In the following poem, a chariot
team, now dedicated in statue form, compares Berenice's victory with a
rare earlier victory by a Spartan queen, celebrated in an epigram that
survives in inscription (87 Austin and Bastianini):

> When we mares were still living, we won an Olympic crown,
>   oh inhabitants of Pisa, for Macedonian Berenice,
> that crown of much-celebrated fame with which we took away
>   the ancient glory of Cynisca in Sparta.

The section of the papyrus on cures for diseases contains dedications to
Asclepius, the god of healing. Although seemingly literary in nature, the
cure epigrams nevertheless resemble prose accounts of miraculous cures
sometimes erected in sanctuaries of Asclepius, as at Epidaurus. An emaciated figure in bronze, set up by a doctor as a thank offering, represents
the sort of diseased persons he claimed to heal.

Erotic epigrams did not develop directly from inscriptions. As a result,
their claim to belong to the generic category of epigram rests on formal
aspects, namely their brevity (typically two to ten lines) and (usually) the
elegiac meter. In origin, they seem related to the elegies of the sixth-
century poet Theognis, whose treatment of erotic relationships between
men and adolescent boys was connected with a broader political/social
agenda. Since Theognis' poetry was recited at symposia, it is commonly
believed that erotic epigrams, like a few purely sympotic ones, came into
being for recitation at early Hellenistic drinking parties, although their

survival in manuscript reveals that poets also collected their erotic compositions for publication. While collections of sepulchral and dedicatory epigrams contain a multiplicity of voices speaking from one poem to the next, in book sequences of erotic epigrams the reader has the impression of a single voice, perhaps that of the poet, but one malleable enough to fit many lovers in its variety of emotional experiences.

The earliest known erotic epigrammatist is Asclepiades of Samos, who was composing already before the end of the fourth century. In the variety of situations projected in his poems, Asclepiades set out many of the themes that reappear in later Greek epigrams of the amatory type. He defines himself as a lover, not by depicting an obsessive passion for one person, but by showing himself continually subject to desire for a changing array of love objects. He names in his surviving epigrams a number of women with whom he had, or wished to have, affairs – Hermione, Didyme, Philaenion, Heracleia, Nico, Pythias. Although the social status of his women is often unclear, variety is certainly in evidence: one poem is directed to seducing a virgin, another concerns a hetaira who announces her promiscuity in golden letters on her breast band, and yet another presents a young woman looking longingly from her window at a handsome youth. Each epigram represents a unique erotic experience, sometimes not that of the poet at all: a young woman laments that her lover Archeades has deserted her, Lysidice celebrates winning a sexual "horse race" with another hetaira, Bitto and Nannion are lesbian lovers, Dorcion attracts lovers by dressing like a boy. In a small number of epigrams, Asclepiades speaks of love between young males. Here the tone is different, as the poet compliments boys on their physical similarity to Eros or emphasizes mutuality of affection between youths of similar ages. In all these instances, the epigram represents an emotional state connected with a single moment in time, sometimes in a defined dramatic setting. In several epigrams, the lover stands outside the beloved's house at night in stormy weather and hopes, though vainly, to be admitted; poems of this type (cf. the soldier's monologue in Menander's *Hated Man*, Ch. 3.1) are called *paraclausithyra* ("beside the closed door") and occur in Latin poetry as well. One of Asclepiades' most poignant epigrams, apparently composed early in his career, expresses his anguish at his continual, inescapable state of erotic longing (*Palatine Anthology* 12.46):

> I'm not yet twenty-two and I'm sick of living. Erotes,
> > why this mistreatment? Why do you burn me?
> For if I die, what then will you do? Clearly, Erotes,
> > you'll go on heedlessly playing dice as before.

The dice game of the Erotes is an image for the lover's experience of love, which feels like an unpredictable game of chance controlled by some unfeeling divine power.

Although the lover who is always in a state of desire for a shifting array of individuals remains prototypical in erotic epigram, the various composers of the type distinguish themselves through their personal characteristics. Posidippus wrote several erotic epigrams, much influenced by Asclepiades, which are known to us through Meleager's *Garland*; despite close imitation of Asclepiades, he yet presents himself as ever hopeful of escaping love's grip through the power of reason. Callimachus, who seems exclusively interested in young men, often finds his refined tastes, for lovers as well as poetry, in conflict with the promiscuous, even mercenary, nature of the youths he desires. The erotic epigrams of Dioscorides are more explicit, as he lists the physical features that attract him to a woman, describes the fulfillment of the sexual act in mutual orgasms, and explains how he overcomes the difficulties of having sex with his pregnant partner. Likewise, Rhianus of Crete, who was primarily an epic poet (Ch. 3.3), writes rather explicitly about the physical charms of boys, who are a "labyrinth, hard to exit" (*Palatine Anthology* 12.93).

One of the most important of the erotic epigrammatists was Meleager, who included over one hundred of his own epigrams in his *Garland* (ca. 100). He provides an excellent example of a late Hellenistic poet of the Greek East, who attached himself strongly to the tradition of Hellenic culture. As he reveals in his self-epitaphs, he was born in Syrian Gadara, lived as a young man in Phoenician Tyre, and finally moved to Greek Cos. He is famous for his elaborate variations of the earlier epigrams and for his complex imagery, which often reflects the late Hellenistic taste for the expression of eroticism through the allegorical figures of Cupids, bows, torches, butterflies (an emblem of the soul), and the like. He is the first known poet to compose cycles of poems about one love object, imitated in Catullus' cycles for Lesbia and Juventius. Though numerous lovers fill out his poetry, Meleager's primary love objects were Zenophila and Heliodora, apparently hetairas, and his favorite boy-love, Myiscus. His special talent was to convey intensity of emotion through witty play with standard erotic motifs. An example is this expression of desire for exclusive possession of his beloved (*Palatine Anthology* 5.174):

> You are sleeping, Zenophila, delicate flower. Would that I were now
>   the wingless slumber sitting upon your eyes,
> so that the one who enchants even the eyes of Zeus would not
>   come to you and I would have you all to myself.

The Latin erotic elegists, including Catullus, were much influenced by Meleager, and Propertius acknowledges this debt by opening his first book with an adaptation of a Meleagrian epigram. The Epicurean philosopher Philodemus, whose library has been uncovered in a ruined villa at Herculaneum, came from the same Syrian town of Gadara but lived in Italy after about 75. Several of his erotic epigrams are for one Xantho or Xanthippe, who may have been his wife, and, although some of his poems concern hetairas, others seem to express contentment with a single partner. Catullus' poetry, with its famous Lesbia cycle, shows the influence of epigrams by both Meleager and Philodemus, and the Epicurean was likely a literary as well as philosophical mentor for the young Roman intellectuals, including Vergil and Horace, who gathered around him at Herculaneum.

While sepulchral, dedicatory, and erotic remained the principal types, many other topics came to be treated in Hellenistic epigrams. Those that have clearly lost association with an inscriptional context are often called epideictic ("display") poems. Epigrams imitating the labels or tags attached to bookrolls to identify the author and work appear as early as Asclepiades' poems for Erinna's *Distaff* and Antimachus' *Lyde* (Ch. 2.1). Other epigrams are modeled on the inscriptions placed on public buildings or monuments, such as Posidippus' epigrams for the Pharus at Alexandria. Roadside signs that point the way to nearby springs and shady groves where a traveler might rest were early developed by Anyte into charming invitations to spend a leisurely hour in a bucolic type of setting. Bucolic epigrams featuring Daphnis and other characters from bucolic poetry form another small subcategory, some of which naturally, but probably falsely, came to be ascribed to Theocritus. Satiric epigrams, one of the most common types in the imperial period, are found, though in much smaller numbers, already in Meleager's anthology. For instance, after the defeat of Philip V by the Roman general Flamininus at Cynoscephalae in 197, Alcaeus of Messene wrote a series of bitter epigrams criticizing the Macedonian king's cruelty and ineptitude.[17] The possibilities for such minor categories of epigram are myriad, as the Posidippus papyrus has now made us aware. The two opening sections surprised scholars by offering an epigrammatic treatment of material found in earlier prose treatises. The first of these concerns stones of all types, ranging from carved gemstones to boulders hurled ashore by tsunami waves, and the second was on omens, ranging from weather signs to military portents to an epitaph for Alexander's favorite seer.

During the second and first centuries BC important epigrammatists were noted for their ability to improvise verses and to vary compositions, those of themselves or others, by treating the same topic with different words and phrases. Both Antipater of Sidon in the late second century and Aulus

Licinius Archias of Antioch, who in 62 was defended by Cicero in a challenge to his Roman citizenship, were admired by Roman intellectuals for their extemporaneous compositions. The trend toward replicating early epigrams with greater or lesser variation arose at the time when Rome was consolidating its mastery over the East, and it may reflect a cultural need to preserve and retool Greek literary heritage for the new political reality. It is also likely that at this time certain earlier Greek epigrams were identified as canonical, and so worthy of imitation and variation. For instance, both Antipater and a certain Archias, likely the one known to Cicero, composed variations of a poignant epitaph in dialogue form composed by Leonidas (*Palatine Anthology* 7.163):

> – Who are you, lady, who lie under a Parian pillar, and whose daughter?
>   – Prexo, Calliteles' daughter. – From where? – Samos.
> – And who buried you? – Theocritus, to whom my parents
>   married me. – How did you die? – In childbirth.
> – At what age? – Twenty-two. – Childless then?
>   – No, I left behind Calliteles aged three.
> – I hope for you he lives and comes to a great old age.
>   – And I, stranger, that Fortune be good to you.

Although the very similar versions by Antipater and Archias are hardly improvements, the poets apparently prided themselves on their ability to replicate a much-admired epigram. What may seem particularly odd to us are multiple variations by one author, such as Antipater's six couplets on Myron's *Cow* or Archias' four variations of Leonidas' dedicatory epigram on three brothers who were hunters – one of land animals, one of fish, and the third of birds. But this ability to say the same thing over and over again, yet differently, was a sought-after quality in writers and orators of the Roman period, as educated persons ceaselessly tried to improve the great works of the past through imitation. Among the largely "epideictic" epigrams ascribed to Archias are an epitaph for a jay and two epigrams on the mythical figure of Echo. Since the jay imitates the sounds of others and Echo can only repeat what she hears, these epigrams may have functioned in Archias' epigrammatic corpus as emblems of his art of variation.

Meleager, who also practiced epigram variation, admired Antipater of Sidon, for whom he wrote a riddling epitaph; it is less clear whether he knew the Archias whose epigrams have been preserved in the *Greek Anthology*. In his *Garland*, the primary vehicle through which Hellenistic epigrams were transmitted to the modern world, Meleager grouped poems in thematic sequences in which model and variation would usually appear side by side. For the reader of this multi-authored collection, the intertextual connections between earlier and later Hellenistic epigrams were inescapably evident. In the erotic section, Meleager set up a persistent rhythm of earlier epigram followed by one or more variations or adaptations, often his own composition. Some of his epigrams seem designed to occupy a certain place in the *Garland*, almost like a commentary on the models being varied, as in this set:

> Callimachus
> Callignotus swore to Ionis that he would not ever
>   care for anyone, male or female, more than her.
> He swore it. But what they say is true, that lovers' oaths
>   do not penetrate the ears of the immortals.
> Now he burns with desire for a youth, and of that girl,
>   as of the Megareans, he has no word or thought.
>   Asclepiades
> Lamp, Heracleia swore three times in your presence to come,
>   but she has not come. Lamp, if you are a god,
> take vengeance on that deceptive girl. When she's playing at home
>   with her lover, go out and don't furnish them light.
>   Meleager
> Sacred night and lamp, we both, he and I, took no other
>   witnesses to our oaths except you two.
> He swore to love me and I swore not ever to leave him.
>   We have a common witness.
> But now he says that running water has carried away his oaths,
>   and lamp, you see him in the arms of others.
>   (*Palatine Anthology* 5.6–8)

Meleager has borrowed the address to the lamp as witness of the oath from Asclepiades, but he adapts it to the voice of someone who has been betrayed, someone like the Ionis of Callimachus' epigram. It is a startlingly effective variation of two epigrams, combining Callimachus' objective look at a pair of lovers with Asclepiades' subjective presentation of a male lover's voice, to produce a rare interior revelation of a woman's erotic longing. As this example shows, Meleager's compositional technique was intimately connected with his editing skills.

While the brevity of epigram form confined it to the lowest echelons in literary canons, ancient poets who collected their epigrams into poetry books often did so with the recognition that even slight poems when arranged with design might rival lengthier compositions. But as the Latin epigrammatist Martial later points out, the reader of an epigram book has a tendency to read selectively. By nature, collected epigrams are subject to rearrangement, whether through reading practices or removal to new collections, and thus they are continually subject to new, different interpretations. It is an essential paradox of the epigram genre that this form most closely tied in origin to a physical site of inscription became, from its adaptation to literary contexts in the Hellenistic age, the most moveable of poetic types. Already in Meleager's *Garland* skill at composition and skill at arranging seem to have been given equal weight in creating the aesthetic appeal of the anthology.

3.7   Dramatic Poetry

The main types of dramatic poetry that were performed in classical Athens – tragedy, satyr play, and comedy – continue throughout the Hellenistic period, both as revivals of older plays and as new compositions. Although a great number of plays of the Athenian type must have been written during the three centuries before the birth of Christ, very little of this original dramatic material survives. Likewise lost, apart from a few fragments and representations on vases, are phlyax plays, parodies of mythological or tragic stories that developed in southern Italy from a combination of a native comic tradition and the importation of Athenian drama. Mime, a less sophisticated type of performance primarily in prose, also became increasingly popular in the Hellenistic age. Theocritus and Herodas elevated this genre to a higher literary status by composing metrical mimes that were collected into a bookroll for a reading public. In typical Hellenistic manner, purely dramatic forms for performance were mixed with other literary types to create innovative hybrid genres. Examples include Theocritean *Idylls* that combine mimelike speech by characters with narrative framing (6, 7, 11) and Callimachus' hymns dramatizing ritual acts (*Hymns* 2, 5, and 6). Another example, discussed below, is Lycophron's *Alexandra*, a long dramatic monologue written in the enigmatic style of oracles.

   In the early Hellenistic age, Athens ceased to be the primary site for the production of plays. Tragedies, satyr plays, and comedies were staged at festivals throughout the Hellenic world, and companies of performers known as the *technitai*, "artists," of Dionysus put on productions at various locales. Among the most important of these festivals were the Soteria established to commemorate the salvation of Delphi from the Gauls in 279/78 and the Dionysia that were taking place on Delos by the end of the fourth century. In Egypt, bands of Dionysiac artists based at Alexandria and elsewhere gave performances supported by royal patronage. In 274 dramatic *technitai*, led by the poet Philicus of Corcyra serving as the priest of Dionysus, marched in the great procession put on by

Ptolemy Philadelphus. The king showed his generosity toward those engaged in intellectual and artistic pursuits by exempting dramatic performers (as well as teachers and other festival victors) from a personal tax levied on Ptolemaic citizens.

By at least the Augustan age, a canon of the best Hellenistic playwrights had been formed. This group was known as the Pleiad, named after a constellation consisting of seven stars, although the ancient lists of best composers vary, giving us more than seven names. The most likely original members of the group, all from the heyday of poetic creativity under Ptolemy II, are as follows: Alexander of Aetolia, who also engaged in the scholarly editing of tragedies in the Alexandrian Museum; Lycophron of Chalcis, who edited the comic texts in Alexandria and wrote at least twenty tragedies; Homerus of Byzantium, son (or, less likely, father) of a female poet Moero; Sosiphanes of Syracuse, who is credited with seventy-three tragedies; Sositheus of the Alexandria in the Troad, who excelled at satyr plays; and Philicus the Dionysiac priest, who wrote forty-two tragedies. Very little is known of the plays composed by the Pleiad. We do have titles of tragedies by Lycophron, some of which are on the traditional mythical themes of Attic tragedy, such as his *Andromeda*, *Heracles*, *Laius*, *Oedipus*, and *Pentheus*. The *Elephenor*, concerning a minor Homeric hero who led the Greek contingent from Lycophron's native Chalcis in Euboea, illustrates the Hellenistic interest in promoting local traditions, while his *Cassandreis* was seemingly a rare historical play about the city of Cassandrea, established in 310. Lycophron also composed a satyr play entitled *Menedemus* in which he praised, in a jocular fashion, the Eretrian philosopher of that name who lived at the court of Antigonus Gonatas. Fragments are preserved in which the wine-loving Silenus complains to the satyr chorus about the frugality and sobriety of Menedemus' symposium, where guests are served a watery cup of cheap wine, slightly soured, and dessert consists of "moralizing conversation" (Athenaeus 10.420b–c). Another satyr play entitled *Daphnis or Lityerses*, by Sositheus, concerned the bucolic Daphnis best known from Theocritus' *Idylls*, who went to rescue his beloved, a nymph named Thalia or Pimplea, from the brigands who had kidnapped her. He came to the land of a brutish harvester Lityerses, the bastard son of the legendary king Midas of Phrygia; this Lityerses challenged strangers to a reaping contest and then cut off their heads. All ended happily when Heracles arrived to save Daphnis, subjected Lityerses to his own version of harvesting, and reunited the lovers. The plays of the Pleiad were likely performed at the new Panhellenic festivals, such as the Ptolemaica established in Alexandria by Ptolemy Philadelphus to honor his father. They were probably also published in bookrolls for interested contemporary readers.

The *Exagoge* (*Exodus*) by a Hellenized Jew Ezechiel, surviving in fragments consisting of 269 lines, is our best-preserved Hellenistic tragedy.
Written probably in the second century, and probably in Alexandria, the
play concerns the story of Moses and the escape of the Israelites from
Egypt. The tragedy opens with a prologue spoken by Moses, who recounts
his genealogy, his exposure as a baby and rescue by the pharaoh's daughter, and his life as a young man up to the point of his flight from Egypt
after killing a man in a quarrel. Now in Libya, he meets the seven
daughters of Raguel at a well and protects them from harassing shepherds.
Raguel then betroths Moses to his daughter Sepphorah, and the play
contained a now lost scene in which her earlier suitor Chum protests. In
another scene, probably set in mountainous pasture lands, Moses sees the
burning bush and encounters God, who gives him a rod with which to
work plagues on the Egyptians and instructs him in how to celebrate
Passover. After a substantial missing section, an Egyptian soldier acting
as messenger to the pharaoh describes how Moses parted the waters of the
Red Sea so that the Israelites might escape and how the pharaoh's army
was destroyed. Here is a sample of that speech, dramatizing a famous
section of the Old Testament book of *Exodus* (224–42):

> Then their leader Moses, taking
> the staff of God, with which before he had devised
> for Egypt evil signs and portents,
> struck the surface of the Red Sea and cleaved it
> to its depth. They all then with their strength rushed swiftly
> along the briny path, and we immediately went forward
> upon their trail. Running forward with a cry, we met
> pitch blackness. Suddenly our chariot wheels
> would not turn and were held as if bound fast.
> From heaven a great flash as of fire became
> visible to us: God, it seemed, was present
> as their helper. When they reached the sea's shore,
> a great wave roared near us, and someone seeing it
> cried out: "Let us flee homeward
> Before the hands of the Highest One.
> For he is their helper, but he works
> destruction on wretches like us." Then the passageway
> through the Red Sea was awash and our army destroyed.

In a final scene the Israelites have reached a desert on the other side of the
Red Sea, and a messenger describes to Moses a nearby valley lush with
meadows and springs. The messenger also saw there a marvelous bird,
assumed to be the phoenix, the symbol of renewed life.

The *Exagoge* demonstrates a fascinating combination of Hellenic and Jewish influences and may have been composed for a mixed Jewish and pagan audience. It dramatizes, with certain liberties, the Moses story as told in *Exodus*. The Septuagint, the translation of the Hebrew scriptures into Greek, was completed by various hands during the Hellenistic period, a process that began in the third century, quite possibly under the sponsorship of the Ptolemies, as recounted in the *Letter of Aristeas* (Ch. 4.3). Ezechiel's play shows knowledge of both the Greek version of *Exodus* in the Septuagint and the tradition of Midrashic interpretation. In form and language, the tragedy is purely Greek. It may have been divided into five acts, as was the norm for New Comedy and perhaps Hellenistic tragedy, and it has typical features of Attic drama, such as a prologue to remind the audience of the main character's history and messenger speeches to recount scenes of action and death. Ezechiel was also influenced by specific plays of Aeschylus, especially the *Persians*, and by Euripides. The romance with Sepphorah, given interest through the rivalry with Chum, is a typical Hellenistic extension of features developed in Euripidean drama, as the description of the lush meadow where the Israelites will find respite seems related to Hellenistic fascination with pastoral motifs.

Another dramatic form practiced in the Hellenistic period was phlyax plays, which originated in southern Italy and were apparently imported to Alexandria, in a newly sophisticated form, during the reigns of the first two Ptolemies. The word *phlyax* was a local Italian term for mime actors who wore masks and used stage props, and there was a long tradition in Doric communities of simple farces by such performers. South Italian vases produced throughout the fourth century depict stage performances, usually on mythical and tragic topics, by grossly padded, comic actors, who are performing phlyax plays or, in some cases as it seems, reproductions of Attic comedies in a local manner. The names of three composers of these plays are known – Rhinthon, Sciras, and Sopater. Rhinthon, the son of a potter from Tarentum, flourished under the first Ptolemy. He is said to have created hilarotragedy, "happy tragedy," an adaptation of phlyax performance to tragic plots. The result was a more light-hearted version of old Attic tragedies. The epigrammatist Nossis, from neighboring Locri, composed a laudatory epitaph for Rhinthon, whom she calls a Syracusan; there she labels him "a small nightingale of the Muses" and speaks of dry laughter as characteristic of his "phlyax tragedies" (*Palatine Anthology* 7.414). He wrote thirty-eight plays, which included such mythical titles as *Amphitryon*, *Iphigeneia among the Taurians*, *Medea*, *Orestes*, *Telephus*, and *Meleager the Slave*. *Meleager* is also the only surviving title from the phlyax plays of Sciras, also from Tarentum; the one fragment from this play parodies Euripides. Sopater, from Paphos on Cyprus, is called both a parodist and a writer of phlyax plays, which suggests the parodic quality of these dramatic performances. He lived from the time of Alexander the Great to the age of Ptolemy Philadelphus. In addition to mythical titles like *Hippolytus* and *Orestes* (probably tragic parodies), we know of plays entitled *Bacchis* (a hetaira name), *Wooers of Bacchis*, and *Marriage of Bacchis*, perhaps a trilogy based on New Comedy plots. In some plays Sopater made fun of contemporary figures such as philosophers and military men. In one called *Lentil Soup* (suggesting a Cynic context), a person who possesses an ornate silver cruet is compared to Thibron, a Spartan mercenary commander of the Alexandrian era, and in a fragment of *Gauls* someone threatens to expose Stoic claims to endurance by roasting three such philosophers.

A feature of later Euripidean tragedies was the solo performance of songs by a main character, often female. These arias, accompanied by emotional music, replaced to some degree the choral songs of traditional tragedy and were later extracted for separate performance. The development of this kind of monodrama stands behind a curious and little-understood Hellenistic dramatic work, Lycophron's *Alexandra*. Alexandra is another name for Cassandra, the daughter of the Trojan king Priam, who was cursed by Apollo with the ability to deliver accurate prophecies that were never believed. In this work of nearly 1,500 tragic trimeters, Cassandra utters obscure predictions that summarize the "future" events of the *Iliad*, as well as the return voyages of the Greeks and the adventures of the Trojan hero Aeneas, who escaped the destruction of his city to settle in Italy. Lycophron's poem has been notorious since antiquity as a "dark" work because of its complex style and riddling manner of speech. Proper names are throughout replaced by circumlocutions or metaphors, as, for instance, Paris abducting Helen becomes a "winged firebrand rushing to the snatching of a dove, who is the hound of Pephnos" (86–7), the last being a place in Helen's native Laconia. The reader's difficulty in understanding the allusions of the "mad" Cassandra is compounded by Lycophron's fondness for lesser-known myths, and the running commentary that provides us a comprehensible paraphrase of the text was clearly necessary already for ancient readers.

The *Alexandra* has technically the form of a messenger's speech, since in the opening and closing lines a guard assigned to observe Cassandra reports to Priam about her enigmatic prophecies. Since the guard claims, improbably, that he can repeat the exact form of her ravings, the poet raises, through the use of this frame, the question of accuracy and interpretation in prophecy and, one suspects, in poetry as well. The prophecy itself may be summarized as follows: the story of the Trojan War and the fall of her homeland, ending with her own rape by the lesser

Ajax (31–364), accounts of those Greeks who will suffer or die in their attempts to return home, including a long summary of the adventures of Odysseus (365–1089), accounts of other Greeks who suffer only after reaching home, including the murders of Agamemnon and Cassandra herself, who accompanies him home as his slave and concubine (1090–1225), an account of the journey of Aeneas to Italy ending with references to the Sibyl at Cumae (1226–82), a list of conflicts between Asia and Europe, ending with historical events, most importantly the Persian Wars, Alexander's triumph over the East, and an uncertain later Hellenistic conflict (1283–1450), and Cassandra's final lament for the uselessness of her prophecies (1451–60). The poem is remarkable for its scope and emotional intensity. This distressed maiden manages to offer, from the point of view of her own personal involvement, summaries of the Trojan cycle of epic poems, including the *Iliad* and the *Odyssey*, important Greek tragedies such as Aeschylus' *Agamemnon*, Herodotus' history of conflict between East and West, and even the stories that will later form the subject matter of Vergil's *Aeneid*. In literary terms, then, Lycophron's poem is a *tour de force*, which attempts to rewrite the masterpieces of Hellenic culture in the dark, allegorical style of Sibylline prophecy.

The identity of the author of the *Alexandra* is much disputed. Our sources generally identify him as Lycophron from Chalcis, who was a member of the Pleiad and did scholarly work under Ptolemy Philadelphus. If this is the case, then the Hellenistic conflict referred to in lines 1446–50 is apparently the campaign of Pyrrhus, the king of Epirus, against the Romans in southern Italy in the 270s, and the poem can be dated to Ptolemy II's reign. But others believe that Cassandra's praise of the Romans as "holding the scepter and monarchy of land and sea" (1229–30) could not have been written so early; these scholars insist that the author was another, unknown Lycophron and that the Hellenistic conflict mentioned is probably the defeat of the Macedonian Philip V at Cynoscephalae in 197. It only adds to the problem that the poem does not reveal the court for which it was written, but it is unlikely to have been the Alexandrian one since there is little about Egypt or Ptolemaic concerns. The emphasis on Troy as the single most important factor in the later history of the Greeks and the Romans points toward the Attalids, who had physical possession of the site of Troy and by the beginning of the second century had formed a strong alliance with the rising power in the West. At the same time, overt praise of the Romans and the remarkable emphasis on the adventures of both Greek and Trojan heroes in Italy, including a detailed account of the achievements of "pious" Aeneas (1226–80), suggest that the poet expected his monodrama to reach Roman ears. Cassandra's prophecies are clearly presented as a Trojan precursor of the prophecies of the Sibyl at Cumae (1278–80, 1464–5), whose predictions gathered into the Sibylline books provided sacred guidance for the Roman state.

Mimes were comic dramatic skits in which one or more players enacted a scene from everyday life, often from the lower levels of society. The emphasis was on character depiction rather than plot, and the subject matter and gestures were often indecent. From as early as the fifth century, troupes of mime actors performed prose texts to musical accompaniment in marketplaces and at symposia. The one known pre-Hellenistic writer of mime was Sophron of Syracuse, who wrote Doric mimes in a rhythmical prose during the fifth century. He was much beloved by Plato, who likely made his mimes known to the wider Hellenic community, and was later imitated by his countryman Theocritus. Sophron wrote separate mimes for male and female characters, and surviving titles sometimes indicate whether the mime belonged to the men's class ("Messenger," "Fisherman to the Farmer," "Tunny Fisher") or the women's class ("Sewing Women," "Women Who Claim to Exorcise the Goddess," "Women Viewers of the Isthmia," "Mother-in-Law").

A few fragments of popular mime from the Hellenistic and imperial periods survive on papyrus. The most interesting of these, from the second century, is known as "The Maiden's Lament"; it has been preserved as a personal copy written on the back of a document bearing the date 173.[18] This mime, which consists of a young woman's complaint to the lover who has abandoned her, seems more dignified than popular versions would likely be. In a category of mime known as the *magōdia*, one actor performed both male and female parts;[19] playing tambourines and cymbals, he parodied comic scenes by behaving indecently as he acted at one time the parts of unfaithful women, adulterers, and pimps and at another time the part of a drunken man going on a revel to his beloved. The "Maiden's Lament," however, is elevated by composition in lyric meters, as in solo performances in later Euripidean plays, and by its more serious, if not truly tragic, tone. In a reversal of the usual *paraclausithyron* in which a male lover is locked out by the woman he desires, here a young woman first utters her lament as she travels through the dark streets to her lover's house and then begs for reconciliation when she reaches his door. She is in a state of high agitation, complains of the pain of her rejection, and admits to intense feelings of jealousy. There are clear similarities to Simaetha's lament for her abandonment in Theocritus' *Idyll* 2, and a few erotic epigrams (*Palatine Anthology* 12.153 by Asclepiades, 5.8 by Meleager) are also composed in the voice of a woman unhappy in love. Despite these parallels with contemporary literary forms, the diction consists of koine forms typical of ordinary speech. The "Maiden's Lament" no doubt offers us an example of the sort of popular mimes performed throughout the Hellenistic world, but the individual who had enough interest in it to make a personal copy may have recognized an unusually high artistic quality.

The *Mimiambi* of Herodas (also spelled Herondas), known from a single bookroll published in 1891, clearly obtained literary status and a reading public even if few ancient references to the author remain. The papyrus, written in the second century AD,[20] contains seven mostly complete poems, while an eighth and the beginning of a ninth have been put together from scraps. Each of the poems is given a title, as typically for Sophron's mimes. What we have, then, is the first part of a collection of Herodas' *Mimiambi*, and titles known from elsewhere indicate that additional poems have been lost from the end of the roll. Biographical information about Herodas is lacking from ancient sources, but his name indicates origin in a Doric community. Based on internal references, the composition of the *Mimiambi* can be placed in the 270s and 260s. He was thus a contemporary of Theocritus, with whom he shares an interest in elevating the popular genre of mime, and Callimachus, with whom he shares an interest in reviving the tradition of archaic iambic poetry; he also knew the poetry of Erinna and Nossis, to whom he alludes with satiric intent. The settings of his poems include Cos and Asia Minor, while the first *Mimiambus* contains praise of Egypt under the stewardship of Ptolemy II. He may have been interested in obtaining Ptolemaic patronage, although whether he was successful is unknown.

The *Mimiambi* offer a typical Hellenistic mixing of genres. The subject matter is that of mime, in which characters are realistically depicted in settings of everyday life. For instance, the first poem features a procuress, a role known to have been played by the magodists, and the fourth about two women who visit a temple of Asclepius recalls Sophron's "Women Viewers of the Isthmia." But unlike mimes that were normally in koine prose, Herodas' character skits are composed in a meter and dialect derived from the archaic writers of iambic poetry. Satirical poetry in the iambic meter was produced in the Ionic areas of Asia Minor and the Aegean islands during the seventh and sixth centuries. Its main practitioners were Archilochus of Paros and Hipponax of Ephesus. Sometimes referred to as blame poetry, compositions in iambic verse often featured biting wit, poking fun at specific individuals. As epic celebrated the achievements of heroes and stands behind later tragedy, so iambic poetry was composed by supposedly lower-status persons to deflate the pretensions of the powerful; it was thus related to the rise of comedy. Herodas made the brilliant choice to cross the contemporary prose form of mime with the old-fashioned metrical and dialectal sound of the iambographers. Both Archilochus and Hipponax used their vernacular dialects, and

Hipponax employed a metrical line called the choliamb ("limping iamb"), which ends abruptly with a sharp reversal of flowing conversational iambs. Herodas makes allusion to his reuse of this meter for dramatic depiction in the first *Mimiambus* where a faithful young woman rejects a procuress's persuasion by threatening to make her "sing a limping song with a limp" (71). The audience expected to understand this dramatized allusion to Herodas' iambic model was one steeped in Greek literary tradition, not the commonplace audience of popular mime.

Scholars have disputed whether Herodas wrote to be read in book format or whether his mimes were composed for performance. His sophisticated allusions to the older poetic tradition and his competitiveness with other Hellenistic poets indicate that he had serious literary aspirations for his *Mimiambi*, and there are indications that the papyrus contains a poetry book with a programmatic arrangement, perhaps originating with the author himself. This of course does not exclude performance, whether by a single actor playing diverse roles or by a small troupe. The setting for performing such allusive poems, however, was surely not the public stage where bawdy humor and vulgar gestures were the rule, but rather social gatherings of the intelligentsia or even festivals offered by monarchs of cultured tastes, like Ptolemy Philadelphus.

The first *Mimiambus*, entitled "Procuress or Matchmaker," dramatizes the visit of an old woman named Gyllis to Metriche, whose lover has been absent in Egypt for ten months. The slimy Gyllis has come to persuade the young woman to give her favors to another youth who saw her at a local festival and now desires her. The sketch ends with Metriche's firm refusal and the gift of a cup of wine to Gyllis before she is sent on her way. The second poem, entitled "Brothel Keeper," consists of a speech to a Coan jury given by Battarus, who accuses a young man of attacking his brothel and carrying off one of his girls. Like the procuress Gyllis, Battarus is a thoroughly despicable character, entirely focused on cash and an admitted *cinaidos*, or effeminate homosexual.[21] Despite the brothel keeper's hostile attack, the ancient audience would easily recognize the accused as the stereotypic youth of New Comedy, mad with desire for an unattainable young woman, and the focus of audience identification. The third, entitled "Schoolmaster," depicts a mother's visit to a schoolmaster, Lampriscus, in order to have her ill-behaving son flogged for his misdeeds. Metrotime's exasperated description of her son's misbehavior provides the reader with a picture of a charming delinquent, just making the transition from childish dice games to more adult gaming, negligent of his studies, and disrespectful to his parents. The schoolmaster, with the help of mute servants or students, administers the flogging, and the mime ends with Lampriscus accepting the boy's promise to reform even as the doubtful Metrotime demands yet more punishment. While the conversation between mother, child, and schoolmaster represents the type of everyday scene typical of mime, the motif of physical abuse was surely familiar from New Comedy where the punishment of slaves, whether depicted or only threatened, added coarser comic elements to the plays.

The fourth, entitled "Women Dedicating and Sacrificing to Asclepius," is the best known of the *Mimiambi*. It represents a visit of Cynno and Phile to the temple of Asclepius in Cos for the purpose of setting up a commemorative plaque and sacrificing a cock as a thank offering for curing disease. The poem opens with the dedicatory prayer spoken by Cynno, and while the temple attendant completes the sacrifice, the women have the leisure to view art works dedicated by wealthier persons and now on display in the temple. Works by famous artists, the sons of the sculptor Praxiteles and the painter Apelles, are viewed there, as well as Hellenistic pieces still known in copies, such as a statue of a boy choking a goose. Time and again, the women marvel at the realistic quality of the art works, as in this speech by Phile (59–62, 66–71):

> That naked boy there, if I were to scratch him,
> Wouldn't it make a wound, Cynno? The flesh laid on him
> is pulsing up like a warm spring, in that little painting. . . .
> That ox, and the man leading it, and the woman with him,
> and that hook-nosed man, and the one with ruffled hair,
> don't they all have the look of life and the light of day?
> If I hadn't thought it was something a woman shouldn't do,
> I would have screamed in fear that the ox might harm me.
> He has such a look in his side-glancing eye.

After a series of such reactions, punctuated by typical abuse of the two slaves with them, the mime comes to an end with the return of the temple attendant, who presents Cynno with the slaughtered cock to be taken home for consumption. Admired for its charmingly realistic depiction of women's conversation and often compared to Theocritus' *Idyll* 15, the poem is also important for the information it provides about the verbal content of dedicatory acts and typical reactions to works of art.

The fifth *Mimiambus*, entitled "Jealous Person," depicts a woman in a state of fury because she suspects her slave Gastron of having sex with someone else, a slave girl. Bitinna first orders him bound and sends him off to the executioners for torture, but then, relenting somewhat, she calls him back and decides upon the lesser punishment of tattooing on the forehead. In the end another slave, Cydilla, for whom Bitinna has warm, maternal feelings, persuades her to postpone the punishment for several days. The reader of course realizes that Bitinna's anger will abate in the meantime and that this quasi-familial relationship between mistress and her slaves will continue as before. The representation of women's sexual behavior as secretly driven by unrestrained lust continues in the sixth and seventh poems, which form a pair. The character of Metro appears in both, and in both she is in search of a well-made dildo. In the sixth, entitled "Women Who Are Friends" or "Women in Private," Metro visits her friend Coritto to find out who made for her a scarlet dildo that "Nossis, daughter of Erinna" (20) now has in her possession. The discrediting of the female poets Erinna (Ch. 2.1) and Nossis (Ch. 3.6) by expropriating their names for women engaged in such practices may owe something to the tradition of the archaic iambographers. Archilochus famously reacted to a broken engagement by shaming the father and attacking the girl as sexually promiscuous. But Herodas' maliciousness toward female poets seems to concern professional rivalries and points to the difficulties that women encountered in attempting to win public recognition through their writings. He implies that the devotion between women – a hallmark of the poetry of Erinna and Nossis – derives from a private life focused on sexual pleasure. At the poem's end Coritto reveals that the dildo maker is a certain Cerdon, and in the seventh *Mimiambus*, entitled "Shoemaker," Metro leads a group of women friends to visit a cobbler named Cerdon. He produces his wares, and the women negotiate prices. The reader senses that Cerdon is offering more than just shoes, and the terms "Nossises" and "Baucises" (a reference to Erinna's girlhood companion) for types of shoes continue the malicious smear of prominent women poets.

The more fragmentary eighth poem, entitled "Dream," casts the poet himself as a character of mime. Awaking his slaves in typically abusive fashion, he then relates his dream to a trusted servant named Annas. Despite loss of significant portions of the text, the dream clearly involves Dionysus as the god of poetry and Hipponax as Herodas' principal model; fellow poets who disparage his work are represented as goatherds tearing to shreds a goat that he had apparently won as a Dionysiac prize. The herding imagery points to the bucolic mimes of Theocritus, and there is a certain similarity as well to Callimachus' first *Iambus* where Hipponax returns from the dead to berate the scholars of Alexandria for their bitter quarreling. While Herodas may have remained outside of the inner circle of Alexandrian poets sponsored by Philadelphus, he clearly was aware of the major poetic trends of the day.

The discovery of the *Mimiambi* on a papyrus bookroll in Oxyrhynchus shows that Herodas was still read, at least in Egypt, in the second century AD. His poetry was admired by at least one Roman author as well. In a letter written about 100 AD, Pliny the Younger compliments a friend on his composition of Greek epigrams and mimiambs in Alexandrian style: "How much human feeling is there, how much elegance, how sweet, pleasing, bright, and accurate they are. I would have thought I were reading Callimachus or Herodes [the Attic spelling] or even better if it exists" (*Epistles* 4.3.4). As Pliny recognized, Herodas shared with Callimachus the best qualities of the early Hellenistic age – a taste for refined elegance in the service of realism, and for sweet pleasure in the service of human truth.

3.8 Parodic and Philosophical Literature

Hexameter parodies of the Homeric epics are attested as early as the fifth century, and parody of tragedy became popular in Attic Old Comedy, especially in Aristophanes' reworkings of Euripides. Parodic literature of both the epic and dramatic types flourished in the Hellenistic period and is important as one of the pathways through which the allusive tendency characteristic of Alexandrian poetry developed. Because parody easily takes on a critical or satiric tone when directed toward historical figures or ideas, it also became a common tool in the philosophical or moralizing literature of the age. Modeling themselves more on Socrates than Plato and Aristotle, the major figures in the Cynic movement and in the Skeptic approach to philosophy spread their beliefs through their manner of living, through witty repartee preserved anecdotally, and through popular sermons on ethical themes. These oral and performative methods of instruction found their way into creative literary forms. The hectoring tone of their sermons seems to underlie the moralizing iambic poetry of Phoenix of Colophon and Cercidas of Megalopolis, while their use of the comic in the service of the serious, with parody as a ready tool, reappeared in the satires of the Cynic Menippus and in Timon's *Silli* (*Lampoons*), a satirical history of philosophy from the Skeptic perspective. All these practitioners of philosophical verse provided models for the more intricately literary compositions of the Alexandrians.

Etymologically, the Greek word *parōdia*, "parody," means "song to the side," suggesting that a parodic work is defined by its imitation of, or allusion to, another work. The most commonly parodied works were the Homeric epics, studied rigorously by schoolchildren and so known practically verbatim by most educated Greeks. Recognition of parody as a genre seems to belong to the fifth century, when Hegemon of Thasos, nicknamed "Lentil Soup," won a victory on the Athenian stage with a parody entitled *The Battle of the Giants*.[22] The most famous writer in the

genre was Euboeus of Paros, who wrote four books of *Parodies* in the time
of Philip II of Macedon. From that period or somewhat earlier comes a
partially extant parody by Archestratus of Gela in Sicily entitled *Life of
Pleasure*, in which the author recounts how he traveled throughout the
Hellenic world to research the most delicious symposium fare. Jokes in
Archestratus typically involve substituting the name of a fish or other
delicacy into a line from the *Iliad* or *Odyssey*. The symposium, where
men enjoyed food, wine, and sex, was a particularly appropriate topic
for Homeric parody because the Greeks commonly viewed it as a symbol
of peaceful pleasures, in contrast to the hardships of war, which formed
the topics of epic. Another parodist of this type, one who lies within our
period, is Matro of Pitane, a town of Mysia in Asia Minor, who wrote
parodies on symposium themes at the end of the fourth or the beginning of
the third century. Athenaeus preserves the first 122 lines of his *Attic Dinner
Party* as well as a few others. Matro's parodic technique is illustrated by
the opening of this poem:

> Tell me, Muse, of the dinners much-nourishing and very many
> which Xenocles the rhetor served us in Athens.

This plays off the beginning of the *Odyssey*:

> Tell me, Muse, of the man much-contriving who in very many places
> wandered after he destroyed the holy city of Troy.

The parodist's trick is to keep the shape of Homer's line, with some words
maintaining the same position, but to deflate the familiar heroic ambiance
by substituting references to a contrasting realm, here luxurious pleasure
instead of the pain of heroic wandering. Again and again, Matro replaces
a Homeric character with one of the extravagant dishes served, as in this
reworking of formulaic epic lines on Achilles' sea-goddess mother
(534.33–4 Lloyd-Jones and Parsons):

> Then arrived a daughter of Nereus, silver-footed Thetis,
> a fair-haired squid, a dreadful goddess using human speech.

Matro's inherently comic parody apparently also had a satiric edge, since
the host Xenocles and one of his most prominent guests, Stratocles, were
wealthy and influential Athenians who in the late fourth century supported Demetrius Poliorcetes and his notoriously luxurious manner of
living. The marshaling of sumptuous dish after sumptuous dish, as if the

whole Greek army was being served up, is surely meant to poke fun at these pretenders to grandeur.

The best-known Homeric parody, the *Battle of the Frogs and Mice*, lies just beyond our time period, perhaps in the Augustan age. A papyrus of the second or first century, however, contains some forty lines from the beginning portion of a Hellenistic precursor, the *Battle of the Weasel and the Mice*.[23] In fact, the later *Battle of the Frogs and Mice* makes allusion to this earlier poem as its model when it introduces the mouse who is to be drowned by a frog as one who has just escaped a weasel. The mock-epic narrator of the *Battle of the Weasel and the Mice* begins, traditionally, by calling upon the Muse to tell him of the "quarrel" (compare the "quarrel" between Achilles and Agamemnon) that led the mice to stand in chilling war against the weasel. It involves Trixus or "Squeaky," the best of food snatchers among the mice (compare Achilles, "best of the Achaeans"), who was caught and crushed by the weasel. His grieving wife, who used to beg him to stay away from the predator (compare Andromache, wife of Hector), hears the dire news from a mouse messenger, named Son of Snatcher. The reader is treated to the scene of her grief, complete with groans and tearing of cheeks. After a brief change of scene to note the feast of the gods on Olympus (compare the council of the gods in *Iliad* 1), the mice assemble for battle and the weasel prepares to face them. As an elderly mouse with the amusing name "Miller" (compare the wise old Nestor advising the Greeks at Troy) begins a speech of counsel to the warrior mice, the papyrus breaks off. If the plot followed the same narrative pattern as in the *Battle of the Frogs and Mice*, then we may guess that the mice had initial success until the gods took pity and came to the aid of the weasel. While these animal parodies can be enjoyed by persons unfamiliar with the Homeric epics, in antiquity even a basic education would have prepared one to appreciate most of the parodic elements. One life of Homer preserves the (obviously false) story that he composed the *Battle of the Frogs and Mice* for the children of a patron. Claiming what appeals to children as suitable for high literature, we remember, is one of the ways in which Hellenistic poets introduced the previously marginal into their sophisticated texts, and Callimachus points out at the opening of the *Aetia* that his detractors accuse him of composing "like a child."

Another comic/satiric author was Machon, who was born in Corinth or Sicyon but worked perhaps in Athens and certainly in Alexandria, where he died probably after the middle of the third century. An epitaph by Dioscorides (*Palatine Anthology* 7.708) praises him as a writer of comedies, whose plays, produced beside the Nile, rivaled those of the old Athenians, and Athenaeus (6.241f) reports that he instructed the Alexandrian grammarian Aristophanes in the genre of comedy. What survives, however, is not his comic dramas but over 400 lines from his *Chreiai*, a collection of witty, sometimes obscene sayings by well-known persons of the fourth and early third centuries – musicians, parasites (that is, spongers at dinner parties), and prostitutes, often in conversation with prominent men such as Demetrius Poliorcetes and king Ptolemy (whether Soter or Phila-delphus is unclear). A *chreia* was a brief statement of something said or done by a historical figure, and they came to be used in the Greek educational system to teach students how to write, the *chreia* serving as a theme to be developed into a more elaborate composition. Prose collec-tions of such sayings and deeds became popular in the fourth century, as a way of documenting the lively oral culture of the contemporary Greek world. So, for example, Zeno, the founder of Stoicism, gathered the *chreiai* of Crates of Thebes, who like other Cynics delivered his message about the uselessness of wealth and power through wit and performance. Machon's *Chreiai*, written in the iambic trimeters typical of dramatic speech, versifies similar prose collections, those concerned with colorful celebrities remembered for their witty repartee.

Machon's work is basically a series of jokes, mostly about gluttony, sex, or bad music, and the best way to convey the character of the work is to provide some examples. The dithyrambist Philoxenus prayed to have a throat three cubits long so that it would take him a long time to swallow tasty food (fr. 10 Gow [1965]). When the comic poet Diphilus was dining with the courtesan Gnathaena, he commented on the coldness of the wine, and she explained that it was so cold because she always poured in his prologues (mocking their reputation for stylistic frigidity). The section of Machon's work offering anecdotes about Gnathaena contains two versions of this anecdote (fr. 16), a shorter and longer, illustrating the expandable nature of *chreiai*. Many of the anecdotes about clever prosti-tutes use obscene humor, often playing on untranslatable sexual slang. When a youth who spent the night with Gnathaena asked her in the morning for anal sex, she replied, "You dare ask for my ass when it's time for pigs to go to pasture?" (fr. 16). The joke hinges on the slang use of "piggy" for vagina. Another anecdote turns on the ancient use of per-fumes in sexually charged symposium settings, and one needs to remem-ber that perfumes were made from olive or nut oils combined with fragrances from flowers. When Demetrius Poliorcetes presented the het-aira Lamia with a variety of perfumes and she rejected them, he jerked himself off and asked her to compare the scent of *that*. When she objected to the putrid smell, he countered, wittily, that even so the perfume was made of "kingly nuts" (fr. 13). Some of Machon's clever hetairas even know how to parody tragedy in the comic manner. When Lais once saw Euripides sitting in a garden with his table and stylus, she inquired why he called his Medea a "doer of shameful deeds" (*Medea* 1346). He asked if she wasn't also a "doer of shameful deeds," and she countered by quoting back to him a line from his *Aeolus* in which a character defends brother–sister incest: "What is shameful if it doesn't seem so to those who do it?" (fr. 18). The anecdote makes use of Euripides' reputation for moral relativism, as it exalts the intellectual sharpness of a woman who belongs to the lowest echelons of social status. If composed for recitation at the Ptolemaic court, where reigned brother–sister monarchs, the witty story would even have offered a delicately ironic defense of the royal marriage. As so often with humor, the repeated demonstration of the superiority of the underdog spurs the comic force of the *Chreiai*, and it is also this exaltation of the "low" over the "high" that situates Machon comfortably in the Alexandrian tradition.

Under the fifth-century democratic government, the Athenians prided themselves on their willing acceptance of *parrhasia*, "freedom of speech," a quality that often manifested itself in scurrilous or degrading attacks on public figures, as in Old Comedy. Many of the persons featured in Machon's *Chreiai* are practicing a form of *parrhasia*, which differs from that in Old Comedy partly because it is placed in a private or semi-private setting. Friendly mockery was a common feature of symposium culture and added to the festive atmosphere enjoyed by all. But Machon mentions that one of his subjects, a clever cithara player named Stratonicus, paid with death for his excessive license after he commented on the audible fart made by the wife of a Cyprian king at a dinner party (fr. 11).

Likewise, the Hellenistic monarchs seemed to have tolerated *parrhasia* only if it did not give too much offense, or threaten their basic political ideology. The best-known case was that of Sotades of Maroneia in Thrace, an obscure figure who is credited with the invention of cinaedic poetry, mimelike verses written for performance in the persona of an effeminate homosexual. He was also, as it seems, the first to compose poetry of literary quality in the so-called sotadean meter, a line-by-line ionic verse used for scurrilous mockery. Known titles include *Descent to Hades* and *Adonis*, concerning the handsome youth loved by Aphrodite and popular with Arsinoe II, who identified with the goddess. We also have lines making fun of a farting flute player (fr. 2 Powell, p. 238) and some fragments from an *Iliad* in sotadeans (fr. 4a–c Powell, p. 239). But his most famous line, written on the occasion of Ptolemy II's marriage to his sister Arsinoe, goes as follows: "Into an unholy hole do you thrust your prick" (fr. 1 Powell, p. 238). After a series of tactless jabs – at Ptolemy, Lysimachus, and other kings – this line finally brought on vengeance, although sources differ as to whether Sotades was merely imprisoned or dropped into the sea in a lead jar by one of Ptolemy's admirals. The evidence suggests that, following the pattern of earlier Greek culture, the absolute monarchs of the early Hellenistic age were willing to maintain a pretense that the famous freedom of the Greeks, hard won in the Persian Wars, still continued, and so tolerated a certain amount of personal mockery, especially in the semi-private setting of the symposium. But there were limits to this charade of egalitarianism, and even the good-natured, literature-loving Philadelphus decided that Sotades had to pay for his "untimely" free speech.

Wit and parody, delivered orally on the spot and later captured in collections of *chreiai*, were a principal means of instruction for the Cynics, who followed "the dog" Diogenes of Sinope, and for the Skeptics, who followed Pyrrho of Elis. A few practitioners of these philosophies did, however, produce writings of literary quality. One such was Crates the Theban (ca. 368/5–288/5), who demonstrated his allegiance to the teachings of Diogenes by the unconventional life he led in Athens. Although he was from a wealthy family, he sold his property and distributed the proceeds to the poor, reportedly after seeing a tragedy about Telephus, a Mysian king who adopted the garb of a beggar. His wife Hipparchia, who also came from a wealthy family, of Maroneia, was so entranced by Cynic ways that she demanded Crates as her husband and shared his chosen life of poverty. The various anecdotes about Hipparchia show that she understood clearly how absolute devotion to philosophical thought, accompanied by abandonment of possessions and conventional behavior, freed a woman from societal restrictions. By modern standards she would be called a feminist, since she combined social theory with revisionist practice.[24] A work by Crates entitled *Epistles* apparently attempted serious philosophy in Platonic style, and he is also credited with composing tragedies, though these were perhaps parodies of tragedies. A hexameter fragment from his *Paignia* is a take-off on philosophical attempts to envision an ideal state, as Plato did in his *Republic*. In it Crates describes an ideal city Pera, "Wallet," named after the leather pouch in which homeless Cynics kept their meager possessions (351 Lloyd-Jones and Parsons):

> There is a city Pera in the midst of wine-dark vanity,
> Fair and fruitful, filthy all about, possessing nothing,
> Into which no foolish parasite ever sails,
> Nor any playboy who delights in a whore's ass,
> But it produces thyme, garlic, figs, and bread,
> For which the citizens do not war with each other,
> Nor do they possess arms, to get cash or fame.

Crates' literary means of doing philosophical mockery is, once again, parody of Homer, specifically of lines in which Odysseus gives an imaginary description of Crete (*Odyssey* 19.172–4):

> There is a Cretan land in the midst of the wine-dark sea,
> Fair and fruitful, with sea all about. In it are many people,
> Countless in number, and nine hundred cities.

For Crates useless desire for wealth was associated with harmful desire for sensual gratification, especially purchased sex, and from an iambic work entitled *Ephemeris*, "Daily Accounts," comes mockery of one who pays a talent (a huge sum) for a prostitute and only three obols (a pittance) for a philosopher (362 Lloyd-Jones and Parsons). Other fragments include a parody in elegiacs of Solon's "Hymn to the Muses" (13 Gerber), in which wealth is valued as necessary for the good life (359 Lloyd-Jones and Parsons), and philosophical parody of an epitaph for the Assyrian king Sardanapallus, in which the dead monarch advises the living to expend their wealth on food, drink, and sex (355 Lloyd-Jones and Parsons). Crates' verse criticism of what traditionally constituted the good life resembles ideas promulgated by other Cynics in prose sermons known as diatribes, recited in a hectoring tone. The diatribes of Bion of Borysthenes, now lost, had an important influence on the later satiric tradition, and something of their flavor is preserved in the moralizing treatises of Teles, who composed in the second half of the third century.

Among the Skeptics the most prolific author was Timon of Phlius (ca. 320–230), who first studied with the ethical philosopher Stilpo of the Megarian school, before devoting himself to Pyrrho, the founder of Skepticism. Like so many of the intellectuals of the era, he led a somewhat unsettled life, working some years in the area of the Hellespont as a sophist before ending up at Athens. He is reported to have had contacts with both Antigonus Gonatas and Ptolemy Philadelphus.[25] Various kinds of verse are attributed to him, including epic, tragedy, comedy, and cinaedic poetry. But his most important work was called *Silli*, or *Lampoons*, written in three books of which sixty-five fragments in 133 hexameters survive. The *Silli* act as a parodic history of philosophy, in which Timon abuses the whole range of Greek thinkers for their dogmatism. The view that all previous philosophers were in some way misguided is a natural consequence of the basic Skeptic tenet that truth is unknowable and settled belief is to be suspended. The first book of the *Silli* was written as a monologue in Timon's own voice, but in the second and third books the late archaic philosopher Xenophanes of Colophon responded to Timon's questions, first about old philosophers and then in the third book (called "Epilogue") about contemporary ones. Xenophanes was chosen for this role of interlocutor partially because his own lampoons, reportedly also called *Silli*, provided Timon with a literary model, and perhaps because he was the first to theorize the difference between opinion and knowledge. The motif of an earlier literary figure, returned from the dead to report on others in the world below or to criticize contemporaries, seems to have been adopted by a number of early Hellenistic poets. Callimachus brings back the blame poet Hipponax in the first of his *Iambi*, and an account that the Eretrian philosopher Menedemus dressed as a Fury from Hades to observe the sins of the living is likely taken from a lost work, perhaps one of the lost "serio-comic" satires of the Cynic Menippus of Gadara, written in prose sprinkled with poetic quotations (and later imitated in Latin by Varro).

Parody was, again, basic to Timon's mockery. The opening line of the *Silli* – "Tell me now, you crowd of agitated sophists" (775 Lloyd-Jones and Parsons) – reworks a common epic line in which the poet calls upon the Muses to reveal to him the mythical past he cannot know. By substituting quarrelsome philosophers for Muses, Timon suggests that their claims to have right knowledge rely on the arrogant assumption that they have taken over a function earlier reserved to these divine figures. Further, while Pyrrho demonstrated that Skeptic thought had led him to a calmness associated with inactivity, Timon here accuses other philosophers of agitation or "excessive activity."

In addition to this general abuse, philosophers were mocked one by one. For instance, Timon repeats a common misrepresentation of Epicurus' philosophy by suggesting that he advocated a life devoted to sensual pleasure: "gratifying his belly, the most greedy thing of all" (781 Lloyd-Jones and Parsons). Cleanthes of Assus, who succeeded Zeno as head of the Stoic school in 263, is satirized with a line about Odysseus taken almost verbatim from the *Iliad* (3.196), from the scene in which Helen identifies the Greek leaders for the Trojan elders (815 Lloyd-Jones and Parsons):

> Who is this one who walks up and down the rows of men like a ram?
> A simmerer of words, a stone from Assus, a cowardly rock.

It appears that Xenophanes, dead for two centuries, here plays the Priam role to ask Timon/Helen to identify his contemporary philosopher, Cleanthes/Odysseus. The mockery seems also directed at Cleanthes' theory that poetry was useful for the philosopher because its linguistic density could clarify complex thought. The reference to the Stoic as a "simmerer of words" alludes to his statement that logic "simmers" and so calms the emotions, and Timon may be accusing the rocklike Cleanthes of composing dry, passionless verse that appeals to the intellect rather than the heart. Surviving poetry by Cleanthes, including a "Hymn to Zeus" (fr. 1 Powell, pp. 227–8), lends credence to this suggestion since it versifies Stoic ethical belief but has none of the mocking wit characteristic of Cynic and Skeptic poetry. Timon's most famous slur, however, was directed at the scholars working in the Alexandrian Museum, who are represented as cloistered pedants, feeding and quarreling (786 Lloyd-Jones and Parsons, quoted in Ch. 1.5). Although it is not clear whether these disagreeable scholars are compared to birds, zoo animals, or some other creatures, what is clear is that the hothouse atmosphere of the Egyptian scholarly scene, sponsored by Ptolemaic largess, leads to rivalry and bickering rather than the internal tranquility that master Pyrrho claims to have found.

Among serious moralizing writers was Phoenix of Colophon, who composed more than one book of *Iambi*, lacking the satiric/parodic bite of Cynic and Skeptic writers. Biographical information is scanty. Since he composed a lament for his native city destroyed by Lysimachus, who was dead in 281, he apparently flourished in the early decades of the third century. His poems, surviving through quotation in ancient authors and in a mixed (apparently private) papyrus anthology of the third/second century, include a reflection on an epitaph for the Assyrian king Ninus (elsewhere called Sardanapallus) emphasizing the impermanence of wealth (fr. 1 Knox in Rusten [1993], pp. 458–60), a ritual begging song spoken in the persona of a crow (fr. 2 Knox in Rusten [1993], pp. 462–4), a complimentary reference to the early astronomer Thales, which has a parallel in an anecdote about the Seven Wise Men told in Callimachus' first *Iambus* (fr. 6 Knox in Rusten [1993], p. 476), a complaint against the extravagant use of wealth as the goal of life, addressed to a Posidippus who just may be the epigrammatist (fr. 3 Knox in Rusten [1993], pp. 464–6), and a lament for one Lynceus, perhaps a comic writer and collector of anecdotes from Samos, the brother of the historian Duris (fr. 4 Knox in Rusten [1993], pp. 472–4). Phoenix was, then, a well-connected writer of the early generation of Hellenistic poets, and likely influential in bringing a philosophical/moralizing tone to the work of the Alexandrians.

Cercidas of Megalopolis, an important Hellenistic city of Arcadia, was also a moralizing poet, but of the later third century; he composed *Meliambi*, or lyric-iambic verses, of a strikingly innovative quality. Unlike most poets or philosophers of the era, Cercidas was an active participant in the political life of his native city. He secured Macedonian support for the Achaean League and led his fellow citizens to defeat the Spartans in the battle of Sellasia in 222. He was also remembered as a law-giver for the

Megalopolitans and, in keeping with his intellectual bent, legislated a requirement that schoolboys learn to recite by heart the Catalogue of Ships from the *Iliad*. His *Meliambi* represent a unique adaptation of lyric or song meters to the comic, conversational rhythms of iambic composers. Written largely in the Doric dialect appropriate to a central Peloponnesian audience, the verses are filled with novel compounds, reminiscent of late classical dithyramb, and forceful expressions.

The papyrus that preserves his *Meliambi* ends with an identification of the work as that of "Cercidas, the dog," meaning that he was a Cynic.[26] This philosophical allegiance is confirmed by a meliambic fragment in which he praises the first Cynic Diogenes as the "offspring of Zeus and a heavenly dog" (fr. 1 Knox in Rusten [1993], p. 434), and his poetry, to the degree that it can be reconstructed from the torn papyrus, seems to versify the type of ethical instruction offered in Cynic diatribes. Yet his active political life fits badly Diogenes' model of homeless withdrawal from society, and it seems likely that Cercidas was moving toward the integration of Cynic thought into community life. His moralizing verse is also heavily influenced by his belief that earlier literature can provide a guide for right living. *Meliambus* 2 Knox (in Rusten [1993], pp. 410–16) is an attack on avarice and an encouragement to use wealth for good purposes; Cercidas there adapts a line of Homer (*Iliad* 8.72) to lyric meter, to support his claim that Zeus will measure on the scales of justice those who pride themselves on their wealth and honor. In *Meliambus* 3 Knox (in Rusten [1993], pp. 416–20) he paraphrases Euripides on the two blasts blown from the cheeks of Eros, one producing a tranquil sea of love and one a raging storm of passion; the poet recommends calm sailing through use of moderation as a rudder of persuasion. In *Meliambus* 4 Knox (in Rusten [1993], pp. 422–4), written in his old age, he declares his life-long passion for literature: "All the delicate creatures of the Muses were stored in your vitals, and you, my soul, have been a fisher of the Pierides [Muses] and their keenest hunter" (7–11). His poems also contain references to other philosophical systems. *Meliambus* 6 Knox (in Rusten [1993], pp. 428–32), the last poem (if not two poems) in the papyrus anthology, is addressed to one "Stoic Callimedon" and mentions both Sphaerus, who succeeded Cleanthes as head of the Stoa, and the Stoic founder Zeno. At one point it also advises against "skepticism," apparently in rejection of the satirical, exclusively critical approach of Pyrrho's followers, like Timon. The poem's principal subject, however, appears to be criticism of later Stoics for falling away from their founder's teachings, especially in misusing erotic relationships with youths for personal gratification rather than for philosophical guidance. Remains of iambic poems on papyri from the Hellenistic anthology that also preserves verses by Phoenix ("Cercidea"

Knox in Rusten [1993], pp. 446–54) are attributed to Cercidas by some, though uncertainly. These *Iambi*, largely critical of avarice, are more conventional in language and theme. The poet, who addresses an otherwise unknown Parnus, claims for himself a life of simplicity and frugality much in the tradition of Cynic behavior.

While the theatrical lives of Cynic and Skeptic philosophers spawned satiric and moralizing literature, much of it in verse, the dominant philosophical schools of the Hellenistic era produced a rich body of prose works, now mostly reduced to tatters. The number of volumes composed by Peripatetics, Academics, Stoics, and Epicureans surely ran into the thousands. Many of these were dry and technical, intended only for serious philosophers, although others were composed for neophytes or those with only a casual interest in philosophy. The majority of Hellenistic philosophical works were treatises dealing with a single topic, having titles like *On the Soul*, although there are also collections of tenets of a philosopher or a school, called doxographies, often in combination with biographical information. The livelier genre of dialogue, in the Platonic manner, fell out of fashion, but some of Cicero's philosophical works, which adapt Hellenistic philosophy for a Roman audience, return to the dialogue form, perhaps to illustrate the type of debates engaged in by adherents of the various schools, either in person or in their written arguments. The sheer volume and complexity of Hellenistic philosophical literature worked against its survival. By late antiquity, the doctrines of the Stoics and Epicureans had become a matter of only historical interest, and so were sufficiently preserved in summaries or through biographical accounts, such as Diogenes Laertius' *Lives of the Philosophers*. For this reason, we know a significant amount about the tenets of the Hellenistic philosophies, and yet the works of their major practitioners survive, for the most part, only in fragments gleaned from later texts.

The Peripatetics were especially prolific, because Aristotle set up his school as a research institution, in which the students investigated and documented nearly all branches of learning. Theophrastus (ca. 371–ca. 287), a native of Eresus on the island of Lesbos, worked closely with Aristotle and became his successor. His interests, which included the life sciences, human behavior, meteorology, logic, and literary criticism, are exemplary of the range and technical nature of much Peripatetic writing. Among his surviving works, which may or may not belong to the period after Aristotle's death in 322, are *History of Plants*, *Plant Explanations*, *On Odors*, *Metaphysics*, *On the Senses*, *On Fire*, *On Stones*, and *On Winds*. His *Characters*, which applies the Peripatetic fascination with taxonomy to analyzing personality types, is his best known work for modern readers; in the seventeenth century it offered an important ancient model for the genre of character drawing. Satyrus of Callatia in modern Romania, a Peripatetic of the late third century, also wrote an *On Characters*, but his most important work was his *Lives*, offering in multiple books biographies of famous political figures, orators, philosophers, and poets. As shown by a large extract from the life of Euripides, found on papyrus,[27] his accounts were filled with anecdotes and quotations, and often presented material from literary works as if historical fact. Other early Peripatetics influenced the establishment of the Museum and Library in Alexandria. Demetrius of Phalerum, who produced works dealing with popular tales, fables, and rhetoric, attended the court of Ptolemy I Soter after his exile from Athens in 307, and Strato of Lampsacus, known for his work on physics and cosmology, lived there as well. Another Peripatetic, Praxiphanes, who worked on grammar and literary criticism, tangled with Callimachus. His name appears in the scholiast's list of Telchines, or critics of Callimachean poetics, and Callimachus wrote a lost treatise entitled *Against Praxiphanes*. Clearly, then, Peripatetic ideas were influential in the formation of Alexandrian scholarly culture, although the hostility of Callimachus suggests that independence of mind and desire for freedom from the ideas spawned in fourth-century Athens may have developed in the second generation of the Ptolemies.

The Stoics developed a holistic philosophy, with the three divisions of logic, physics, and ethics. This division, like other basic tenets of Stoic philosophy, goes back to Zeno of Citium, a list of whose works is provided by Diogenes Laertius (7.4). His most famous and controversial work, the *Republic*, displayed evidence of his early interest in Cynicism through its description of an ideal state free from many conventional practices. The main source for the orthodox positions of the Old Stoa, however, was the writings of the prolific Chrysippus (ca. 280–207) of Soli in Cilicia, who is said to have composed over 700 works. His tendency to quote extensively from other authors, including poets like Euripides, helped make possible such productivity. Chrysippus was famous for the brilliance of his logic, but it is also of interest that he found literary texts and artistic works to be valuable sources for philosophical speculation. In the later Hellenistic period, Stoicism was renewed in a form congenial to the developing Roman world by Posidonius, a native of Apamea on the Orontes who taught at Rhodes. He displaced logic from its central position in earlier Stoic thought as the basic tool of philosophy and awarded this role instead to the deductive processes of science and historical observation. Unfortunately, Posidonius' great achievement in integrating human reasoning with the physical nature of the universe is known only through quotations and summaries. Of the titles attributed to him in many fields of learning, the two best known were *On Oceans*, in which he determined terrestrial geographical zones through mathematical calculations and astronomical observations, and *History*, an account of events throughout the world from 146 to the 80s in which he argued for the importance of personal moral character in determining historical events.

The only complete surviving philosophical works of the Hellenistic period are Epicurean. In Book 10 of *Lives of the Philosophers*, Diogenes Laertius preserves certain texts composed by Epicurus himself: three so-called letters, which are actually brief summary treatises, and a set of *Key Doctrines*, essentially a catechism of fundamental beliefs that Epicureans should memorize. The *Letter to Herodotus* (an otherwise unknown Epicurean) is an epitome of Epicurus' philosophy of nature, intended for the serious student who cannot devote himself to the thirty-seven volumes of *On Nature* (fragments of which survive from Herculaneum). The *Letter to Pythocles*, addressed to a young favorite, summarizes Epicurus' views on astronomy and meteorology. The *Letter to Menoeceus* is the most carefully written of the three, presented in a fine Attic style, with some care taken for balanced clauses and periodic sentence structure; it was intended to win adherents by explaining Epicurus' basic views on how to achieve happiness, namely, by not fearing death (since it is a state of nothingness) and by living a good life based on avoidance of pain and moderate pleasures. Although it was not unusual for Hellenistic prose treatises to have an opening address to a primary recipient, the strong bonds of friendship fostered among members of the Epicurean sect may be reflected in these personalized summaries. *Key Doctrines*, on the other hand, consists of an objective list of basic principles, likely excerpted from Epicurus' longer, specialized works. Although Epicurus shows little interest in literary topics, there is no reason to believe that he was actively hostile to poetry or imaginative prose. While the master attempted to win over new recruits by clear explication of his moral philosophy in a fine prose style, the Roman poet Lucretius, in the six books of his *On the Nature of Things*, showed that the techniques of Hellenistic didactic poetry could be adapted to the presentation of Epicureanism with great effectiveness.

The Villa of the Papyri at Herculaneum has given us knowledge of the writings of another Epicurean philosopher, Philodemus of Gadara (ca. 110–ca. 40). Before its destruction by the volcano, the villa housed well over 1,100 papyrus rolls, in both Greek and Latin, and most of those that have been recovered are philosophical treatises in Greek, primarily Epicurean; it provides our best evidence for the working library of a late Hellenistic philosopher, evidently Philodemus. From Cicero we learn of his close friendship with Lucius Calpurnius Piso Caesoninius, Caesar's father-in-law, and it has been supposed that the magnificent villa on the bay of Naples was the property of this Piso, known as a philhellene and man of literary tastes. More than forty bookrolls, all fragmentary, have been identified as containing works by Philodemus, and computer techniques for reading the charred papyri continue to increase our knowledge of these treatises.

As a young man, Philodemus had studied in Athens with Zeno of Sidon, who was perhaps the most important Epicurean philosopher after Epicurus, and in many cases his writings closely follow Zeno's teachings. As a result, his works are not so important for their originality of thought as for the information they contain about the development of philosophy during the Hellenistic age and as evidence for the form in which it was transmitted to the Romans. The texts by Philodemus that have been partially recovered may be classified as follows: summaries of earlier philosophy (*Arrangement of Philosophers* in ten books, *On the Stoics* criticizing Zeno of Citium and others, and *On Epicurus*); a defense of the Epicurean method of inductive argumentation entitled *On Phenomena and Inferences*; theological works including *On Piety*, which defended Epicurus as a pious man who respected the gods and behaved justly; ethical works including *On Vices and Opposing Virtues* in ten books, *On Frank Speaking* concerning how to heal the soul with honest speech, *On Death* dealing with therapies for grief, and *On Anger* setting out Epicurean views on channeling anger effectively; and works on speech and music, including *On Rhetoric*, *On Music*, which attacks the view that music affects character, *On Poems* (see Ch. 4.4), and *On the Good King According to Homer*, which shows how the proper exegesis of Homer can benefit rulers. While Philodemus does not challenge or greatly expand the teachings of his master, he proves himself skillful at argumentation and displays wide learning in the areas of philosophical thought and literature. His more technical works are often argumentative and written without regard for stylistic grace, but works like *On Death*, perhaps constructed to persuade nonbelievers, have some rhetorical flair. Philodemus' voluminous writings digest the best of Hellenistic thought for a mixed audience of native Romans and Greeks living in Italy; as such they foreshadow the nature of much imperial literature.

3.9   Polybius

The historian Polybius is the most important prose writer to fall within the Hellenistic period. His *Histories*, composed in forty books, documented the rise of Rome to world domination in the period from 220 to 146. As the writer of a universal history dealing with events throughout the known world, Polybius followed the model of Herodotus, but as a historian who focused on the accurate reporting of political events within his own lifetime or that of his acquaintances, he is much indebted to Thucydides. His *Histories*, though not distinguished for their literary style and now read mostly by historians, are nevertheless remarkable on several levels. They contain our fullest account of the events of the second century, when the Romans crushed their western competitor Carthage and bent the kingdoms of the Greek East to their will; as a highly self-conscious historian, Polybius provides abundant information about his predecessors and Hellenistic theories of historiography; and his analysis of governmental systems constitutes a model for the representative democracies of the modern world. In addition, he provides within his *Histories* a significant amount of autobiographical information, so that we have, for once, substantive knowledge of how a Hellenistic writer's life experiences shaped his literary accomplishments.

Born about 200 and dead by about 118, Polybius was a citizen of the prominent Hellenistic city of Megalopolis, located in the region of Arcadia in the north-central Peloponnese; the same city had been the homeland of the philosophical writer Cercidas (Ch. 3.8). From the middle of the third century Megalopolis had played a major role in the Achaean Confederacy, a union of Peloponnesian states that shared the same laws, weights, coinage, magistrates, and courts. As Polybius tells us (2.37.9–11), the goal of the league was not self-aggrandizement but a desire to maintain independence from the overlordship of Macedonian monarchs and, later, after the Roman defeat of Philip V and Perseus in the second century, of Rome itself. Polybius was born into the aristocratic elite of his city and, by virtue of both family status and natural talent, was headed for local political distinction. His father Lycortas served as *stratēgos*, "general," of the Achaean Confederacy, the league's highest office. As a youth in 182, Polybius was chosen to carry the funeral urn of Philopoemen, the great Achaean statesman and general who dismantled Sparta's walls and resisted Roman interference. Elected *hipparchos*, "cavalry commander," of the Confederacy in 170/69 at the age of thirty, Polybius seemed on his way to a distinguished military and political career on the model of the much-admired Philopoemen. But fate took a different turn. The Achaean Confederacy was entering its last two decades, a period during which the Romans deprived it of independent action. After the Roman defeat of the Macedonian king Perseus at Pydna in 168, one thousand hostages from pro-Macedonian or neutral families were deported to Italy to assure compliance to Roman dominance throughout Greece. Among them was Polybius.

While the other hostages lived dull lives in small Italian towns, Polybius had the good fortune to remain in Rome and to form friendships with influential Romans. Most important among these was Scipio Aemilianus, the future destroyer of Carthage in the Third Punic War. Polybius became Scipio's friend and political mentor when the young Roman was only eighteen and through this connection gained access to the intellectual elite in Rome, including Scipio's friend Laelius. The group of philhellenes gathered around Scipio is often referred to as the Scipionic circle; it included the Latin comic playwright Terence, the Roman satirist Lucilius, and, in the 140s, the Stoic philosopher Panaetius, a Greek from Rhodes. It was during his period of exile, from 168 to the restoration of the hostages in 150, that Polybius began his *Histories*. In his early years he had received a solid education that brought a familiarity with major Greek poets, though he seems to have lacked the capstone experience of serious philosophical study. For those who would pursue the active career of military commander, as he intended to do, he stresses the importance of scientific and technical studies, especially geometry, astronomy, and geography, while in his life of forced leisure he devoted himself to hunting and history. During this period he must have read earlier historians voraciously and made extensive use of the archival and eyewitness sources in Rome. Having gained the trust of rising Roman political leaders, Polybius had extensive privileges and freedoms. Early on, he helped in the escape from Italy of Demetrius I of Syria, the son of Seleucus IV, who returned to enjoy some years of *de facto* rule in the Seleucid East. In the late 150s he apparently accompanied Scipio to North Africa, Spain, and Gaul, made a crossing of the Alps in the footsteps of Hannibal, and was later, after his release as a hostage, present at the destruction of Carthage in 146. He also sailed beyond the Pillars of Gibraltar into the Atlantic and eventually visited Alexandria and Sardis. After the demolition of Corinth in 146, he acted as a Roman agent in Greece to facilitate the political settlement there and received civic honors from his native city, including a marble statue. The work on his monumental *Histories* continued after his return to Megalopolis, and he was apparently making changes to nearly the end of his life. It is reported that he died by falling off a horse at the age of eighty-two.

Polybius composed other works that no longer survive: an early appreciative biography of Philopoemen; a work on military tactics; a study of the equatorial region; and a history of the Numantine War, which ended in 133 with Scipio Aemilianus breaking the Celtiberian resistance in Spain. His *Histories*, epitomized already in antiquity, is the only Hellenistic historical text that substantially remains for us. Of the forty original books, only 1–5 survive intact. An ancient abridgment preserves continuous narrative sections of Books 6–18, but of the others only fragmentary excerpts still exist. Polybius' original purpose was to explain "how and by what kind of constitution nearly the whole world was brought under the rule of the Romans in less than fifty-three years, a unique event in history" (1.1.5). To give background to his principal subject, his first two books deal with events just preceding the period when Rome came to dominance: the struggle over Sicily between Rome and Carthage in the First Punic War (264–241), how Rome began to interfere in Greece to put down Illyrian piracy, and the invasions of the Celts into Italy. The main narrative in Books 3–30 covers the period from the 140th Olympiad (220–216), when Polybius argued that the Romans first decided upon universal aggression, to 167, when they brought the Macedonian monarchy to an end. Later, however, he decided, as he tells us in the so-called "second prologue" (3.4–5), to extend his account (Books 31–40) to the year 146 in order to explain how the Romans governed their subjects and what effects their rule had on the dominated peoples. The events of this period culminated in the final destruction of Carthage, Rome's principal rival in the west, and the crushing of the Greek confederacies marked by the razing of Corinth. Despite the tremendous work involved in adding ten books to his already lengthy history, Polybius' decision was motivated by his status as an eyewitness to many of the major events of the period, in his capacity as Scipio's friend and even at times as an active political agent of Rome in the reorganization in Greece. As a result of his personal participation, he believed that he had privileged access to the "truth" about this historical period.

Polybius conceived his history as *universal* in scope; it was thus distinguished from more limited histories concerning an individual's life, a single war, or one city. He makes it clear that only with Roman domination of the inhabited world did true universal history become possible. Such a historical narrative, he claims, is organic, that is, like the body of a living creature. Specialized histories focus on only part of the body and cannot provide a view of the whole living creature: they therefore misrepresent the truth of the events that took place. Polybius also calls his history *pragmatic*, by which he means that he deals with prominent people, important places, and military and political events, rather than with chronologies, genealogies, and fabulous or mythical events. Since prose historical accounts did not begin in Greek culture until the second half of the fifth century, historians who wished to discuss earlier events generally had to depend on legends, family memories, and archival lists. The establishment of chronologies for earlier periods was difficult, and genealogies were important in that endeavor. Polybius' rejection of this type of history was connected to his focus on relatively recent historical events, for which there were written accounts, documentary evidence, and eyewitnesses. His method of organization for his pragmatic history of universal scope was to discuss each Olympiad, or period of four years (between Olympic games), in terms of the events that took place in different geographical arenas moving from west to east – first Italy in its interaction with Carthage and Spain, next Greece, and then Ptolemaic Egypt and Seleucid Asia. This organization was designed to show how, for the first time in the history of the world, the political events in all these places were interconnected (a *sumplokē*, "weaving together," in Polybius' terminology), as events moved from their beginning (*archē*) through a fixed duration of time to the single end (*telos*) of Roman domination.

Polybius' intended audience was the aristocratic elite of Greece and Rome, especially men of action. As he states at the outset, "the truest education and training for a life of political involvement is study of history, and the clearest and unique method of learning how nobly to endure changes in fortune is to remember the reversals that have happened to others" (1.1.2). Much in contrast to the scholarly poets in Alexandria or the philosophical wits in Athens, Polybius was the product of a more traditional intellectual environment, in which old-fashioned aristocratic values still held sway; in fact, Cercidas' moralistic and participatory philosophy may have informed the education system under which he was trained. The Achaean leadership centered in Megalopolis challenged Macedonian militarism by a devoted defense of homeland that drew upon the Spartan values of heroic achievement and noble sacrifice. The code of conduct Polybius had learned from men like Aratus of Sicyon (an Achaean *stratēgos* and historian of the third century), Philopoemen, and his father Lycortas, one that emphasized action over contemplation, found a match, somewhat ironically, in the value system of his Roman masters, as they entered their period of expansion beyond the confines of Italy. While most of the Greek world had moved away from heroic idealism to greater cynicism, skepticism, and a nostalgic longing for past greatness, the cultural climate of remote Arcadia maintained many of the elements of an earlier era; as a result, Polybius found Roman culture, with its emphasis on pragmatism and devotion to duty, especially in the military realm, not uncongenial, and the Romans found in him a compatible guide to Greek practice and thought. What made possible, then, Polybius' unifying view of this crucial historical period was his personal admiration for Roman conduct and achievement mixed with his sorrow at the catastrophe befalling Greece.

As he frequently mentions, the force that drives human affairs and produces constant changes is Tyche, or Fortune, and it is this force that has shaped the arc of events, conceived as an organic body, of Rome's rise to overlordship of the world. What remains unclear in Polybius' view of historical causation is how the unavoidable force of Fortune interacts with human choice and action. Through intelligence, training, and character, human beings are able to affect the course of history, although uncontrollable chance remains a factor as well. For Polybius, one purpose of writing history was to make moral judgments, to provide praise or blame for the behavior of nations and human beings, in terms of how nations are constituted and how individuals react to inevitable reversals. The famous analysis of the three main forms of government in Book 6 – monarchy, aristocracy, and democracy in relation to their degenerate corollaries of despotism, oligarchy, and mob rule – has the goal of praising the Roman constitution as a uniquely successful combination of all three. Praise or blame for individuals is based not just on political success or failure but also on innate qualities, including ability to deal with misfortune. Scipio Aemilianus became Polybius' primary hero because of his extraordinary skills as a military commander and his nobility of character, best exemplified in his sympathetic identification with the Carthaginians as he is destroying their city. One of Polybius' main villains is Philip V of Macedon, who is soundly criticized for his cruelty and dissipated lifestyle; Polybius judges him to deserve his ultimate defeat. The relationship between Fortune and morality is perhaps made clearest in his statement that he has appended ten books on the aftermath of Roman dominance in order to show, with reference to both conquerors and the conquered, "that what seems the greatest success has resulted for many in the greatest misfortune if they did not use it properly, while for not a few unexpected misfortunes have resulted in some measure of advantage if they have reacted nobly" (3.4.5–6). In the latter group he likely counted himself, since surely he viewed the paramount misfortune of his life, to be exiled to Rome, as the means by which he came, in his later years, to expend his best efforts in helping his countrymen adjust to Roman rule.

One striking feature of Polybius' *Histories* is the pervasive intrusion of the narrator, often to provide criticism of earlier historians. In the fourth, third, and second centuries were produced many now lost works of history, and Polybius' comments provide essential, though one-sided, information about some of the most important of them. His main point is that history, in contrast to imaginative literature, has truth as its goal. The worst offenders against the writing of historical truth are those who deliberately present falsehoods through personal bias or self-interest. Examples of these are Philinus of Acragas in Sicily, criticized for his pro-Carthaginian history of the First Punic War (1.14, 3.26), and Fabius Pictor, the first Roman to write history (though in Greek), who is criticized for attributing the Second Punic War to the personal ambition of Hannibal, whom Polybius admired for his expert generalship and endurance of misfortune (1.14, 3.8–9). Polybius also recognizes other reasons for historians' deviation from the truth, such as ignorance, inexperience (especially of military affairs), focusing too narrowly on a circumscribed topic, and the presentation of fabulous events or legendary material. He considers fourth-century Ephorus of Cyme, who combined events in Greece with those in the barbarian East, as the first universal historian but criticizes him for including accounts of colonies, foundations, and genealogies as well as for his lack of military knowledge (5.33, 12.28.10–11, 34.1.3–5). In other words, Ephorus' history did not have the pragmatic cast of Polybius'. The most important historian after Ephorus was Timaeus of Tauromenium, who in the first half of the third century produced a long history of the western Mediterranean, with focus on his native Sicily; this history terminated about 264, the date at which Polybius' begins his historical preamble (Books 1–2). Polybius devoted almost the entirety of Book 12 to criticism of Timaeus, disliked for his inclusive historical approach, his Sicilian biases, and his bookish method of research: not a man of action, Timaeus wrote his history in libraries during his fifty years of exile in Athens. While Timaeus may exemplify in a historical mode the Hellenistic spirit of diligent scholarship, Polybius represents a kind of throw-back to the active political life of the earlier Greek *polis*, a mode of life that, paradoxically, made him particularly well suited to build bridges to Roman culture.

Polybius also objects to what he calls tragic history. The main problem with this type, he claims, is that it confuses two different literary effects, enthrallment (*psychagōgia*), directed purely to pleasure, and instruction (*didascalia*), useful in the active life. For Polybius, as we have seen, the purpose of history is to provide practical benefit for that elite class of serious persons who may be in the positions of power in their nation. Aristotle had famously asserted that poetry was more philosophical and serious than history because it provided general truths while history only reported particular facts (*Poetics* 9.3). But certain historians, prominently Duris of Samos who in the early third century wrote a history of Macedonia, developed a narrative style that incorporated elements of tragic plots and emotional descriptions designed to arouse pity in the readers. Polybius prefers to single out as an abuser of the tragic style Phylarchus, whose history of the period from 272 to 220 was critical of the Achaean leader Aratus of Sicyon and supportive of Cleomenes of Sparta. He claims that Phylarchus detailed the sufferings of the people of Mantinea in order to accuse Aratus and the Macedonians of cruelty in enslaving them (2.56.7–8):

In his eagerness to provoke his readers to pity and to make them sympathetic to his account, he introduces a picture of women with hair disheveled, clinging and beating their breasts, as well as the tears and lamentations of men and women as they were led away in the company of their children and elderly parents. He does this sort of thing throughout his entire history in an attempt to make dreadful events appear vividly before our eyes.

After labeling Phylarchus' style "ignoble and womanish," he explains why it is not appropriate to the writing of history (2.56.10–12):

> A historian should not provide a thrill by exaggerating historical events nor should he, like a tragedian, seek for probable words and calculate all the events incidental to his subject, but rather report in full what was actually said and done, even if it should be rather ordinary. For the goal (*telos*) of history is not the same as that of tragedy, but the opposite. The tragedian should thrill and charm (*psychagōgēsai*) his audience through the plausible words of characters, but the historian should instruct (*didaxai*) and persuade serious readers for all time by reporting true deeds and words, since in the first case the plausible even if false compels its viewers through illusion, while in the other case truth compels by benefiting those serious about learning.

Polybius here reflects a debate about the purpose of literature, whether to instruct or entertain, that extended throughout the Hellenistic period and involved both poetry and prose. Interestingly, his own narrative method is not immune to the tragic style, as his concept of the rise of Rome as an unexpected interaction of events with an organic beginning, course, and end is remarkably similar to Aristotle's description of a tragic plot. Polybius' concept of history as driven by an unknowable Fortune, in control of both national groups and individual men, whose worth is also somehow determined by their noble or ignoble behavior, seems shaped by the same tragic world view that underlay the Greek vision of life.

Polybius describes his style as "austere" or "dry," which he claims is suitable for the type of reader he wishes to attract, namely, a man of affairs interested in nations, cities, and dynasts (9.1). During the Hellenistic age a florid prose style marked by wordplay and emotional effect developed in Asia Minor; it became known as the Asianist style and was generally condemned by literary critics and rhetorical theorists. Although no complete work of this type has survived, ancient sources single out Hegesias of Magnesia (mid-third century), an orator and author of a *History of Alexander*, as a typical exemplar of the turgid phrasing, confused images, and ineffective pathos that marked the Asianist manner.[28] Polybius' style easily fits into the opposite category, called the Atticist style after the

classical orators of Athens. Although his diction consists mostly of standard koine words and he strives primarily for clarity rather than symmetry
of phrasing or rhythmical effect, he does use some literary devices to
add emphasis to key points in his narrative. There are a number of
extended similes, such as the comparison of a battle in Sicily between
the Carthaginians and Romans to a boxing match between two well-
matched fighters (1.57.1–2), the comparison of defective forms of government to woodworms that eat away timber (6.10.3–4), or the comparison
of Timaeus in his reliance on library sources to the man who thinks he can
become a painter by observing the works of old masters (12.25^{e}7). Despite
his criticism of historians who make up speeches such as their characters
would have delivered, he too often highlights political decision-making by
giving the opposing speeches of statesmen, and it is unlikely that these, if
written versions ever did exist, remained at his disposal. All the major
players in his *Histories* receive character sketches that sum up the author's
view of their strengths and weaknesses, and there are a number of gripping
descriptions of events, despite his determination to avoid tragic-style
manipulation of the reader. One example is the description of Hannibal's
crossing of the Alps with men and animals, including elephants (3.50–6).
Criticizing tragic historians who even bring in the gods to help Hannibal
(like the *deus ex machina* who ends a tragedy), he points out that, though
the crossing was difficult and cost many lives, it was far from an impossible human endeavor: Hannibal had Celtic guides to show the way, and
Polybius personally retraced the journey. The vividness of his description,
then, has first-person authority.

Polybius often repeats, for the sake of *emphasis* (a Greek term suggesting
both clarity and vividness), his fundamental belief in the benefits conferred
by history and in the historian's responsibility to the truth. Modern
scholars of historiography recognize that even when events are reported
as accurately as possible, selection of details, limits of knowledge, and
personal opinion prevent the historian from attaining absolute historical
truth, and as a result Polybius' persistent claims that his universal history
surpasses all others in truthfulness can seem naïvely self-serving to the
modern reader. At the same time, however, he successfully uses these
narrative digressions to insert types of information absent or less prominent in earlier historical writers. He believes it important that the reader
comprehend not only the chronological relationship between events
but also the spatial relationship between places. He therefore provides
geographical outlines of the world and its divisions, as in his summary of
the relative positions of Europe, Asia, and Africa (3.36–8) or in his
description of northern Italy with emphasis on the Celtic settlements in
the fertile Po Valley (2.14–16). He also describes in detail the physical

layout of certain cities and sites in order to enhance the reader's ability to visualize the events there. Book 34, surviving only in fragments, was apparently dominated by such geographical topics. Polybius also includes digressions on military tactics or practices and scientific or technical advances. His explanation for the superiority of the Roman legions, with their maneuvering flexibility, over the Macedonian phalanx, with its fixed formation, is masterful (18.29–32), while his explanation of the military machinery invented by the famous mathematician Archimedes to save Syracuse from its Roman besiegers shows a personal interest in mechanics (8.3–7). His long, complex explanation of recent advances in fire signaling as a means of quickly conveying military information over great distances (10.43–7) suggests that he may have been personally involved in these technical innovations. When Polybius speaks about new material necessitating a fresh historical account, part of what he had in mind were these geographical, scientific, and technical topics.

Polybius' single most important achievement as a historian was his ability to grasp how the rapid rise of Roman power, mostly within his own lifetime, brought into existence the world dominance that the Hellenistic monarchs had vainly hoped for in pressing their claims as heirs of Alexander's short-lived empire. From the very beginning of his writings in the 160s and 150s, he directed the structure and themes of his *Histories* to conveying this fundamental insight. The quality of his work is shown not only by its survival, when so many other histories of the period are lost, but also by his influence on later writers, Greek and Roman. The philosopher Posidonius (Ch. 3.8), who headed the Stoic school in the first century, began his own (lost) *History* where Polybius left off, and his attempt to integrate all fields of knowledge into one comprehensive vision of culture extends Polybius' historical approach into a wider, holistic arena. The geographical writer Strabo, of the Augustan age, identifies Polybius as a major source and quotes him frequently, and the Latin historian Livy relied upon Polybius' account of the second century, through not always with accurate understanding. In continuing the tradition of universal history, Diodorus Siculus, whose work was completed about 30 in Rome, followed closely Ephorus for Greek material and Polybius for the later Roman era. Although the "Machiavellian" nature of Polybius' *Histories* is disputed by many current scholars, it appears that Machiavelli himself was aware of Polybius' analysis of constitutional types. If Polybius' work is now known primarily to specialists of the ancient world, in the eighteenth century it was widely read by educated men. As a result, his admiring account of the Roman form of government likely influenced the formulation of the United States Constitution with its system of checks and balances among branches of government.

3.10   Technical Prose Writing

Plato was fond of illustrating philosophical problems through analogy to practical crafts, or *technai*. The usefulness of this method stemmed from Plato's separation of banausic craftsmen, who had specialized knowledge gained through hands-on experience (such as shipbuilders or shoemakers), from philosophers, whose knowledge was more abstract and comprehensive. But in the early Hellenistic era writings on technical matters by intellectuals who understood their subject through reason, not just practice, became increasingly commonplace and valued. This change owed much to the example of the Peripatetics, who followed Aristotle in accumulating and organizing information about various natural and human subjects. In Stoic philosophy *technē*, or art, was even considered a natural and important part of the universe. The Stoics conceived Nature as a fire capable of *technē*, and Zeno (Ch. 3.8), the Stoic founder, defined *technē* as "a system of perceptions exercised for a purpose serviceable for living."[29]

Important technical writings were produced during the Hellenistic era in the fields of mathematics, astronomy, mechanics, medicine, and geography, while pseudo-scientific writings on wondrous phenomena, known as paradoxography, were also produced. Since writings of this sort were valued for their content rather than their style, it is often the case that the most important treatises are known only through summary in later authors or, in some cases, in Arabic translation, and the works that do survive may not have been the most influential or original texts on the subject. Since our concern is with literary studies rather than the history of scientific advances, the discussion here will focus on the manner of presenting technical material in textual form, rather than the content. Interestingly, technical writings tend to have similar characteristics from one author to another, as well as across disciplines. For instance, the combination of clear and concise verbal explanation with visual illustration in the form of a diagram or drawing is typical of treatises in all the areas except paradoxography. In addition, many of these treatises open with an address to a patron, such as a king, or to a friend or fellow scientist to whom the treatise is sent, and valuable information about the writer's purpose and difficulties is often revealed in these introductions. The material presented, whether in multiple books or in monograph form, tends to be organized in catalogue fashion, as the author proceeds from one proposition or example to another.

Theoretical mathematics began in Greece in the fifth century and made important advances during the fourth. Plato's insistence in the *Republic* that decades of mathematical education were essential training for a philosopher shows that the logical processes involved in understanding mathematical problems were in his day considered fundamental to developing the mind. Greek mathematics was geometrical in focus, and it remained concerned with problems of plane and solid geometry and with absolute numbers rather than algebraic expressions. Eudoxus of Cnidus (ca. 390–ca. 340), who worked in Athens and likely with Plato, is an important forerunner of the Hellenistic mathematicians. His theory of proportions and his work on the relationship of cones and pyramids to cylinders and prisms were the starting points for Hellenistic advances in geometry, while his application of mathematics to the motions of heavenly bodies was the basis for Hellenistic mathematical astronomy. His work is mainly known, however, second-hand, such as through Aratus' poetic adaptation of Eudoxus' astronomy in his *Phaenomena* and Hipparchus' commentary on that poem. Our earliest extant treatises on mathematics belong to the Hellenistic age and were produced by three great mathematicians: Euclid, Archimedes, and Apollonius of Perge.

Almost nothing is known of the life of Euclid, the most celebrated mathematician in western history. He most likely flourished during the reign of Ptolemy I, but certainly after Eudoxus and before Archimedes, who mentions him. He was probably trained in Athens, the center of mathematical studies in the later fourth century, and the mention of his students at Alexandria by a later source opens the possibility that he worked in Egypt. His fame rests on the thirteen books of the *Elements*, which became the basic text of geometry for well over two millennia.[30] Because the purpose of the *Elements* was to transmit knowledge, the relationship between content and author is quite different than it would be for a Hellenistic poet and his poetic text. Euclid freely incorporates, without acknowledgment, material and method from earlier mathematicians, especially Eudoxus, and his own text, as transmitted in manuscripts, had acquired in antiquity accretions and spurious material, provided to enhance the reader's learning. Because the *Elements* is such a fundamental text, not only for pure mathematics but also for such allied fields as astronomy, mechanics, and geography, it deserves a more detailed treatment than other technical works.

The sequence of topics in the *Elements* is as follows: Books 1 and 2 on rectilinear figures, Books 3 and 4 on circles, Book 5 on proportions (from Eudoxus), Book 6 on application of proportions to plane geometry, Books 7–9 on number theory, Book 10 on irrational lines (which Thomas Heath calls "the most remarkable, as it is the most perfect in form, of all the Books of the *Elements*"[31]), Books 11–13 on solid geometry, ending with the inscription of polyhedra in a sphere. The *Elements* lacks a personalizing introduction. Euclid begins Book 1 with definitions (such as "a line is a breadthless length"), postulates (such as "all right angles are equal to one another"), and common notions, also called axioms (such as "if equals are added to equals, the wholes are equal"). Additional definitions appear at the beginnings of other books as needed, particularly Book 11, where solid geometry is introduced. After this preliminary matter, Euclid proceeds to the propositions, which follow a standard form that must have preexisted his formulation. Each proposition is accompanied by a diagram, and these are often "updated" in modern editions and translations to reflect current mathematical procedure rather than ancient drawing techniques (of course the drawings in the manuscripts are hand-drawn copies by scribes). The classic form of a proposition contains as many as six parts, which are illustrated here with reference to Euclid's first proposition in Book 1.

1 "Enunciation" of the problem: "On a given straight line to construct an equilateral triangle."
2 "Setting-out" of the data: "Let AB be the given finite straight line."
3 "Specification" or restatement of the problem in terms of the data: "Thus it is required to construct an equilateral triangle on the straight line AB."
4 "Construction," meaning any additions to the figure: "With center A and distance AB let the circle BCD be described; again, with center B and distance BA let the circle ACE be described; and from the point C, in which the circles cut one another, to the points A, B let the straight lines CA, CB be joined."
5 "Proof": "Now, since the point A is the center of the circle CDB, AC is equal to AB. Again, since the point B is the center of the circle CAE, BC is equal to BA. But CA was also proved equal to AB; therefore each of the straight lines CA, CB is equal to AB. And things which are equal to the same thing are also equal to one another; therefore CA is also equal to CB. Therefore the three straight lines CA, AB, BC are equal to one another."
6 "Conclusion," which states what has been proved in accordance with the enunciation: "Therefore the triangle ABC is equilateral; and it has been constructed on the given finite straight line AB. Being what it was required to do."

Here we have the basic technique found in mathematically based texts and adopted, as appropriate, to other technical forms of analysis: the accumulation of a body of accepted knowledge, such as definitions, postulates, axioms, and proved theorems; reasoning by means of deduction; and use of visual aids in the form of line diagrams or, in other disciplines, drawings and paintings. The virtues of this technical style are clarity and economy, which means stating all that is logically required and nothing more. While the purpose is instruction, the style of presentation has an austere beauty that can be aesthetically appealing.

In contrast to Euclid, much more is known of Archimedes' life, from Polybius and other reliable sources. Since he died in the Roman siege of his native Syracuse at the age of seventy-five, his dates (287–212) are relatively secure. His father was an astronomer named Phidias, and he was acquainted with, perhaps even related to, king Hiero II and his son and successor Gelon. The introductions to his works reveal that he corresponded with other leading mathematicians of the third century, such as Conon of Samos and the polymath Eratosthenes of Cyrene, both of whom worked in Alexandria, and it is reasonable to suppose that at some point in his life he traveled, perhaps to the Egyptian capital. His fame rested as much on his mechanical inventions as on his theoretical mathematics. Polybius gives a fascinating account of how his devices wreaked havoc on the Roman attackers during their siege of Syracuse and paralyzed the soldiers with fear (8.5–7): he made clever catapults that were effective for both long and short range, he invented machines with arms extending out over the city walls to drop large stones on Roman scaling ladders, and he created an iron hand capable of grabbing the prow of a ship, lifting the vessel, and then releasing it into the water, with disastrous results. One famous anecdote concerns his ability to move a huge ship belonging to Hiero II (see Ch. 3.4) by operating a pulley with his own hand. He is reported to have said on this occasion: "Give me a place to stand, and I will move the earth." Another anecdote concerns a problem posed to him by the same king – namely, how to determine if a gold crown had been adulterated with silver. According to Vitruvius (9.1.9–10), he discovered, while in his bath, a solution involving displacement of water and ran naked through the streets shouting *eurēka, eurēka* ("I've found it, I've found it"). He was also credited with the "snail shell," or Archimedean screw, that was used to raise water, a musical organ operated hydraulically, and star globes, which Marcellus, the commander during the siege of Syracuse, took to Rome as personal booty.

Despite his incredible facility at constructing mechanical devices, Archimedes reportedly engaged in this practical activity only at the urgings of Hiero, since he considered his machines the "diversions of a geometry at play" (Plutarch, *Life of Marcellus* 14.8). He viewed mechanics as an ignoble endeavor and preferred the "beauty and excellence unmingled with necessity" (Plutarch, *Life of Marcellus* 17.6) of pure mathematical reasoning. As a consequence, Archimedes avoided writing on mechanical subjects, though he reveals in the introduction to *Method to Mechanical Theorems*, addressed to Eratosthenes, that he often first worked out his theorems by mechanical means and only later developed the mathematical proofs that were the subject of his published works.

In geometrical mathematics Archimedes' principal achievements involved determining the surface area of spheres and cones through ratios to plane surfaces. The importance of these discoveries is indicated by the symbolism of his tomb, which bore a cylinder circumscribing a sphere, together with an inscription giving the ratio between the two (uncovered by Cicero in a state of neglect, *Tusculan Disputations* 5.64–6). This and other relationships between planes and curvilinear surfaces are proved in the two books of *On the Sphere and the Cylinder*, for which also survives a commentary by the Alexandrian Eutocius of the fifth century AD. The introductions to these two books, addressed to an obscure mathematician Dositheus, reveal something of his method of developing and publishing proofs. He mentions that since he had earlier sent some puzzling problems to Conon of Samos, the solutions for these, provided in these treatises, should have gone to him as well. But since Conon had since died (sometime after 245), Archimedes is sending his finished proofs to Dositheus as someone who loves mathematics and can understand them. A similar statement in *Quadrature of the Parabola*, lamenting the loss of Conon and making it clear that Dositheus was considered a poor substitute, suggests the intellectual isolation of this incredible genius, who worked, though in a wealthy city, outside the great intellectual centers of the day. His other extant prose works are *Measurement of the Circle*, *On Conoids and Spheroids*, *On Spirals*, *Equilibriums of Planes or Centers of Gravity of Planes*, *On Floating Bodies*, and *The Sand Reckoner*. This last, addressed to Hiero's successor Gelon, is perhaps Archimedes' best-known work. It is concerned with the inadequacy of the traditional Greek system of arithmetic notation to accommodate extremely large numbers. Archimedes demonstrated the utility of a new notation of his own invention by arguing that if the sphere of the universe, with the sun at its center (in accordance with the theory of Aristarchus of Samos), were to be completely filled with grains of sand, his system would still include some numbers larger than the number of grains of sand.

The third great mathematician of the Hellenistic age was Apollonius of Perge in Pamphylia, who flourished during the reign of Ptolemy IV Philopator in the last quarter of the third century. He studied Euclidean geometry in Alexandria and later went to Pergamum. Of his principal work, entitled *Conics*, Books 1–4 survive in Greek and Books 5–7 in Arabic translation, while the eighth book is lost. His studies on the sectioning of cones became standard down to modern times, and he is credited with designating the three conic sections by the names *parabola*, *ellipse*, and *hyperbola*. Of interest, once again, are the introductions to the individual

books. In the introduction to Book 1, addressed to Eudemus of Pergamum, he explains that he had given an earlier version of his work to the
geometer Naucrates because he was leaving Alexandria but that now
he was sending a corrected version of the first two books and would
send the other books after they were finished. Book 4 begins with an
address to king Attalus I, since, as Apollonius explains, the more mathematically knowledgeable Eudemus was by then dead. From these introductions, like those of Archimedes, we gain a fascinating glimpse of the
publication methods of ancient writers and of their relationships with
patrons and other intellectuals. It is clear that preliminary versions might
circulate among a small group of acquaintances as a form of prepublica-
tion and that, as a result, authors could have difficulty making sure that
the final, authorized version was the only one passed on to posterity.

Similar insight can be gained from *On Burning Mirrors* by Diocles
(ca. 200), who lived in Arcadia and was apparently a contemporary of
Apollonius. His work, surviving in Arabic and in a few Greek extracts,
was a series of somewhat unrelated propositions concerning mirrors,
conics, and a standard problem of how to double a cube. In the introduction he states that Pythion the Thasian geometer wrote to Conon of Samos
about how to find a mirror surface such that the rays of the sun reflected
from it would meet the circumference of a circle; in addition, he states that
the astronomer Zenodorus, when he visited Diocles in Arcadia, set him
the problem of how to find a mirror surface that would reflect the sun's
rays so as to cause burning. Diocles promises solutions to both these
problems, though not necessarily original solutions. From these introductions, like those of Archimedes, it is evident that theoretical mathematicians did not work in research groups supported by monarchs in their
capitals, but often alone with only occasional contact, in person or by
correspondence, with persons capable of understanding their work.

Greek astronomy developed as a branch of mathematical geometry.
The astronomers of the Hellenistic age were aided by knowledge of
Babylonian observational records of the heavens, but their great contribution was to go beyond observation to apply abstract geometrical models of
spherical objects to the physical universe. For most Greek thinkers of the
era, the universe was a sphere holding fixed stars, "wandering" planets,
the sun and moon, with a spherical earth at its center. Once again, the
surviving treatises are not necessarily the ones we would most like to have
but those deemed useful during the medieval period. For instance, one set
of texts comes from a manuscript of the ninth or tenth century AD, known
as the "Little Astronomy,"[32] containing treatises that were likely preserved because they were used in schools for elementary astronomical
instruction.

In this manuscript we find the earliest extant astronomical works in Greek: *On the Moving Sphere* and *On the Risings and Settings of the Stars*, both by Autolycus of Pitane (ca. 360–ca. 290), and Euclid's *Phaenomena*. Both apply the classic form of the geometric proposition to problems of astronomical spheres, and the *Phaenomena* offers a proof that a spherical earth lies at the center of the cosmos, based on reasoning rather than true observation. Aristarchus of Samos, who was working in the early third century as shown by his observation of the summer solstice in 280, is famous for anticipating Copernicus' heliocentric theory of the universe. That he did so is guaranteed by the preface to the *Sand Reckoner*, where Archimedes, like almost all other ancient astronomers, rejected Aristarchus' novel idea that the earth revolved around the sun. Unfortunately, the only extant treatise by Aristarchus, *On the Sizes and Distances of the Sun and Moon*, presupposes the usual geocentric view in its presentation of geometrical and arithmetic measurements for heavenly bodies. It is unclear whether this is an early work, composed before the development of the heliocentric theory, or whether Aristarchus did not consider his radical concept necessary to his work on astronomical measurements. Hipparchus (second half of the second century), who came from Nicaea in Bithynia and lived mostly at Rhodes, was another serious and important mathematical astronomer. He founded trigonometry and discovered the precession of the equinoxes, that is, why equinoxes occur earlier in each successive sidereal year. While his technical work is known from an important mathematical textbook called the *Almagest* by the great mathematician Ptolemy who worked at Alexandria in the second century AD, his only extant treatise is a *Commentary on the Phaenomena of Aratus and of Eudoxus*. In this work he shows how closely Aratus follows Eudoxus and criticizes some of the astronomer's views. Last chronologically among the extant Hellenistic treatises are three elementary works on astronomical spherics (bound with Euclid and Aristarchus in the "Little Astronomy") by Theodosius of Bithynia (ca. 100). These are *Spherica* in three books, concerning great and small circles on the sphere, *On Geographic Places*, containing twelve propositions about the appearance of the sky as seen from various places on earth, and *On Days and Nights* in two books, containing thirty-one propositions on the lengths of the days and nights at different times of the year at different latitudes of the earth.

While royal patrons of the Hellenistic era seem not to have been drawn to abstract mathematics, they displayed more interest in its practical applications. Of course talented engineers had long been recognized for their work on public projects or in the service of wealthy rulers, but now in the Hellenistic era advances in mechanics came to be described in technical writings, composed either by the inventors themselves or by those who educated themselves in engineering. As Hiero encouraged Archimedes to adapt his purely intellectual achievements to perceivable bodily form useful to ordinary people, even earlier the Alexandrian native Ctesibius produced remarkable mechanical devices that came to the notice of the Ptolemies. Said to have begun as a practicing barber, Ctesibius had an extraordinary talent for pneumatics: his inventions included a pump with plunger and valve, the water organ (a musical instrument involving forcing air into pipes containing water), an accurate water clock that kept time at night and could be adjusted to seasonal change, and some kind of catapult. Hedylus of Samos (or Athens) composed an epigram celebrating a drinking horn, or rhyton, made by Ctesibius in the shape of the Egyptian god Bes, the "dancer," and dedicated in a temple of Arsinoe II (4 Gow and Page [1965]);[33] the technical trick here was to make a vessel that offered its own musical accompaniment to the dancing figure when wine was poured from its spout. Ctesibius' *Commentaries* on his inventions are lost, but his descriptions are paraphrased by the Hellenistic writer Philo of Byzantium, the Roman architectural writer Vitruvius, and Hero of Alexandria in his *Belopoeica* (*On Making Missiles*) of the late first century AD.

The earliest extant work of mechanics is Biton's *Construction of War-Machines and Artillery*, written for a Pergamene king, probably Attalus I, so that he could better defend against the engines of his enemies. Biton stresses the importance of applying technical knowledge about measurements and proportions in the construction of the devices, as well as the proper selection of wood. The work describes six machines built by specific individuals and often for specific purposes: four non-torsion catapults (the type in use until about 240), a *helepolis* or siege-tower that was designed for Alexander the Great, and a *sambuca* or scaling ladder, used by marines assaulting from ships. The drawings accompanying the text, now badly corrupted, were probably of high quality and essential to understanding the technical descriptions. The other extant writer on mechanics of the Hellenistic age is Philo of Byzantium (ca. 200), who wrote a *Mathematical Compendium* in nine books. Extant are Book 4 on catapults (in Greek), Book 5 on pneumatics (in Arabic adaptation), and (in Greek) parts of Book 7 on defensive preparations and Book 8 on siege tactics. In the book on catapults, Philo cites the mathematical theories of the famous fifth-century sculptor Polyclitus in stressing the need for accuracy in numbers, to be obtained only gradually through successive calculations (50). He claims that Alexandrian craftsmen were the first to discover the essential element in constructing these machines, namely, the diameter of the circle that holds the spring, and that they did this because of patronage from kings who loved fame and craft. He stresses that excellence in construction cannot be determined by theory alone but requires experimentation.

Ancient medicine had its starting place in a series of treatises preserved under the name of Hippocrates, the famous Coan physician of the later fifth century. Since these works are often inconsistent, they likely represent an anonymous tradition of medical writing from the classical age. Only in the early third century can we begin to identify medical researchers who composed treatises about their own theories and discoveries. Advances made in medicine during the Hellenistic age, as in other fields, involved a combination of theoretical reasoning manifest in taxonomy and close observation based on experimentation. The great experts in the field, influenced by the philosophical work of the Peripatetics in life sciences and Stoic ideas of nature as a perfect, unfailing *technē*, also borrowed concepts and techniques from mathematicians and engineers.

Unfortunately, no complete work survives from the hand of the three most important medical figures of the third century: Praxagoras, Herophilus, and Erasistratus. The earliest of these was Praxagoras from Cos, the site of a major sanctuary of the healing god Asclepius and a school of medicine going back to Hippocrates. Praxagoras was an important anatomist, who made observations about the connection between the brain and the spinal cord and was the first to draw a distinction between veins and arteries. He was the teacher of Herophilus from Chalcedon (ca. 330–ca. 260), who made fundamental discoveries about human anatomy through dissection of the body. Earlier physicians had been hindered by a Greek taboo against cutting the human body, even if deceased. Crucial to Herophilus' work, conducted in Alexandria, were the devotion of the early Ptolemies to scientific knowledge and their sense of freedom from traditional Greek prohibitions. Famously (and notoriously), the Egyptian monarchs provided Herophilus with cadavers for dissection and even condemned criminals for vivisection. In his *Anatomica*, lost except for three fragments, Herophilus detailed the results of his direct observations of the functioning body. His achievements include understanding the anatomy of the brain, the discovery of the nerves, including the optic nerve, a clearer understanding of how the lungs function in respiration, a theory of pulse rhythm, and a scientific study of female organs. His view of the pulse utilized arithmetic progressions and the musical theories of fourth-century Aristoxenus of Tarentum. His contemporary Erasistratus, from Iulis on Ceos, who had perhaps been a student of Theophrastus in Athens, worked in Alexandria and/or in Antioch at the court of Seleucus I Nicator. He too performed dissections and vivisections on criminals received from "kings." One of his lasting achievements was to provide a good description of how heart valves function. Perhaps influenced by

Ctesibius' work on pneumatics, he developed a mechanistic view of the human body as a large machine consisting of many smaller ones. The heart, for instance, was conceived as the living equivalent of a water pump. Plutarch associates Erasistratus with the belief, held by the Stoics, that nature is "accurate (*akribēs*), a lover of *technē*, unfailing, and uncomplicated" or, more colorfully, in the physician's own words, that nature holds "nothing tawdry" (*Moralia* 495c).

Herophilus and his followers were considered "rationalists," because they sought medical causes through inductive and deductive processes. In contrast arose the "empiricists," who focused on what could be learned through the hands-on practice of medicine; with them dissection again became taboo. The founder of the "empiricists" was Philinus of Cos, who worked ca. 240, and was once a student of Herophilus. His six books against the Hippocratic lexicon of the Herophilean Bacchius are lost. The sole complete surviving medical treatise of the Hellenistic age was written by another empiricist, Apollonius of Citium, who worked in the first century. In his commentary on the Hippocratic treatise *On Joints*, in three books, he sets out methods of setting dislocated or broken joints through textual explanation accompanied by illustrations. Book 1 concerns the shoulder, Book 2 the elbow, wrist, and vertebrae, and Book 3 the thigh, knee, and ankle. The remarkable diagrams illustrate various methods of repairing dislocated joints, involving such techniques as manually pulling the joint into place, strapping patients to boards and ladders to readjust the joints, and even hanging them upside down (figure 3.1). He argues that because the Herophilans lack hands-on experience and rely exclusively on reason, they are prone to mistakes. As an example, probably following Philinus, he criticizes Bacchius for not understanding the meaning of Hippocrates' words through his inexperience with patients.

Geography as a branch of learning also came into its own in the Hellenistic age. This was a result of applying geometrical mathematics to obtain relatively accurate measurements of distances on the earth and to the accumulation of knowledge about remote regions of the inhabited world through the writings of travelers. As a consequence, geographical works tend toward alliance either with mathematics and astronomy or with the ethnographical aspects of histories, which often bordered on the fabulous. No work of the three most important geographers of the age – Eratosthenes, Agatharchides, and Artemidorus – has survived in complete form, but much is known of them from later sources, most especially Strabo, who used all three as primary sources in his *Geographia* of the Augustan age.

Eratosthenes of Cyrene (ca. 285–194), a student of Callimachus, was invited from Athens by Ptolemy III Euergetes to become the royal tutor to

Figure 3.1   *Illustration of physician's assistants treating a patient, from a 10th c. AD manuscript (Laurentianum 74. 7) of Apollonius of Citium's commentary for On Joints.*

his son and head of the Alexandrian Library. He was a man of great learning, a true polymath, nicknamed "beta" because he was second best in many areas of endeavor. His *Geographica*, in three books, was the first mathematical geography and the first attempt to give an account of the entire inhabited world, in both physical and ethnographical terms. In a mathematical work, *On the Measurement of the Earth*, Eratosthenes estimated the earth's circumference by calculating the distance between Syene in upper Egypt and Alexandria as one-fiftieth of the whole, based on a triangle constructed from shadows cast on sundials on the summer solstice in each place. His geographical work extended this type of measurement to determining the length and breadth of the known world. His calculations were later severely criticized by the astronomer Hipparchus, in three books entitled *Against Eratosthenes*, because he often relied on estimates rather than exact numbers, but the utility of Eratosthenes' practical application of mathematics to unknown distances was defended by Strabo. Among other interesting features of Eratosthenes' *Geographica* were his rejection of Homer as an accurate source of geographical knowledge on the basis that as a poet his goal was enchantment not instruction, his recognition of major geological changes over time from the presence of shells at great distances from the sea, and his division of the earth into segments, called "seals," by fixing intersecting coordinates obtained by astronomical observation (a system replaced by Hipparchus' division of the globe into 360°). His third book contained a projection of the terrestrial sphere on a plane surface, namely a map, but now known only through description in later sources.

While Eratosthenes created the discipline of scientific geography, the writing of descriptive geography, based on travelers' accounts, had been practiced since the fifth century and continued in the Hellenistic period. The best-preserved example is *On the Erythraean Sea*, in five books, by Agatharchides of Cnidus (ca. 215–after 145). Agatharchides was associated with the Ptolemaic court, where he assisted important officials, including the Peripatetic scholar Heraclides Lembus. His description of the Red Sea, culled from royal reports of earlier explorers and eyewitness accounts, was his last work, curtailed because of political disturbances in Egypt, probably the expulsion of the intelligentsia in 145. About one-fifth of the work is preserved in verbatim excerpts, from Books 1 and 5. The first book seems to have focused on Ptolemy II's Nubian campaign and the interest of the Alexandrian monarchs in hunting elephants to train for military purposes. Book 5 was more ethnographical, cataloguing the remote tribes and unusual animals that lived along the shores of the Red Sea, particularly in the relatively unknown south. Agatharchides focused sympathetic treatment on the miseries endured by many of these groups, such as the Nubian gold miners, the destitute and uncivilized fish-eaters, or the root-eaters who were regularly attacked by lions. In one passage (21) he explains how to create sympathy in readers by vivid description and criticizes the frigid, paradoxical language of the Asianist Hegesias. Artemidorus of Ephesus (ca. 100) wrote eleven books of geography, now lost, but often cited in antiquity. While he relied on Agatharchides as a source for the geography of the East, he knew the West first-hand through voyages along the Mediterranean shores and outer Spain. A recently discovered papyrus contains the introduction to his second book, in which geography is said to be more important than philosophy; it is followed by an account of Spain accompanied by an unfinished map, a procedure consistent with the formal features of technical writing.[34]

A corollary to the scientific treatises of the Hellenistic age is provided by the paradoxographical works. The word *paradoxography* refers by etymology to what is "incredible" and it is often paired with terms for the "wondrous" or "unique." One scholar has defined paradoxography as the "semi-scientific study of the origins and causes of contemporary wonderful happenings ... whether in relation to natural phenomena or historical or mythological events steeped in ritual."[35] Among the lost prose works of Callimachus are two wonder books – *On Wondrous and Unbelievable Events in the Peloponnese and Italy* and *A Collection of Wonders Throughout all the World Place by Place*. How Callimachus' research on paradoxological happenings, or *thaumata*, connects with the interests of his patrons is suggested by an anecdote told by Lucian in *Literary Prometheus* (4), which indicates that Ptolemy Philadelphus had a taste for the rare and wondrous. The king had brought to Egypt, for display in a spectacle offered to his Egyptian subjects, a completely black Bactrian camel and a man of two colors, divided precisely into a white half and a black half. Contrary to Ptolemy's expectations, the audience reacted with fright to the camel, despite its jeweled bridle and purple cloak, and with laughter and repugnance to the man, as if he were a monster. The king then realized that his subjects did not share his own sense of wonder at "novelty," but preferred the traditional beauty of harmonious form. As Theophrastus explains in his *Inquiry into Plants* (2.3), unusual natural phenomena, such as when a plant changes the kind of fruit it produces (black figs instead of white ones), were explained by seers as portents, perhaps signaling some horrific event; viewed so, they would of course evoke fear or disgust in common folk. While Theophrastus believes in rational, scientific explanations for such phenomena, such as the effects of bad weather, Ptolemy apparently found such "wonders" a source of entertainment, a kind of aesthetic object pleasing for their novelty alone. It was in this cultural atmosphere that paradoxographers began to compose their prose catalogues of wonders.

Three collections of marvels, preserved in a ninth- or tenth-century manuscript,[36] are most likely by Hellenistic authors. In form, they simply catalogue events or natural phenomena, often culled from scientific works, especially of the Peripatetic school, or from the more colorful historians of the classical age. All of them make truth claims, although their subject matter is defined by its incredible nature. Occurrences are typically cited because they are unique (*idion*), specific to one place or time. The manuscript of the *Collection of Paradoxical Stories* gives as its author Antigonus, often identified (without firm basis) with the third-century Antigonus of Carystus, who wrote *On Animals* and biographies of philosophers and perhaps served the Attalids as a bronzeworker. The Antigonus who wrote paradoxography cites among his sources Aristotle's *History of Animals* and Callimachus' prose works on rivers, stones, and other such matters; poets, including prominently Philitas of Cos, are also quoted as reliable sources. Antigonus is concerned with the odd (and often mythically or ethically significant) behavior of animals and with unique natural features of rivers, fountains, plants, stones, and the like. Another work from this manuscript is entitled *On Amazing Stories Heard*, and is falsely attributed there to Aristotle; it supplements its catalogue of wondrous natural phenomena with reports concerning places in the West connected to Greek myth, such as Cumae as the home of the Sibyl. The third work, *Wondrous Stories* by someone named Apollonius, begins with stories of shamanistic figures of Greek history, including Epimenides of Crete, who acquired prophetic powers after sleeping for fifty years, and Abaris, who supposedly came from the Hyperboreans (a fabulous people who lived in the farthest north) and predicted natural disasters. A variety of wondrous natural phenomena follows, with frequent citation of the sources from which the information was culled. It is not surprising that an age fascinated with scientific reasoning and experimentation should also feel, at times, the need just to marvel at the unexplainable and unverifiable.

4

Topics in Hellenistic Literature

Hellenistic literature is enjoying a wave of aesthetic appreciation and scholarly interest that contrasts sharply with typical assessments made in the past. During the eighteenth-century Enlightenment, the classical period of Athenian culture came to embody an ideal of ordered beauty, so that literature composed after the death of Alexander was viewed as imitative and decadent. This trend continued during the period of nineteenth-century Romanticism, when literary critics developed a largely negative, and somewhat paradoxical, opinion of Hellenistic literature as concerned with passions, but only bizarre ones, or, alternately, as stripped bare of emotion by a focus on scholarly allusion rather than life. Typical of such attitudes, as they continued into the earlier twentieth century, is this description of the post-Alexander era as "a period when creative imagination and healthy political interests were all but dead, when learning flourished rather than letters, and when speakers and writers were no longer guided by true Attic theory and practice."[1] In recent decades much has changed, and positive assessment of Hellenistic literature has never been higher than today. The papyrological discoveries of the twentieth century, which added so significantly to our corpus of texts, as well as a series of excellent scholarly editions and commentaries after mid-century[2] were important as basic steps in stimulating these changing attitudes. More recently, the successful application of modern critical approaches has widened the frame of reference through which this body of literature is viewed. As a result, we have come to understand how Hellenistic literature formed an integral part of a fascinating cultural era

that is not only a worthy heir to high classicism but also strongly reminiscent of our own diverse and technically specialized culture.

4.1   Learning and Innovation

One of the broad themes addressed by both past and recent scholars has
been the relationship of Hellenistic literature to the earlier Greek literary
tradition. Hellenistic writers evince a clear "anxiety of influence."[3]
Quintilian (*Training in Oratory* 10.1.54) tells us that textual scholars
working in the Alexandrian library, namely, Aristophanes of Byzantium
and Aristarchus of Samothrace, set up canons of literary greats, excluding
writers of their own era who had not yet stood the test of time. Homer was
almost universally viewed as the best poet ever, but there were also lists of
those judged to be best within various genres, such as the nine lyric poets,
the ten Attic orators, and the three tragedians. Aristotle in the *Poetics*
offered another model of judgment, that of formal development toward
a goal or *telos* of perfection, which he identified for tragedy in Sophocles'
Oedipus Tyrannus. Similar developmental models were set up for the visual
arts, especially sculpture and painting, with, again, a *telos* reached in the
classical period. When the best in every field was thought to have been
already achieved, aspiring poets (and artists) found themselves in a difficult psychological position. Even in the early fourth century the epic poet
Choerilus of Samos complained that the poetic arts had run their course
"so that we are left behind in the race, and there is no place for the person
who peers about to direct his newly yoked chariot" (317 Lloyd-Jones and
Parsons). By the third century this anxiety about the accomplishments of
the past had come to manifest itself in a longing for the lost greatness of
earlier Greek culture, often now expressed in works that recrafted literary
language and forms to suit contemporary culture. In exploring this difficult relationship of Hellenistic literature to its archaic and classical predecessors, scholars have devoted particular attention to the poetic use of
allusion, the pervasiveness of genre innovation, and the general learned
quality of the poetry.

   The "art of allusion," as it has been called, has long been identified as
a primary characteristic of Hellenistic poetry. While earlier literature
contains traditional phrasing and echoes of other texts, Hellenistic poets
often included allusions that were meant to recall specific passages, the
context in which they occurred, and even scholarly discussions of them.
This intensified use of allusion in Hellenistic literature has to do with the
poets' greater awareness of the tradition of Greek literature as something
to be preserved in a new setting, and with their expectation that their

audience would, at least in part, consist of highly educated individuals. In the past, scholars have cited the allusive nature of Hellenistic poetry as one of its more cerebral, even musty qualities, a signal that it was a literature intended only for other scholars. Certainly, many Hellenistic allusions do involve rare and problematic words, especially those that appear but once in Homer, the so-called *hapax legomena* ("once-said words"), and it was this obscure diction that the Hellenistic glossographers and textual commentators studied and debated. The poets of the age sometimes display their erudition by using choice words in such a way as to indicate their opinion about some scholarly controversy (for example, see Ch. 2.2). But scholars are now coming to understand that rare vocabulary was also chosen for more poetic purposes, such as beauty of sound or contextual resonance. For instance, the critic Andromenides, writing probably in the third century, explains that the splendid quality of Homer's *Iliad* 17.52, "braids which were plaited with gold and silver," consists not in the mention of gold and silver but in the dense sound of the words *plochmoi*, "braids," and *esphēkōnto*, "plaited" (Col. 23–4, 185–6 Janko). Significantly, *plochmoi* is a Homeric hapax, next appearing in Apollonius (2.677). In choosing to adorn his poetry with this unusual word, Apollonius may have been not only asserting his scholarly knowledge of Homeric diction but also striving for a euphonic effect. Similarly, he adopts the Homeric hapax *amēchania*, "helplessness" or "despair," as a persistent epithet for his hero Jason. Although scholars have often remarked on the "modern," Hellenistic nature of this heroism of uncertainty, by choosing a "once-said" word Apollonius evokes the resonance of the specific Odyssean passage in which it occurs (*Odyssey* 9.295), where Odysseus, trapped in the Cyclops' cave, despairs as the monster devours his men. The allusion to this passage invites the reader steeped in Homer, as even marginally educated persons were, to compare the two epic heroes, and perhaps to recognize that while Odysseus perseveres in his homecoming, his men all die, whereas Jason's continuing despair results in a safe homecoming for the great majority of the Argonauts. Allusions, then, can set up complicated interpretive puzzles, based on similarity and difference between famous earlier passages and the new Hellenistic ones.

Other allusions involve broader contextual similarities, which sometimes provide clues to the aesthetic models for Hellenistic poetry. An important example is an opening passage in the *Theogony* where Hesiod describes how the Muses breathed into him poetic knowledge as he was herding his sheep on Mt. Helicon. In these lines Hesiod provides an imaginative description of the almost supernatural powers that seemed to belong to the oral poet, who was, in preliterate Greece, the main source of information about a distant past, still knowable through the aid of the divine Muses. During the Hellenistic age the place of Hesiod's investiture as a poet, the peak of Helicon near his hometown of Ascra in Boeotia, functioned as a cult site where the Muses were worshipped. As patrons of the arts, the Ptolemies provided financial support for the buildings and festivals there. Hellenistic poets were keen to show both their indebtedness to Hesiod, who in his didactic poetry associated the divine workings of the universe with the ethical lives of ordinary persons, especially farmers like himself, and their own changed circumstance, and consequently, the scene on Mt. Helicon was remade to characterize the new means by which poets acquired their craft. In a very fragmentary passage immediately following the prologue to the *Aetia*, Callimachus claims that as a youth he was transported, apparently in a dream, to Helicon where he asked questions of the Muses; in response, they supplied him with information about customs and rituals for his poem. We as readers are of course aware that the conversation with the Muses is a fiction, designed to place his modern subject matter, often derived from prose sources, in a poetic tradition. Likewise, in *Idyll* 7 Theocritus describes an encounter between the urban poet Simichidas, who seems a self-representation of the poet, and the rural singer Lycidas, who exchanges bucolic songs with Simichidas. Here the famous Heliconian spring called Hippocrene, from which Roman (and probably Hellenistic) epic poets were said to drink, is replaced by a local Coan spring called Bourina, mentioned also by Philitas, though in an unknown context. All this suggests a pastoral reworking of the Hesiodic investiture. Although the knowing Lycidas, the best of country singers, has some marks of divinity, he is identified in the poem as unmistakably a goatherd, one who guides Simichidas toward more beautiful song by his own example. Among the new sources of poetic inspiration, Theocritus seems to say, is the song of ordinary people. In addition, Theocritus here plays with the paradox that while Hesiod was turned from shepherd into poet, Simichidas must reverse that course and become like a herdsman in order to gain poetic skill.

Hellenistic poets also allude to each other, and these verbal echoes sometimes suggest agreement or disagreement about poetic principles. The epigrammatist Posidippus composed several epigrams, mostly erotic, as poetic variations of epigrams written by his older contemporary Asclepiades of Samos, perhaps to mark his respect for the innovative Samian. In contrast, a fragment of Callimachus seems to poke fun at Asclepiades' epigram on Antimachus' *Lyde* by labeling Lyde, woman and poem, "fat" (fr. 398). At the same time, similarities between epigrams of Posidippus and Callimachus' poetry suggest that these two poets were engaged in rivalry or dissent. The identification of Posidippus as one of the Telchines who criticized Callimachus' poetry, by a scholiast to the *Aetia* prologue, supports this impression. So, for instance, an epigram on the Milan papyrus (22 Austin and Bastianini) in which cranes fly from Thrace toward Egypt reverses the image in the *Aetia* prologue of cranes flying from Egypt to Thrace (fr. 1.13–14). Since Callimachus' cranes represent, through the length of their flight, the type of long poetry he avoids, there is all the more reason to think of an intended allusion, particularly if the prologue was written late in his life after the publication of Posidippus' epigram. If Callimachus' crane image is somehow critical of the Macedonian epigrammatist (although length can scarcely be the whole issue since Posidippus specialized in short poetry), Posidippus seems, likewise, to have alluded to Callimachus' poetry with critical intent. In the second line of Callimachus' "Bath of Pallas," a participant in the goddess's ritual bath mentions that she has heard "the ponies just now neighing" (*Hymn* 5.2). These are the horses conveying the sacred image of Athena, in that solemn moment when the procession approaches. But Posidippus parodically reworks the phrase to a very different purpose. In an epigram in which a prostitute celebrates her victory over another prostitute in a contest to see which one could first bring her partner to climax, the young men being "ridden" are described as "ponies just now neighing" (*Palatine Anthology* 5.202). The wording of this risqué poem is exactly that in the "Bath of Pallas," and surely it is here Posidippus who alludes, in a kind of spoof, to Callimachus' hymnal poetry.

Scholars have also studied how Hellenistic poets remade the literary tradition to accommodate new contexts and interests through genre innovation. Literary genres had developed in earlier Greek culture in accordance with the needs and conventions that attached to the occasions on which they were performed, either public ones like festivals or private ones like symposia. But though many performance occasions continued in the Hellenistic age, authors asserted their independence from the literary past by remaking genres in terms of length, subject matter, tone, and purpose. Scholarly studies of specific instances of Hellenistic genre adaptation generally rely on detailed analysis of how composers reuse the diction and settings of their models to point up the central differences in tone or purpose. Examples can be culled from almost every author and genre. Epic narrative was adapted to the shorter form now called epyllion, with an accompanying shift in focus away from the heroic values of older epic toward personal pathos, often of female characters (Callimachus' *Hecale*, Moschus' *Europa*), and epic discourse was reworked as mimelike dialogue in Theocritus' urban and rustic *Idylls*. Objective narrative elegy was recast in Callimachus' *Aetia* where the subjective, intrusive voice of the poet directed the topics and manner of telling in accordance with his personal preferences. The robust, satiric tone of archaic iambic poetry was adapted to criticism of the philosophical, moral, or aesthetic positions of others, as in Timon's *Silli* or Callimachus' *Iambi*, and combined with subliterary, prosaic form of mime in Herodas' *Mimiambi* to produce realistic portraits of contemporary life. In losing its musical accompaniment, lyric verse received new life in written form, including, for instance, epistolary poetry (Theocritus' "Distaff," *Idyll* 28). Epigram was freed from *in situ* inscription to take on new subject matter or to play fictively with its own form, as when inscriptions are embedded within book epigrams or other literary forms. Historical narratives, especially the more fantastic and pathetic forms, began in the late Hellenistic period to develop into romantic stories of novel length, although surviving examples from papyri all date to the first century AD or later.[4] The *Letter of Aristeas*, which narrates the creation of the Septuagint, has some of these characteristics, since it contains a lengthy section of symposium discussion between Ptolemy and the Jewish scholars that can scarcely be accurate historically. Despite the wide variety of generic innovation, what is common throughout is a focus on previously marginal figures, such as women, children, and low-status or even non-Greek persons, and on the emotional lives of individuals rather than topics of broader social and political significance.

An important means of Hellenistic genre innovation was the mixing of genres, often known by the German expression "Kreuzung der Gattungen."[5] Even as the social system that supported performance occasions was changing and disintegrating, philosophical thinkers, especially the Peripatetics, were defining genres and analyzing what was appropriate to them. Archaic and classical authors had followed the conventions appropriate to their forms, which were often dictated by the performance environment, but now scholars developed rules for what was appropriate in genres. For innovative and bookish poets like Callimachus, these rules may have seemed more provocation than guide, and as a result, examples of poems that combine generic forms are easily found in his poetry. The so-called "Victory of Berenice," the opening episode in Book 3 of Callimachus' *Aetia*, is a particularly complex example, consisting of a frame containing a story within a story. The frame itself adapts the genre of lyric epinician to an elegiac celebration of Queen Berenice II's victory in chariot racing at the Nemean games. As Pindar often includes a mythical narrative in his odes praising victors, so here Callimachus embeds the story of Heracles' visit to Nemea where he killed a lion (his first labor) and established the games. But the actual account of Heracles' heroic adventure is deflected in favor of the story of Molorchus, a poor man who entertains Heracles in his humble dwelling. The further twist is that Molorchus has performed a heroic deed of his own, since he defeated the mice that were stealing his food – by inventing the mousetrap. In this "mock-heroic" tale embedded in and displacing the story of Heracles' labor, we have an adaptation of both lyric (epinician) and shorter epic narrative (note the similarity to the *Hecale*) to create a new form of elegy.

The title *Eidullia*, "Little Genres," given to a collection of Theocritus' poetry signals that the combination of different literary types, both within and across poems, was the innovative basis for defining the generic identity of the poems as a group. Likewise, in *Iambus* 13 Callimachus defends himself against those critics who find fault with his *polyeideia*, "variety of form." He disagrees with the idea that the gods have allotted one poet the ability to compose elegy, another epic, and yet another tragedy (fr. 203.31–2), and rejects the claim that writing in Ionic, Doric, and a mixture of dialects is too daring (fr. 203.17–19). Over the course of his career, Callimachus demonstrated the flexible nature of his poetic talent, as he composed in different genres, in a variety of meters, and in several dialects. By enunciating his rebellion against generic rules in the last of his *Iambi*, he calls attention to the mix of generic forms within the book itself. Written in the limping iambic meters of the collection are, to name selective types, fables (*Iambi* 2, 4), an epinician (*Iambus* 8), a birthday poem or *genethliacon* (*Iambus* 12), and two poems about statues, based on epigrammatic motifs (*Iambi* 6, 9). As a result, the book of *Iambi* becomes itself, through its internal "mixture of genres," an example of the poetic practice Callimachus is defending. In rejecting the unity associated with a single poem in a single generic form, Callimachus creates a new unity, in which diverse poetic types are tied together by a recognizable personal voice, that of the creative artist himself.

The use of prose sources rather than the mythical tradition has long been recognized as another aspect of the erudite innovation of Hellenistic poets. Throughout the post-Alexander period, it was commonly accepted that the purpose of poetry was to give pleasure, in the service of which falsehood might be advantageous, while the purpose of prose was instruction, based on truth. This dichotomy, however, begs for contradiction or at least qualification, and one of the impulses of the age was to blur the line dividing the material deemed appropriate to poetry and to prose. The ancient social role of the poet as purveyor of knowledge found new life in the composition of didactic poetry, cast in the Hesiodic mold, but the subject matter of this poetry was now the new scientific knowledge, based on reason rather than tradition. In addition, poetry in other genres, such as elegy, hymn, and epigram, sometimes now included material of a technical, mathematical, or scientific nature. While the adaptation of poetic form to subject matter taken from prose treatises seems, at first blush, a recipe for inhibiting aesthetic effect, the phenomenon must be understood in the context of the new aesthetics of rationalism taking hold in Hellenistic culture.

In the hands of the best poets of the age, material taken from scientific and technical manuals could be transformed into a compelling poetic vision. Callimachus' description of the nautilus shell dedicated by a young woman to Arsinoe in her temple at Zephyrium (14 Gow and Page [1965]) was based on Aristotle's account of the animal's behavior (*History of Animals* 622b5–15). But by giving voice to the dead mollusk, whose shell survives in the temple along with its dedicatory epigram, Callimachus sets up a series of enticing dichotomies (male–female, alive–dead, goddess–mortal, spoken–written) that lift the poem beyond its specific cultural usages. Likewise, Posidippus' section on stones, which apparently opened the epigram book preserved on the Milan papyrus, owes much to treatises like Theophrastus' *On Stones*, which listed the origins and properties of hard objects obtained from the earth. By reworking such prose material as epigrams about the beauty of the stones and the individuals who possessed them, the poet celebrates the physical reality of the terrestrial globe, as if offering an introduction to the other epigram sections about various human activities. Eratosthenes' lost *Hermes*, a hexameter poem that was perhaps both hymn and epyllion (frs. 1–16 Powell, pp. 58–63, with 397–8 Lloyd-Jones and Parsons), contained an account of the young god's first ascent into heaven, during which he marveled at the musical harmony of the spheres and, in a preserved fragment (fr. 16), gains a panoramic view of the earth's globe with its five zones. Eratosthenes thus converts into traditional narrative form his specialized understanding of geography and astronomy. Likewise, epigrams explaining wonders, especially the regeneration of one species of animal from the carcass of another, offered by Archelaus of Egypt to one of the Ptolemaic kings, poeticize a belief espoused in Peripatetic works on life sciences. The epigrams, apparently gathered into a collection, were given a quasi-philosophical point, about the continuity of life through "natural" processes, by one introductory line: "Lengthy time seals everything through [transformation into] other things" (129.1 Lloyd-Jones and Parsons). Apollonius' narrative structure for the journey of the Argonauts, involving a day-by-day account of their progress along the coast of the Black Sea and the inhabitants they encountered, is reminiscent of prose geographies, of which Agatharchides' *On the Erythraean Sea* is a partially surviving example (Ch. 3.10). Again, the poet suggests a broader vision, one that connects the way things were at the dawn of Hellenic civilization with the way the things are in his own day, through aetiology and covert references to the role of Egypt in the Greek mythical tradition. Theocritus, with his interest in personal relationships and the pastoral realm, may seem removed from the scientific sphere, but in fact his poetry also reflects the impulse of the age. His view of love as a disease for which song is

possibly a cure may signal a personal interest in medicine (cf. the section
of epigrams on "cures" in the Milan papyrus). Not only was his friend
Nicias a student of the famous physician Erasistratus, but also his father
bears the same name as the Coan physician Praxagoras. Family connections may explain why Theocritus spent time in Cos, where Hippocrates'
medical school flourished. His precise, almost scientific knowledge of
plants, especially those of the eastern Mediterranean, has been noticed,
so that the early Hellenistic interest in botany, best preserved in Theophrastus' *History of Plants*, may have contributed to his wonderful pastoral
landscapes (often set in Sicily or southern Italy). If the technical almost
slips from view in these poets, it nevertheless had a profound effect on
their ability to create an imaginative vision that moves beyond the particularity of fact to suggest the universal.

Didactic poetry written to popularize the prose writings of serious
scientific thinkers was normally composed in epic hexameters, but in a
few instances authors created innovative generic hybrids based on technical prose sources. In his prose *Chronological Tables*, now lost, Eratosthenes set out a chronology of events from the fall of Troy to, apparently,
the death of Alexander, which used, for the first time it seems, the four-
year periods between the Olympic games, called Olympiads, as the basis
for much of the timeline. Then, toward the middle of the second century,
Apollodorus of Athens made a versified version, also lost, of Eratosthenes' important chronological work. Apollodorus was primarily a
researcher rather than a poet, and he worked in Alexandria with the
Homeric scholar Aristarchus until the dispersion of 146, when he fled to
Pergamum. His lost *Chronica*, covering 1,040 years from the fall of Troy to
his own lifetime, was not composed in the expected epic meter, but in an
iambic meter of the comic type. Heavily influenced by Apollodorus' work
is an extant but anonymous poem, in 747 comic iambs, called *Circuit of the
Earth* and addressed to a king Nicomedes of Bithynia, probably Nicomedes II Epiphanes, whose reign began in 149. This work is a fascinating
hybrid of geography, chronology, and ethnography, and has been called
an ancient "archaeology" of the world.[6] In the lengthy preface, the author
justifies his choice of "comedy" on the basis that in this mode a person
may speak briefly and clearly (the desired qualities of didactic poetry and
learned prose) and yet attract the soul (*psychagōgein*) of the right-thinking
critic (the desired quality of poetry). He explains that Apollodorus, who,
though not named, is identified by certain biographical facts and a summary of his work, used comic meter for the sake of clarity and to make his
work memorable, since "charm runs throughout a work when research
and metrical speech intertwine" (43–4). Toward the end of the prologue,
the anonymous poet gives a list of the prose sources from which he took

information, a poetic "bibliography" that begins with Eratosthenes' *Geographica* and ends with the great historian Herodotus. Another "prose" feature incorporated throughout is the frequent naming of a specific source for some fact, as if the poet felt the need to provide versified footnotes.

Another kind of generic experiment was offered, though rarely, by serious researchers who chose to present their ideas, not in prose, but in poetry. Not simply assuming the popularizing role of didactic poets, these scientific experts seem, rather, to be offering themselves as the successors of the old "masters of wisdom," the great poets of earlier eras. One such instance is Archimedes' *Cattle Problem* (201 Lloyd-Jones and Parsons), an elegiac poem of forty-four lines on the mathematical problem of indeterminate analysis. The subject chosen for illustrating the problem comes from the *Odyssey*, where Homer tells how Odysseus' men encountered on Sicily "seven herds of cattle . . . of fifty each" (12.129–30) belonging to the Sun. Archimedes, a Sicilian himself, used the exact number of cattle given by Homer to formulate a complex computational problem involving how many bulls and how many cows in each herd were of a certain color. Enunciating this problem in good elegiac couplets with a few puns thrown in (if the addressee succeeds in learning how many bulls and how many cows of each color there were, he would be "not unlearned in *numbers* but not yet *numbered* among the wise") is both a technical and a poetic *tour de force*, which suggests, in part, that a mathematical genius like Archimedes may have conceived himself on some level as the legitimate successor to Homer. Not, then, just a clever way to present a logical problem, the use of elegiac meter and the choice of Homeric subject matter may indicate a rejection of the typical Hellenistic dichotomy of purpose between prose and poetry with the assignment of utility to one and pleasure to the other; rather, perhaps, Archimedes offers pure reason, in the form of mathematics, as a new means of achieving a unity of poetic form and content.

Another example is offered by an epigram of eighteen lines on the famous geometric problem of duplicating a cube, composed by Eratosthenes (fr. 35 Powell, p. 66) and quoted by him in a letter to his patron Ptolemy III Euergetes. The letter begins with some lines from an unknown "writer of tragedies," in which king Minos orders that a tomb built for the hero Glaucus be doubled in size – by doubling the length of each side. Since this is a mistaken way to make a solid object only twice as large, Eratosthenes points out that at least some earlier poets, far from possessing wisdom, were mathematically ignorant. After explaining the history of the problem of duplicating the cube, Eratosthenes then describes a dedicatory monument he set up, consisting of a pillar with a mechanical device in bronze soldered near the top, beneath which was a condensed account of his own solution to the duplication problem, a diagram to illustrate that solution, and then an epigram, which itself contains a miniature history of the problem culminating in Eratosthenes' solution. While at its dedicatory site (perhaps in the royal complex) the epigram provided an account accessible to the casual reader, in the context of the letter it becomes Eratosthenes' answer to the mathematically ignorant tragedian, since he demonstrates, as the tragedian could not, how to duplicate the cube, and he does so in a verse medium.

The sense of despair expressed by the fourth-century poet Choerilus of Samos about the possibility of finding untrodden paths for his poetic chariot gave way in the early Hellenistic era to an understanding that scholarly study of earlier literature could combine with the new rational knowledge of the universe to form a literature of a radically different kind. As a result, Hellenistic literature is often layered, with a charming, sometimes witty, surface accessible to a nonspecialist reader and deeper layers of allusion and learning recognizable to readers with expert knowledge. Scholarly appreciation of this new literary aesthetic, of learning and innovation, has been steadily increasing in recent years as critics come to understand more fully the relationship of the authors to the culture in which they lived.

4.2   Book Culture and Performance

Writtenness has often been claimed as a distinguishing mark of Hellenistic literature. As Peter Bing puts it, "poetry is now chiefly composed and experienced in writing."[7] Certainly authors do often mention, or thematize, writing in their poetry, and it is in the third century that poets first collected their own poems for publication in book format. A greater expectation that literature would be read on papyrus rolls surely affected its character since the possibility of rereading supported the addition of complex allusions or scholarly references and readers could now respond to textual elements with the eye as well as the ear. Modern scholars have often connected this bookish tendency in composing with the work on texts that went on in the Alexandrian Museum and elsewhere, and certainly scholarly and theoretical material did find its way into the literature of the age. As a result, claims have sometimes been made for a sharp division between literature composed to be performed for the masses and that written for the educated elite. Recently, Alan Cameron has challenged certain aspects of this view.[8] As he points out, substantial evidence exists for performance of literature in the Hellenistic age, both publicly and privately. He also challenges the division between popular and elite literary cultures by arguing that even sophisticated poets like Theocritus and Callimachus recited their poetry at times in public settings, such as the new Ptolemaic festivals. While an increased awareness of, and self-consciousness about, the importance of writing in the creation of texts is clearly a defining mark of Hellenistic literature, Cameron's arguments have created a more balanced picture. He has been particularly successful in dispelling the old idea that Hellenistic poets were focused exclusively on an almost fetishized literature of the past, known from the dusty papyrus rolls in their library, and that therefore their compositions were to be studied only in relationship to these earlier works, not for any possible connection to the realities of their own society. At the same time, other scholars were studying more closely the growing body of evidence that, from the first half of the third century, poets collected their poetry into carefully arranged books, where the authorial ordering enhanced the levels of meaning derivable from the texts. The truth is that while old ways of performing before an audience continued, composers were now acutely and self-consciously aware of the new written settings in which their texts would be primarily encountered.

Undeniably, writing, reading, and the materiality of texts were prominent topics in the poetry of the Hellenistic age. In the *Aetia* prologue Callimachus claims that when "I first set my writing tablet on my knee," Apollo appeared to offer him advice on how to compose poetry (fr. 1.21–2). The reference to the young poet's writing tablet is programmatically meaningful, shaped by the sharp contrast with the opening of the *Theogony* where the Muses visit the apparently illiterate shepherd Hesiod. In another example, the epigrammatist Hedylus praises a poet named Socles because, though he "plays more sweetly than Sicelidas [Asclepiades of Samos] by the wine," when thoroughly drunk he departs the drinking party to set down his poetry in writing (6 Gow and Page [1965]). What Hedylus seems to admire is Socles' ability to combine the Dionysiac inspiration of the symposium with the discipline needed to produce polished poetry in writing. The Muses, who provided the oral poet with memory of past events and knowledge of the unobservable, were also remade in new images for the literate age. In the so-called "Seal" elegy (because, like a signet ring used for sealing in wax, it marks the poem with the author's name), Posidippus calls upon the Muses to "write in the golden columns of my tablet" and hopes that after death he will be honored with a statue in which he is depicted "unrolling a book" (118 Austin and Bastianini).[9] The Muses are now partners with the poet in the process of creative writing, and the poet, like his audience, experiences literature in bookrolls. Asclepiades of Samos, in an epigram on Antimachus' *Lyde* (*Palatine Anthology* 9.63, quoted in Ch 2.1), thematizes the new dual possibility of performance and reading for the reception of literature. Lyde is *both* the woman celebrated in a long poem by Antimachus *and* the title of his book, a "written text" produced by the collaboration of the poet and the Muses. Likewise, in an epigram by Posidippus, the "columns of Sappho's lovely ode," which "have voice," are said to be *leukai*, a word meaning both "white" and "lucid" (122.5–6 Austin and Bastianini); the dual, ambiguous meaning of this adjective charmingly evokes both the aural effect of the poem when read aloud and its visual effect when seen on the light-colored papyrus.

Elsewhere as well, the distinction between poetry as language and the materiality of writing is blurred for an astonishing poetic effect. The poems that Theocritus sends out to potential patrons in *Idyll* 16 are personified as Charites ("Graces") because the poet hopes to receive in exchange *charis* in the sense of "gratitude," and also because the poems have the poetic quality of *charis* or "charm." In addition, the physical form suggested by personifying the poems as goddesses merges with the physical form they have as bookrolls when, returning from an unsuccessful journey, they bow on cold knees in his coffer. Similarly, Meleager ends his *Garland* with an epigram spoken by the *corōnis* or flourish that marked the conclusion of a work (*Palatine Anthology* 12.257). The information about author and title that usually appears at the end of the papyrus roll becomes here part of the text itself, so that, once again, the poem marks verbally its own material existence in a book.

In other instances, the visual form of the poetry becomes essential to its message. Epigrams, as they were inscribed on tombstones and dedicatory objects, were the only forms of verse that were written to be seen rather than heard in pre-Hellenistic Greek culture. Just as epigrams were adapted to new subjects in the Hellenistic age, so some aspects of their original visual contexts were adapted to aesthetic uses in bookrolls. Acrostics are known from a fair number of Hellenistic stone inscriptions, and this usage, to spell out the name of a deceased or dedicator, may have been the model for acrostics in book poetry, such as Aratus' famous naming of his stylistic preference by spelling out *leptē* (Ch. 2.2, 3.5). The technopaegnia, poems that assume the visual shape of an object to which they refer, are also related to inscriptions placed on the body of a dedicated statue; some of the earliest ones may actually have been composed to fit on an object. But as they have come down to us in the manuscript tradition, their effect depends upon the interpretive tension created by reading the often obscure, puzzling text while experiencing the visual clarity of the shape. Three of these were composed by Simias of Rhodes, a poet and glossographer of the early third century who perhaps created the prototype for later pictorial poems. His "Wings" takes the shape of the wings of Eros, who speaks explaining how his appearance relates to his function as a primeval force of nature (*Palatine Anthology* 15.24); in "Axe" (15.22) the Greek hero Epeius offers to Athena the tool with which he constructed the Trojan horse; "Egg" (15.27), representing the egg of a nightingale, provides an extended metaphor for the development of poetic rhythm and meter on the model of animal song and movement. In book format, the lines of "Egg" must be rearranged to produce the pictorial shape, but the proper order could be maintained if the poem were written on an egg-shaped object that an observer turned round and round in the hand. As a material object, such an egg would have been highly unusual, of special interest to lovers of poetry; it seems probable, however, that from early on the text circulated independently. There are two other technopaegnia of our period, the pseudo-Theocritean "Syrinx" (15.21) in the shape of a herdsman's pipe dedicated to Pan, and Dosiadas' "Altar" (15.26), another mythical object that speaks, claiming that it was made by the Argonaut Jason. Both poems are highly allegorical, written in an obscure style like that of Lycophron, and apparently composed as book poetry, to be seen if not also heard.

At the same time that authors were exploring the new possibilities created when texts were composed for consumption in books, performances of literary texts, both prose and poetry, continued in public and private settings. In all likelihood, recitation of new compositions among a circle of acquaintances, a common practice in Rome, was standard in the Hellenistic age as well, and symposia, where witty conversation and performance of favorite songs and poetic passages had long been practiced, were good places to share experimental works. Aspiring authors no doubt hoped to gain recognition through performance at festivals held in many locations throughout the Hellenistic period, and perhaps even to be noticed by a supportive monarch. These literary performances, like the athletic events taking place at the same festivals, were competitive, divided into categories such as epic, lyric, rhetoric, and encomium. The names of many victors are preserved in honorific inscriptions, and in a few instances the winning poems survive on stone. For example, shortly after the middle of the third century, a lyric hymn to Apollo and one to Hestia were inscribed at Delphi, as part of a series of honors offered to their composer, Aristonous of Corinth (Powell pp. 162–5). There is extensive evidence for itinerant poets who performed their compositions on subjects of local interest as they moved from city to city. In the first century Cicero describes a successful tour of the Greek East made by the poet Archias, a native of Antioch. The leading poets of the third century seem also to have performed at public events. Our biographies of Apollonius say that as a youth he "displayed" his *Argonautica* at Alexandria, his native city, and when it was badly received went into exile on Rhodes; he likely also recited his poetry about the founding of cities, including Rhodes, in the cities thus celebrated. In his *Encomium to Ptolemy*, Theocritus mentions poetic contests held at Alexandrian festivals, which probably included the great Ptolemaica (*Idyll* 17.112–16):

> Not ever did come to the sacred competitions a man of Dionysus
> with knowledge of how to strike up a clear-sounding song
> to whom he [Ptolemy II] did not give a gift worthy of his skill.
> The interpreters of the Muses sing of Ptolemy in exchange for his generosity.

A marginal comment on a fragmentary conclusion to *Idyll* 24 ("Little Heracles") suggests that the poem functioned as a hymn to Heracles (a divinized ancestor of the Ptolemies), performed in a competitive setting. Public performances can be imagined as well for Callimachus' poems, especially certain hymns and lyric poems, and certainly parts of the *Aetia*, particularly the "Victory of Berenice" and the "Lock of Berenice," both of which deal with datable events early in that queen's reign.

An important issue in Hellenistic scholarship involves how the traditional settings for the reception of literature, oral performance and visual inscription, interact with the new importance of writing and books to the literary experience. As mentioned before, even the most famous and sophisticated authors continued to perform for special occasions and to write verses for inscription in a fixed site. But their compositions, like those of earlier poets, were now regularly transferred to papyrus rolls where the settings for performance or inscription were physically absent, but imaginatively present. The experience of "reading" literature, whether by personally looking at the columns of writing or by listening to another read or recite from memory, thus involves an imaginative recreation of another time and place. An essential change in the nature of the literature occurs when poets focus creatively on the consequences of separating the occasion presupposed by the literary work from the actual reception of the work. In a significant number of poems, literary effect is produced by emphasizing for the reader the fictional nature of the performance or the site of reading represented in the poem. Callimachus' mimetic hymns (2, 5, and 6) create this awareness of literary distance because the voices heard in them are those of participants in ritual acts. Since the speaker in the "Hymn to Apollo," as both a native of Cyrene and a director of the chorus, so closely resembles Callimachus himself, the dramatization of the ritual tends to fade from the imaginative view of the reader, for whom the voice praising the god easily coalesces with that of the poet. Likewise, the speakers in the hymns for Athena and Demeter provide extended and objectively told narratives that lead the reader to forget the ritual context and so to hear the narrator's voice as closely aligned with Callimachus' own. In many instances, it cannot be known if Hellenistic epigrams surviving in books were in fact once inscribed, but some epigrams signal their composition as book poetry by making their fictionality explicit. In an epitaph by Leonidas, for instance, a poor man speaks from the dead to request that the passerby deliver him a ritual greeting even though his tomb is entirely hidden from view by brambles and thorns (*Palatine Anthology* 7.656). Since a passerby could not read the obscured inscription and the composer of the epitaph could not have known the stone's future fate, the fictionality of the epitaph is evident. It could be read only in a book, where the reader would have the leisure to appreciate the poet's clever play with the conventions of inscription. In such instances, the book format in which the poem is inscribed has become an essential part of the literary experience.

One of the most important innovations in Hellenistic literature was the invention of the poetry book. Although papyrus copies containing multiple short poems by older poets surely existed previously, the early Hellenistic process of sorting and arranging for scholarly editions produced a model for poets to issue their own short poems in ordered collections. Doing so offered great literary advantages. The poet preserved the particularity of the short poem, where stylistic precision could be practiced, while larger themes could also be addressed, within clusters of poems or through sporadic repetition throughout the collection. As a result, poetry books were a way for the characteristics of brevity and conciseness congenial to many Hellenistic writers to rival, through arrangement in collection, the characteristics of length – weightiness of language and subject, and (in the better examples) unity – characteristics that were associated with higher-status forms, like epic and tragedy. While variety, or *poikilia*, was an accepted aesthetic principle for poetry books, poet-editors also had various means of achieving coherence, such as using a single poetic voice, focusing on certain themes or topics, or creating symmetrical arrangements or other patterns of design. The papyrus discoveries of the twentieth century have given scholars the opportunity to observe the arrangements of poems within previously lost poetry books and, by comparison, to recognize the traces of other such books in the texts preserved in manuscripts.

Callimachus' *Iambi* and *Aetia*, both only partially preserved, provided later Latin poets important models for the organization of collections. The four bookrolls of the *Aetia* were presented as poetry books, since the episodes in them are marked off as separate poems in papyrus copies. Although extensive loss of the text makes it difficult to understand the arrangement of these episodes within the individual books, more evident are the broader principles for unifying the *Aetia* into an integrated set of four poetic books, forming a larger whole. The famous prologue is balanced by an epilogue placed at the end of Book 4, where a reference to Hesiod echoes the scene on Mt. Helicon that is the first *aition*. In a similar way, the opening of Book 3, the "Victory of Berenice," links to the final episode in Book 4, the "Lock of Berenice." This linking from beginning to end is called ring composition, and it was likely used to unify Books 1 and 2 as well, although loss of the sequence of episodes in Book 2 makes this uncertain. But it has been plausibly suggested that Book 1 ended with a personal reference to Callimachus as an old man tended by the boys who are his fans (fr. 41), and Book 2 likely began with a symposium scene in which Callimachus expresses to his dining companion his preference for serious conversation and light drinking (frs. 178–85). If this is correct, then it is evident that Callimachus has used the beginning and end points of his books to link references to his poetic preferences and hopes for success. The architectural design giving the *Aetia* its structure was imitated in Latin poetry books (especially the four books of Vergil's *Georgics*); also influential, especially for the Latin elegists, was the cohesion given the episodic collection by the narrator's personal voice.

The epilogue to the *Aetia* (fr. 112) speaks of passing on to the "prose pasture of the Muses," a reference to the *Iambi* that follow immediately in one important papyrus.[10] It would appear, then, that not only did Callimachus arrange the *Aetia* and *Iambi* as poetry books, but he also issued a comprehensive edition of his poetry in which the works were arranged and linked in an order of his choosing. As the *Diegeseis*, or ancient summaries, show, the *Iambi* were followed by four lyric poems and then the narrative *Hecale*. Despite substantial loss of text, we do know enough about the *Iambi* to see that Callimachus provided them with a studied order. Unlike the *Aetia*, the thirteen iambic poems do not lend themselves to architectural arrangements with complicated sets of ring composition, but rather the odd number of poems and their linear succession offer simpler opportunities for sequencing that seem to fit the somewhat prosaic and acerbic character of the work. Even so, the collection begins and ends with poems that make clear – through the biting criticism voiced by the pedant scholar Hipponax in *Iambus* 1 and the polemical defense of Callimachus' *polyeideia*, "variety of form," in *Iambus* 13 – the relationship of Callimachus' poetry to the earlier tradition of iambography as well as his own theoretical principles of composition. Variety given coherence is the basic principle for organizing the thirteen poems, which represent in iambic form a number of different genres. This generic variety is nevertheless organized, not in sections, but through linked pairs separated by one intervening poem (2 and 4 as fables, 3 and 5 as critical of erotic behavior, and 7 and 9 on statues of Hermes). The organization differences between the *Aetia* and the *Iambi* show clearly, then, how Callimachus' penchant and talent for variety extend even to his techniques of arrangement.

The six *Hymns* probably also descend to us in an order given them by their author, in a more linear sequence appropriate to the dignified topic of the Olympian deities. Callimachus begins with Zeus, moves to his twin children Apollo and Artemis, and then to the longest hymn, that for the island of Delos as Apollo's birthplace. This sequence suggests the importance of familial groupings in the divine world and hints at a reflection of this pattern in the development of the Ptolemaic dynasty. The prominence of Apollo, as god of poetry and prophecy, also hints at Ptolemaic benevolence toward Callimachus, as a poet favored by Apollo. The final two *Hymns*, to Athena and Demeter, form a pair through their mimetic representation of a local festival, their shared use of Doric dialect, and the similarity of their embedded myths, both of which deal with the punishment of young men who offend the goddess. Even though these *Hymns* were likely written for separate occasions and perhaps over a considerable amount of time, they have been gathered into a collection where their interconnected themes reinforce the poet's respectful but ironically witty approach to both traditional Greek religion and to monarchs who are future gods.

For other Hellenistic collections, absolute proof of authorial ordering is not obtainable, but nevertheless likely on the basis of comparison with known poetry books and what can still be determined of a meaningful order. Herodas' *Mimiambi*, for instance, survive on a papyrus containing eight poems with remnants of more (Ch. 3.7). The first poem was apparently chosen for the introductory position in the collection, because it refers to a character's "limping song," thus recalling, metapoetically, Herodas' own "limping" iambic meter. *Mimiambi* 6 and 7 were clearly written as a pair, because they have some of the same characters (women in search of sexual toys), in different but chronologically sequential settings. In addition, *Mimiambi* 8 has a programmatical cast, because in it a first-person speaker, easily identifiable with the poet, speaks of a dream in which he seems to meet Dionysus, patron god of his poetry, and engages in rivalry with a person who disparages his craft. Although the poem would work well at the end of a poetry book, the state of the papyrus prevents certain knowledge of the scope of the collection.

It is even more uncertain whether Theocritus published his own works in a poetry book. The manuscript tradition preserves his poems in three different orders, and the rather meager papyri remnants show that no single canonical order existed even in the early imperial period. The main consistency is the placing of *Idyll* 1 first in all the Theocritean manuscripts and papyri, as the prototypic example of a bucolic poem. Yet the title *Eidullia*, "Little Types," almost certainly goes back to a third-century edition, and it is reasonable to suppose that an epigram identifying Theocritus as the author appeared at the beginning of this early edition (*Palatine Anthology* 9.434):

> The Chian is another, but I the Theocritus who wrote this
> am one of the many Syracusans,
> son of Praxagoras and well-famed Philinna.
> I have dragged in no foreign Muse.

Here the speaker distinguishes himself from his homonym, Theocritus of Chios, an orator of the late fourth century, who would scarcely have been more famous than the Syracusan Theocritus after the third century. The epigram is cleverly laid out as a book tag, or *sillybos*, identifying the author of the roll by parentage, city of origin, and preferred genre, much in the manner of Callimachus' bibliographical *Pinaces*, where homonyms were a special concern. All this points to composition in the third century and even to the ambiance of Alexandria. In addition, the "Theocritus" who speaks boasts that he has dragged in no foreign Muse, an odd way of saying that as Syracusan he writes Doric poetry. The verb for dragging here can also refer to limping, and it is possible that the author is polemically and allusively attempting to distinguish himself from that other writer of poetic mimes, Herodas, who adopted the mask of an Ionic iambographer writing in "limping" iambs, though his name suggests Doric extraction. A significant amount of evidence, then, points to a collection of Theocritus' poetry produced by the author himself, a collection that unfortunately was dismembered and rearranged, probably to highlight the bucolic elements. Even so, the traces left in the later manuscript tradition are consistent with one bookroll consisting of bucolic poems, a second beginning with "Charites" (*Idyll* 16) for Hiero II and ending with the "Encomium to Ptolemy" (*Idyll* 17), and a third starting with the Ionic poems. The "Distaff" (*Idyll* 28) makes an excellent beginning for this third bookroll, since it was composed to accompany a distaff that is sent as a gift on a journey to Ionian Miletus; as such it both suggests Theocritus' general debt to Erinna, whose *Distaff* demonstrated how to adapt epic hexameter to personal themes, and metaphorically announces the movement of the Doric poet to a geographical/literary realm associated with the great lyric poets of the past, especially Sappho. Since the "Distaff" accompanies a gift of such an object for Nicias' wife Theugenis, the female models for Theocritus' "journey" to Ionia are appropriately evoked by this specifically feminine activity of weaving, itself an emblem of poetic composition.

In addition to the author-edited collections discussed above, it is evident that a number of Hellenistic epigrammatists gathered their poems into book format. These in turn became sources for Meleager's *Garland*, where perhaps were assembled only the most famous of earlier epigrams. While such collections by Callimachus and Posidippus are all but certainties, it seems likely, based on the number and nature of surviving poems, that others were made by Asclepiades of Samos, Hedylus, Anyte, Nossis, Leonidas, and Antipater of Sidon. A small collection of twenty-two epigrams attributed to Theocritus descends to us in the bucolic manuscripts, and, though it is unlikely to be the work of Theocritus himself, it has a meaningful arrangement, with a programmatic opening in the form of a dedication to the Muses and Apollo and a tripartite division by subject or type (bucolic, sepulchral/dedicatory, on poets and in nonelegic meters). As is known from long sequences of Hellenistic epigrams in the later Byzantine anthologies, Meleager completely dismantled earlier epigram collections of this type to create his own complex and meaningful order. The *Garland*, likely divided into four or more books (sepulchral, dedicatory, erotic, and "epideictic"), was organized into short sequences on the same theme or topic, and especially in the erotic book later variations, often by Meleager himself, are juxtaposed with their models and connected by verbal links.

With the publication of the Milan papyrus, it is now possible to compare Meleager's method of anthologizing with an epigram collection preserved on a papyrus from the late third century. While most scholars agree (though there are dissenters) that all the epigrams on the new papyrus are by Posidippus, it is more controversial whether the arrangement of the epigrams was that of the author or an editor. The collection is divided into sections of six to twenty epigrams, headed by subtitles of the type "pertaining to omens," "pertaining to dedications," "pertaining to statues." The topics of the surviving sections are as follows: stones (including engraved gemstones), omens, dedications, epitaphs (overwhelmingly for women), statues, equestrian victories (especially by the Ptolemaic queens), shipwrecks, cures, and "characters" (more epitaphs). Two of these categories, dedications and epitaphs, are found in the Byzantine epigram anthologies, but the surprising range of the sections indicates that the literary uses of epigram in the early Hellenistic period were much more varied than previously imagined. Although the sections lack the complexity of arrangement found in Meleager, their underlying themes seem to be highlighted in their opening and closing poems and in some are further emphasized by arrangements. The omen section, for instance, is concerned generally with the issue of how to know what cannot be observed and ends with a godlike Alexander creating a final *sēma*, meaning both "sign" and "tomb," for his favorite seer Strymon. As another example, the statue section conveys the message that Lysippus, Alexander's favorite sculptor, represented the pinnacle of sculptural achievement, carried forward by his successors in the interests of the Ptolemies. More generally, the collection of Posidippan epigrams is thematically focused on the Ptolemaic dynasty, as it defines the Egyptian monarchs as god-kings who mingle among men in various walks of life. It is a message of broad scope, present in no individual epigram, but clearly expressed through the concatenation of topical sections and individual poems.

4.3   Social and Political Background

The older view of Hellenistic literature as elitist (the "ivory tower" view) and aestheticist ("art for art's sake") tells a story of authors who lived in a closed world, where they escaped from a distressing existence in multi-ethnic monarchical societies by composing literature that expresses its nostalgia for the lost Greek past through esoteric language and puzzling literary games. An important, and quite recent, critical trend challenges this view by exploring the relationship between Hellenistic literature and its contemporary social and political setting. These studies are generally influenced, directly or indirectly, by the "new historicism," a critical approach in which literature is grouped with other textual and material evidence to form a fabric of discourse that both reflects and constructs its culture. Correspondingly, scholars are now arguing that Hellenistic literature not only holds up a mirror to the world around it but also participates in the construction of political ideology and the dissemination of new social practices and ideas. Categories of analysis typically used to support this approach include genre or the role of women, colonialism or the interaction of Greek culture with native traditions, and physical displacement or problems of social identity.

In contrast to the political and social satire of Old Comedy, the plays of Menander have traditionally been viewed as nonideological, reflecting the political apathy that beset the Athenian populace when subjected to Macedonian overlordship. Now, however, scholars are suggesting that the conventions of the plot in New Comedy point to ideological concerns of both a social and political nature. David Konstan has emphasized that Menandrian plots often provoke reflection on social issues by complicating audience reaction to a character. In *Grouch*, for instance, Cnemon, who seems rightly punished for his lack of sociability, also presents a view of personal self-sufficiency and attachment to the land that evokes a traditional Athenian ideal of the rugged citizen-farmer. Susan Lape has argued that the stylized romances of New Comedy, which typically involve a rape and the endangerment of a young woman's status as a citizen, have to do with Athenian anxiety about maintaining citizen identity and so preserving democratic culture. By masking the heroines' true civic identity, these plots allot women an element of independence and empowerment, she argues, that introduces into the Athenian imaginary the possibility of a different society with an enhanced role for women and a breakdown of the social stratification maintained by citizenship and marriage laws. Likewise, the braggart soldiers of Menandrian comedy play complicated roles. They clearly offer the Athenian audience an opportunity to enjoy a good laugh at a comic type closely identified with their political oppressors, but at the same time, by acknowledging their tender feelings for a young woman, the soldiers of *Hated Man* and *Girl with Cut Hair* gather audience sympathy for a marital relationship that challenges Athenian citizenship rules. In these new readings of Menander's comedy, the personal has become the platform on which political and social debate takes place.

Scholars have also come to recognize how the imaginative prose and innovative poetry of the Hellenistic era could serve the ideological interests of the new monarchic kingdoms, in which the rulers presented themselves as godlike benefactors of their subjects, eventually to be worshipped as gods themselves. In support of these political ideologies, certain prose authors rewrote traditional Greek mythology and religious stories in novelistic, purely fictional accounts in which the adventures of heroes were rationalized as history and the gods were characterized as extraordinary mortals who had been rewarded with cult. Euhemerus of Messene, who was in the diplomatic service of Cassander and later (after ca. 297) resident in Alexandria, produced the most influential of these. His *Sacred Record*, known only from the historian Diodorus Siculus and an epitome of Eusebius, was a fictional travelogue in which Euhemerus claims that he was dispatched by Cassander on a voyage of exploration to an island in the Indian Ocean called Panchaea. The civilization there was described as a utopia established by priests imported from Crete by Zeus. A temple founded by Zeus when he was still among mortals contained a golden stele on which he had inscribed an account of these events. According to Euhemerus, there were two types of gods, those who were immortal and everlasting, such as the sun, moon, and stars, and those who had acquired deification because of their benefactions to humankind, such as Heracles and Dionysus. These terrestrial deities included Uranus, Cronus, and

Zeus as well as their wives and children. Although Callimachus has Hipponax refer to Euhemerus as "that one who invented the Panchaean Zeus" and who, "babbling, scribbles impious books" (*Iambus* 1, fr. 191.10–11), his rationalization of traditional Greek religion served well the portrait that the early Ptolemies painted of themselves as kings on their way to becoming gods. Similar was the approach of Dionysius Scytobrachion (a nickname meaning "leather arm"), a later third-century author who wrote accounts of the Argonauts and fictional stories of Libyan history. These are, once again, only partially known, from paraphrases in Diodorus Siculus and some papyrus fragments. In Dionysius' version of the Argonautic adventure, the civilizing humanity of Heracles, now the leader of the expedition, was contrasted with the savagery of the barbarians they encounter, and Medea is recast as a virtuous, humane figure who leaves her homeland through necessity rather than for love of Jason. His Libyan stories begin with the Amazons, who conquer and civilize much of the world, and then continue with their successors, the Atlantii, a people ruled by Uranus, the giver of agriculture, and his descendants, who are later divinized. In these fictional stories, the adventures of the Amazons resemble those of Alexander and the rulers of the Atlantii are remarkably like the Ptolemies. Although the rationalizations of traditional religion by Euhemerus and Dionysius Scytobrachion did not become generally accepted in pagan culture, their tales offered a model for the past that supported the contemporary myth-making of the monarchs.

It is now also recognized that the Alexandrian poetry composed to honor the Ptolemaic monarchs and their courtiers, once dismissed as sycophantic and so uninteresting, involves complicated and fascinating poetic techniques for adapting the conventions of earlier Greek poetry to the changed needs of monarchs who have acquired a degree of divinity. In a ground-breaking study, Frederick Griffiths has shown that, in addition to the type of direct praise offered to Ptolemy Philadelphus in his "Encomium to Ptolemy" (*Idyll* 17), Theocritus also found various indirect methods of suggesting the resemblance of the Ptolemaic monarchs to Greek heroes and divinities, especially those who somehow negotiate the divide between human and god. The "Little Heracles" (*Idyll* 24) takes on a clear cultural relevance when it is remembered that the Ptolemies claimed descent from Heracles, a point made sharper by a covert reference to Ptolemy Philadelphus' birth date as coincident with that of his ancestral hero, now divine. Likewise, the "Epithalamium for Helen" (*Idyll* 18), which represents a marriage song for Helen and Menelaus, projects a mythical model for a Ptolemaic marriage, likely that of Arsinoe II and Philadelphus, as it insinuates the possibility that the queen, like Zeus' daughter Helen, has within her the seeds of divinity. Related too is the

"Hymn for the Dioscuri" (*Idyll* 22), since Castor and Polydeuces, brothers of Helen, shared the status of being both mortal and immortal and their cult was of special interest to Arsinoe, who during her earlier marriage to Lysimachus had built an Arsinoeion at their cult site on Samothrace; in Callimachus' "Apotheosis of Arsinoe" (fr. 228 with *Diegesis*) the Dioscuri carry off the body of the dead queen to her new heavenly home. One of the trickier aspects of Ptolemaic ideology was the practice of brother–sister marriage, developed on the model of Egyptian royal practice but also useful for cementing the dynastic line. In "Encomium to Ptolemy" Theocritus reminds his audience that Zeus and Hera offer a divine model for Philadelphus and Arsinoe, and one of Callimachus' most famous poems, the "Lock of Berenice" (fr. 110), develops a complex rhetorical strategy for disseminating a new dynastic myth supporting and characterizing the marriage of Berenice II and Ptolemy III Euergetes. By adopting the voice of the catasterized lock mourning its separation from its beloved queen, Callimachus was able to present a romanticized picture of the passion uniting the royal couple. The overly personal, eroticized, and largely incredible portrait so created would scarcely have been effective in Callimachus' own voice, but was made charmingly acceptable through the poet's ironized ventriloquism of the lock, which assumes the role of a maiden companion, now separated from her friend.

A number of Hellenistic poets and prose authors chose to present obscure or local myths involving the drama of brother–sister passion,[11] and surely the issue of the Greek taboo against sibling marriage, so clearly violated by the Ptolemies, lies behind this trend, whether in support or rejection of the Ptolemaic model. The tragic story of Byblis and her brother Caunus, told later in Ovid's *Metamorphoses* (9.450–665), offers an interesting example, because the tale is connected with the founding of Miletus. An important city of Asia Minor with a population of mixed (Ionian) Greek and Carian origin, Miletus had in the fourth century fallen under the rule of Mausolus, the wealthy philhellene satrap (or Persian governor) of Caria (ruled 377/6–353), who married his sister Artemisia. The story of the incestuous love of Byblis and Caunus existed already in the fourth century, and was likely promoted to justify the sibling marriage in Miletus' ruling family; in that regard it stood as a functional model for the new myths promoted by the Ptolemies, such as that of the lock's catasterism. Byblis and Caunus were the children of Miletus, the eponymous founder of the city located on the southern mainland across from Samos. Some version of their story was told in a prose account by Aristocritus, of unknown date, and in Apollonius' *Foundation of Caunus*, neither extant. But a fragment of Nicaenetus of Samos, a writer of hexameter narrative and epigrams (perhaps late third century), relates how

Caunus, after conceiving a passion for his sister, nobly resisted and fled Miletus to found Caunus, a city that became a refuge for displaced Ionians, and how Byblis so mourned for his return that she was changed into an owl (fr. 1 Powell, pp. 1–2). Other versions, as is evident from Parthenius' account in his *Erotic Stories* (11) (see Ch. 4.5), were more hostile to Byblis, since in these the incestuous passion is hers alone and her brother flees in horror at her proposals. But Parthenius preserves a few lines of his own on the subject that are sympathetic to the girl's plight and document a mourning ritual for Byblis on the part of the maidens of Miletus. We can only surmise how the changing political circumstances of the Hellenistic period and the monarchic allegiances of the authors may have affected these versions of the Milesian founding story. What is more evident is that the motif of brother–sister desire, whether happily fulfilled or ending disastrously, was a common mythical paradigm through which dynastic marriage practices might be promoted or denigrated.

Just as Ptolemaic sibling marriage was based on the traditional union of the pharaohs with their sisters, supported by the myth of Isis and Osiris, some scholars have posited that projections of Ptolemaic ideology in Greek poetry may reflect other native Egyptian practices and images as well. In Susan Stephens's recent formulation, certain Alexandrian texts were designed to be viewed through a dual lens, Greek or Egyptian, so that the stories seem either modifications of traditional Hellenic myths or Greek versions of familiar Egyptian themes. The presence of Egyptianizing elements remains somewhat controversial, because they presuppose native readers capable of comprehending the complex literary language and traditional poetic conventions of their Greek overlords. But works like the *Aegyptiaca* of Hecataeus of Abdera, written under Ptolemy I Soter, demonstrate a tendency in the early Ptolemaic period to recast world history from an Egyptocentric point of view, and the monarchs certainly represented themselves iconographically in the form of Egyptian pharaohs. By the time of the second Ptolemaic generation, the bright intellects gathered around Arsinoe and Philadelphus had, it seems, figured out how to present the political and religious ideology of these monarchs in a form that was seamlessly Greco-Egyptian. For instance, the "Lock of Berenice," which owes something to women's laments such as those in Sappho and Erinna's *Distaff*, also evokes Isis' cutting of a lock in mourning for Osiris, one of the fundamental stories of Egyptian mythology. In the "Hymn to Delos" Callimachus links the flooding of the Inopus river on Delos at the time of Apollo's birth with the annual flooding of the Nile, the time of the birth of the Egyptian god Horus with whom Apollo was often identified. Since Apollo asks his mother Leto to avoid giving birth on the island of Cos as it is destined to become the birthplace for Ptolemy II, there is a correlation, unexpressed yet obvious to anyone with some knowledge of Egyptian traditions, between Ptolemy as Horus/pharaoh and Apollo as the divine Horus. In addition, the structure and purpose of Apollonius' *Argonautica* come much more clearly into view when the voyage of the Argonauts is read against legends of early Egypt and Greek colonization there. A legendary pharaoh Sesoösis (or Sesostris), known to Herodotus (2.103.1–104.1) and Hecataeus of Abdera (in Diodorus Siculus 1.53–8), is represented by Apollonius as the founder of Colchis. This version of Sesostris' great civilizing journey with his troops to the far East not only mirrors in distant mythical time Alexander's eastern conquests but also connects the structure of the world at the time of the Argonauts with Egyptian civilizing actions. In addition, the *Argonautica* ends, seemingly abruptly, with an episode involving Euphemus' dream about his descendants, who will someday found the city of Cyrene in Libya, an old Greek colony in Egypt that replicates the new foundation at Alexandria. In this way Apollonius suggests that this fundamental Greek mythical story of the Argonautic adventure takes place in a world shaped, both in the distant past and in the reader's present, by the civilizing power and military might of Egypt. In Ptolemaic ideology, the kingdom centered at Alexandria is synonymous with the known world, and it takes the poetic synthesis of Greek and Egyptian myth to create an imaginary world where this can be true.

It has also become evident that Hellenistic authors were sometimes writing to please, not only the monarchs themselves, but also their courtiers. These *philoi* or "friends" of the king, as they were called, served as a group of advisors and as administrators of the king's territories. They were wealthy, influential, and cultured men. The Samian Callicrates, son of Boiscus, served as the admiral (or nauarch) of Philadelphus' navy and gained the honorary position of priest of the Sibling Gods. As we learn from epigrams by Posidippus (39, 74, 116, 119 Austin and Bastianini), he established a temple to Aphrodite-Arsinoe at Zephyrium on the coast near Alexandria and dedicated to the Sibling Gods a bronze statue of a chariot and driver with which he was victorious at Delphi. In a similar way, Callimachus in his elegiac "Victory of Sosibius" (fr. 384), written probably in the 240s, celebrates a Nemean victory won by another wealthy and powerful court advisor. The poem provides an interesting parallel to Posidippus' earlier epigrams, since in its sixty or so surviving lines it incorporates several voices, that of Sosibius himself, the Nile, and a votive offering, as if Callimachus has learned how to unite a series of epigrams on a single subject into a coherent elegy. But Sosibius was to become even more powerful after the death of Ptolemy III Euergetes in 221. Together with another counselor, he acted as primary advisor and military leader for Ptolemy IV Philopator in the Fourth Syrian War (219–211), and Polybius lays the blame on him for the native unrest that began in that period. More certainly damning was his willingness to murder members of the royal family. To retain control of the Ptolemaic lands, he murdered the queen mother Berenice, the former wife of Euergetes, and in 204 disposed of Philopator's widow Arsinoe III in order to become regent over their son, Ptolemy V Epiphanes. In stark contrast to Callimachus' early exaltation of Sosibius as heroic victor and generous benefactor of the poor, Polybius (15.25.1) calls him a "false guardian of Ptolemy" and "shrewd instrument" of evil for the king.

Yet other works, while full of praise for the monarchs, were directed, at least in part, at audiences outside of court circles. One important example is the so-called *Letter of Aristeas*, which, though purportedly composed by a Greek courtier of Ptolemy II, was actually written, probably in the later second century and probably by a Jew, to describe the creation of the Septuagint. A significant part of the intended audience was likely the Jewish elite living in Alexandria, although the author also had an eye to pleasing the Egyptian ruler. The work, addressed by Aristeas to his brother Philocrates (hence the modern misnomer *Letter*), is a fictional account, though likely with a historical basis, of the courtier's journey to Eleazar, the Jewish High Priest, to request that a body of scholars travel to Alexandria to translate the Pentateuch into Greek for the Library. The narrator's claim to have been present at court when Demetrius of Phalerum suggested to Ptolemy II the addition of the Jewish holy texts to his massive book collection is shown to be false by the fact that Demetrius was exiled from Egypt at the beginning of Philadelphus' reign. The story of seventy-two Jewish scholars assembling at Alexandria to do the translation is not, however, historically impossible and may reflect, in basic form, the reality of the Septuagint's creation (which gets its name by rounding off the number of scholars to seventy). Modern scholars have come to view the curious combination of fact and fiction in Aristeas' work as serving to create a charter myth for the Septuagint. In this reading, the unknown author's goal was to provide the Septuagint the status of a sacred text in the eyes of the Jewish community, perhaps specifically the Greek speakers living in Alexandria. At the same time, the narrative treats king Ptolemy in a favorable light and uses a sophisticated combination of Greek literary forms to fill out the narrative details and create an intellectual ambiance for the story. For instance, a description of the expensive furnishings made of gold and silver sent by Ptolemy for the Jerusalem temple recalls other descriptions of extravagant displays made by Hellenistic monarchs, such as Callixenus' account of the grand procession of Ptolemy Philadelphus in Alexandria (Ch. 1.5); the purpose may have been not only to suggest the king's respect for the Jewish religion but also to laud his generous use of wealth. A long section reporting the conversation between the monarch and the scholars at a series of banquets is organized in a question-and-answer format like that in collections of *chreiai* preserving the sayings of historical persons (see Ch. 3.8). In the manner of Greek philosophers attendant at court, the Jewish scholars give Ptolemy advice about how to rule well and how to live the good life, almost as if the Jewish faith were another Hellenistic philosophy. As with other parts of the narrative, the banquet section grants to these Hebrew wise men a role within the broader Hellenic world, of which the Jewish state was very much a part.

A new importance for women in the Hellenistic age, as literary subjects, authors, and patrons, has also been the topic of intense scholarly activity. This trend is largely the result of feminist scholarship, which is concerned to recover and value the lives of ancient women, especially in their capacity as writers and agents, and to use gender as a means of mapping cultural practices revealed through literary texts. The prominence of Ptolemaic queens in Alexandrian poetry is a striking and characteristic feature, reflecting their importance in the new ideology of Hellenized Egypt (figure 4.1), but perhaps reflecting as well their own promotion of literary and intellectual activities. The collection of Posidippan epigrams on the Milan papyrus unmistakably represents a Ptolemaic universe in which the queens, more than the kings, are star players. A now-divinized Arsinoe II receives a series of gifts from admiring worshippers in the dedicatory section, and the equestrian section is dominated by the victories of the female members of the house of Ptolemy. The victories in chariot racing by Berenice I, Arsinoe II, and a later Berenice (either the wife of Euergetes or a daughter of Philadelphus), like Callimachus' celebration of Berenice II's Nemean victory at the beginning of the third book of the *Aetia*, have the effect of providing the queens with a heroic status previously reserved for Greek men. As the epigrammatist has Ptolemy Philadelphus say in the closing couplet of this section, "Not do I set up the glory of my father as great, but *this* is the great thing, that my mother, a *woman*, won victory with a chariot" (88.5–6 Austin and Bastianini). The revised mythology of the Amazons, invented by Dionysius Scytobrachion, provides a paradigm of female military victors, whose conquests set the stage for the male rulers who follow. At the same time, the queens are also represented as kindly benefactors, particularly to women and particularly in matters of love. This begins already with Berenice I, who, according to Theocritus, was saved by Aphrodite from the underworld and taken to share divinity in her temple. There "she gently breathes soft desire into all mortals and grants comfort from their cares to those who long" (*Idyll* 17.51–2). Arsinoe II was also identified in her cult at Zephyrium with Aphrodite as goddess of the sea and goddess of love. Epigrams by Callimachus and Posidippus suggest that this Arsinoe-Aphrodite was worshipped by both sailors in need of protection on the seas and young women as they entered a world of marriage and sexuality. In *Idyll* 15 Theocritus shows the enthusiastic response of two ordinary Alexandrian wives to the romantic tableau of Aphrodite embracing the young Adonis, presented for public viewing by Arsinoe in her palace. Callimachus' representation of Berenice II as a bride-queen longing for the absent husband-king in the "Lock of Berenice" continues this presentation of the Ptolemaic queens as both fully sexualized beings and powerful rulers; he even makes oblique reference to the story that, before her marriage to Ptolemy, she engaged in a military situation by riding onto the battlefield and rallying the troops. The historical tradition about Cleopatra VII, who used her sexual relationships with Julius Caesar and Mark Antony in an ambitious attempt to rule the world, follows on the model of the ideology developed to promote the interests of her predecessor queens.

Figure 4.1 *Sardonyx gem with Egyptianizing portrait of a Ptolemaic queen, 2nd or 1st c. Greek, Hellenistic Period, width: 4.9 × 4 cm (1 15/16 × 1 9/16 in.). Museum of Fine Arts, Boston. Francis Bartlett Donation of 1912. 23.592. Photograph © 2007 Museum of Fine Arts, Boston.*

The cultural restraints that had earlier inhibited women from composing literature did not disappear in the Hellenistic age, but they apparently
lessened, at least in some circumstances. In addition, the new emphasis on
book format aided female writers, since written publication got around
social impediments to women appearing in public performances. As a
result, gender affected genre, and the adaptation of the traditional male
author's voice to the female persona contributed to the development of
new literary forms and manners of expression. An early example is Erinna
(Ch. 2.1), whose *Distaff* adopted epic hexameter, traditionally suited to the
male activities of war and adventure, to express a woman's grief for her
lost childhood companion. Erinna, like other women poets, took the lyric
poet Sappho as a model for her lament, but her expression of a subjective
emotional experience, the interior life of a young woman confined to her
loom, in epic-style verse pointed the way for the remaking of old literary
forms for new uses. Likewise, women epigrammatists of the early third
century contributed importantly to the remodeling of inscriptional verse as
a high literary form. Anyte (Ch. 3.6) made use of the traditional women's
prerogative to express grief and longing in order to adapt inscriptional
epitaphs to charming (book) laments for deceased animals (a horse, a
puppy, a cock, a dolphin, and insects). By representing her first-person
voice as that of a woman viewer in the company of other women, Nossis
(Ch. 3.6) linked a series of ecphrastic epigrams in what was surely an early
epigram collection. Since Meleager comments on the eroticism of Nossis'
compositions, we may assume that her expressions of admiration for the
beauty and charm of the women in the paintings suggested, in aggregate,
women's erotic attraction to each other, in the manner of Sappho's lyric
songs. Moero (sometimes spelled Myro) of Byzantium, the wife of a
"philologus" or textual scholar named Andromachus and the mother of
Homerus the tragedian who belonged to the Pleiad, is grouped in the
prologue to Meleager's *Garland* with Anyte and Sappho. Unfortunately,
only two of her epigrams remain. In these, as in a poem on the young Zeus
from a work entitled *Memory* and a lost narrative from a work entitled
Curses, she shows herself concerned with motherly roles, nourishment of
the young, and the tension between a woman's sexual desires and her
loyalty to husband and children (frs. 1–6 Powell, pp. 21–3). Hedyle, the
mother of the Samian epigrammatist Hedylus and the daughter of an
Athenian woman Moschine who wrote iambic verse, authored an elegiac
poem entitled *Scylla*, in which Glaucus, in love with the monstrous Scylla
who ate some of Odysseus' men in the *Odyssey*, brought her gifts of conch
shells and halcyon eggs, both symbols of female sexual productivity (456
Lloyd-Jones and Parsons). It is clear, then, that some women, especially
those belonging to intellectual families, became composers of poetry that

was read and appreciated by contemporary authors and that they often focused on the experiences and concerns of women.

At the same time, and perhaps partially in response to the writings of women poets, fictional female characters assumed a new prominence, whether portrayed positively or negatively, in the writings of male authors. Mythical narratives are often constructed around the female characters, who were commonly marginalized in earlier versions of the story. The familiar myth of Theseus' victory over the Marathonian bull has been completely recast in Callimachus' *Hecale* to focus on his reception by the kindly old woman Hecale and the establishment of rites in her honor. Likewise, Theocritus' "Little Heracles," modeled in part on Pindar's first *Nemean*, expands the narrative to focus on Alcmene's tender maternal care for her infants, her amusing attempt to rouse her husband in the middle of the night, and her consultation of the seer Tiresias in order to provide for Heracles' future. An anonymous hexameter poem entitled *Megara*, which is preserved as "Moschus" IV (Gow [1952a]), presents a later stage of Heracles' life, but again from the perspective of the women who care about him. It consists of a tearful conversation between Heracles' wife Megara and his mother, which occurs after he has slaughtered his children in a fit of madness and before he completes his labors; the source for this episode was likely a classical historian. Although Medea does not appear until Book 3 of the *Argonautica*, the story revolves around her passions and actions, so that the ancient Argonautic myth is reshaped to accommodate Hellenistic interest in the romantic longing of a young girl. Moschus' *Europa* as well refocuses the important myth about the origin of Minoan civilization on Crete, symbolizing the transference of civilization and power from the old cultures of the east to the new societies formed in the west, on a girl's erotic awakening as she encounters a tempting bull. Ordinary women of Hellenistic society play a large role in the poetic mimes of Theocritus and Herodas as well. Even when depicting their foibles, Theocritus seems generally sympathetic to his female characters, whether it be the cautious Syracusans who admire Arsinoe's Adonis festival in *Idyll* 15 or the erotically naïve Simaetha who thinks of bewitching Delphis in *Idyll* 2. In Herodas' *Mimiambus* 1 Metriche's loyalty to her missing lover is offset by the pure wickedness of the old bawd Gyllis, while the poet's emphasis on the sexual appetites of the women in *Mimiambi* 6 and 7 makes his satirical distaste for their kind plain enough. Whether the women who visit the Temple of Asclepius in *Mimiambus* 4 are made laughable by their naïve response to the art objects they view remains a subject of disagreement among scholars. Women figure in good numbers in the sepulchral and dedicatory epigrams preserved in the *Greek Anthology*, as they also appear frequently in the inscriptions of the Hellenistic age. Significant for the new literary interest in women is the Posidippus papyrus, where the sepulchral section is overwhelming about the female dead of all ages while the Ptolemaic queens, much more than the kings, dominate the dedicatory and equestrian sections.

Another topic that has received recent scholarly attention is spatial mobility and displacement and the resulting problems of social and cultural identity. In earlier Greek culture most authors composed for performance in their own *poleis* and worked within the literary traditions of their local regions. Exceptions, such as the lyric poets Pindar and Simonides, who received commissions from wealthy individuals through the Greek world, or Herodotus, who traveled widely in gathering the materials for his *History*, foreshadow the commonplace situation of authors in the period after Alexander. Menander's supposed refusal to accept Ptolemy's invitation to migrate to Egypt marks his position at the border of the Hellenistic age. But in the third century recognition by a monarch, signified by an invitation to his court, became a desired and largely necessary means of literary recognition. In contrast to Menander, the comic poet Machon migrated from Athens to Alexandria, and Theocritus, after failing to gain patronage from Hiero II in Syracuse (*Idyll* 16), came gratefully under Ptolemaic protection. Posidippus managed to maintain his self-identity as Macedonian while composing dozens of epigrams promoting the Ptolemies, and this seeming anomaly likely has to do with the Ptolemies' desire to promote themselves as Macedonian descendants of Alexander, now resident in Egypt. Likewise, Callimachus' focus on Cyrene as his native city has dual and ambiguous implications: as an early Greek colony in Egypt, Cyrene had the distinction of establishing Hellenic culture in Libya, but during the first half of the third century the city had lost its independent status to become an extension of Ptolemaic Egypt. The epigrammatist Leonidas left his native Tarentum to wander in a state of exile and poverty, a common situation in the early Hellenistic world. When the influence of the monarchic courts began to decline in the second century, writers often continued to travel, but now, under the growing political hegemony of Rome, often to places of their own choosing. Meleager's migration from the Palestinian Gadara to Phoenician Tyre to Greek Cos may show an ambitious poet's ability to move away from the periphery toward a center of Hellenic culture even without court patronage (at least in the late Hellenistic period). The Stoic philosopher Posidonius, a native of Syria, was educated at Athens, made a grand tour of the Mediterranean basin, and settled in the city of Rhodes where he educated both Greeks and Romans. Beginning about the middle of the second century, Rome itself became an advantageous destination for some literary figures, at times through forced residence for political reasons (Polybius) or enslavement (Parthenius) and at other times as a voluntary home for ambitious or intellectual elites (Archias).

This pattern of spatial mobility with resulting ethnic tensions and mixed allegiances is easily observed in the literature itself. In Theocritus' *Idyll* 14 one friend advises another to join Ptolemy II's army as a way of escaping a painful love affair, and in Herodas' first *Mimiambus* a young woman's lover is absent on a similar mercenary assignment. The consequences of immigration to Alexandria find poetic representation when the two Syracusan women in *Idyll* 15 encounter frightening Macedonian horsemen in the streets and praise Ptolemy for ridding the city of Egyptian pickpockets; later they spar with a man who complains about their chattering in broad Doric accents. Movement from place to place is often used thematically in Hellenistic poetry, and Daniel Selden has argued that displacement is an essential element in Callimachean poetics, evident in his choice of subjects, his coalescence of Greek and Egyptian, and even his allusive style. In one of Callimachus' epigrams (14 Gow and Page [1965]), for instance, a young woman Selenaea from Smyrna on the coast of Asia Minor dedicates to Arsinoe-Aphrodite at Zephyrium a nautilus shell that she found on the island of Ceos (near Attica). Since the shell symbolically represented female reproductive organs in Greek thought, the dedication is likely an offering preliminary to marriage; at the same time, Selenaea's movements across the Aegean and her acquisition of this nautilus (or "sailor") suggest the scope of Ptolemaic maritime power. Similarly, Phanocles (fr. 1 Powell, pp. 106–7) relates how the head of the murdered singer Orpheus was thrown into the sea off Thrace and floated with his lyre to the island of Lesbos, where the inhabitants buried both; by thus acquiring Orpheus' voice and instrument, the Lesbians became exceptionally skilled at lyric song. In the *Aetia* local legends and customs from all parts of the Greek world flow to Callimachus' Muse, since his sources, which include local histories and dinner conversation with travelers to Alexandria, bring him knowledge from the far reaches of the Black Sea in the east or the cities of Sicily in the west. Discontinuity, an expressed stylistic mark of the *Aetia*, is an appropriate aesthetic principle for such variety of subjects. Imagined travel, such as through dreams or to the underworld, was also a means for authors to connect with sources of inspiration located elsewhere. Examples include Callimachus' dream of transportation to Helicon in the *Aetia*, the appearance of the dead Hipponax in *Iambus* 1, that of the dead Xenophanes in Timon's *Silli*, and Herodas' dream of meeting Dionysus and perhaps Hipponax in his eighth poem. Nossis, resident at Locri in southern Italy, signals her debt to Sappho by asking an imagined traveler (and also the reader of her poetry book) to carry her name to Sappho's hometown of Mitylene on Lesbos (*Palatine Anthology* 7.718). By these and other means Hellenistic writers bridge their displacement in both time and space.

The social bonds with family and ancestral place, which traditionally provided Greeks their sense of self-identity, were in the Hellenistic world often replaced by freely chosen friendships and romantic ties. Theocritus addresses three poems (*Idylls* 6, 11, and 28) to his friend Nicias, who was not only a physician but also a poet (surviving are lines from Nicias' reply to the *Cyclops*, as well as a few epigrams). Callimachus' most tender epigram is a lament for his poet-friend Heraclitus (*Palatine Anthology* 7.80, quoted in Ch. 3.2). Much of the poignancy of the poem stems from Callimachus' sadness that the spatial separation of the old friends had, without his knowledge, changed into the permanent separation of death. Stories about bonding between strangers who have little in common socially, such as Theseus and Hecale in Callimachus' epyllion or Heracles and Molorchus in his "Victory of Berenice," reflect a new sensibility concerning our common humanity. Romantic attraction, confined in earlier Greek literature mostly to portions of lyric and elegiac poetry, permeates a range of genres in the Hellenistic age. While New Comedy generally concerns family life and relationships between citizens, the factor motivating plots is almost always a young man's desire for a girl. Likewise, in Theocritus' pastoral and urban mimes, erotic desire – or how to alleviate its pain – is consistently a major theme. And in contrast to New Comedy where young citizen women seldom appear on stage or express romantic inclinations, the strongest portraits of desire in Hellenistic poetry are often those of women, as, for instance, Simaetha in *Idyll* 2, Medea in the *Argonautica*, and Europa in Moschus' epyllion. Mythological romances are a common topic in Hellenistic elegy, as in the Acontius and Cydippe episode in the *Aetia* and in catalogue poetry such as Hermesianax's *Leontium*, Phanocles' *Erotes or Beautiful Boys*, and Alexander Aetolus' *Apollo*, in which the god predicts and recounts various unhappy love affairs (fr. 3 Powell, pp. 122–3, from Parthenius 14). The *Erotic Stories* of Parthenius, offering instances of often extreme female passion, come from a wide variety of (mostly lost) sources in both prose and poetry, and the roots of the ancient novel, which typically focused on the adventures of a pair of separated lovers, were surely late Hellenistic, even if the surviving examples are all later. The preferred topics of Hellenistic literature reflect, then, new ways in which individuals identified themselves through relationship with others, and our fascination with this literature is largely related to the way in which we find our own personal experiences mirrored there.

4.4   The Critical Impulse in Literature and Art

The three centuries following the death of Alexander were a period of intense theoretical speculation in all known branches of human knowledge. Oddly, however, scholars have in the past treated the philosophical discussions about literature in Plato, Aristotle, and their fourth-century contemporaries as a kind of dead end, in the belief that serious literary criticism was held in abeyance during the Hellenistic era, when the focus of discussion narrowed to the analysis of rhetorical styles and the textual and philological work of grammarians. Quite recently scholars have begun to reassess the nature and extent of Hellenistic literary criticism. This current trend is driven in large part by work on fragmentary texts, especially new editions of Philodemus' literary treatises, which include summaries of the views of earlier critics. These advances in our knowledge of post-Aristotelian literary criticism have revealed complex and sophisticated theoretical debates, particularly about the nature of poetry or the "poetic." At the same time, it has become increasingly evident that early Hellenistic theoretical assessments of art shared with contemporary literary theory a set of conceptual categories and technical terms that provided a parallel understanding of the historical development of style and technique. As a result, some of the most exciting current work in the field involves the interaction of literature with theory, often revealed through analogies to art.

Our own divisions into literature and art, poetry and prose, do not map precisely onto those of the ancient world. There was in fact no word for "literature" meaning both prose and poetry, and no word for "art" meaning visual objects of an aesthetic nature. The central critical term that developed in the classical age to encompass these verbal and visual fields was *mimēsis*, usually translated as "imitation" or "representation." Poetry, as opposed to history, was linked conceptually to statues and paintings, as opposed to objects like houses or ships, because these verbal and visual forms were conceived as mimetic, that is, representative of something. For Plato, literary and artistic objects were mere imitations of the phenomenal world, which was in turn an imitation of the "real" world of the ideal forms; it was on the basis of this distorting gap between literary/artistic imitations and the truth that Plato banned poetry, including Homer, from his ideal society. Aristotle, on the other hand, redeemed poetic *mimēsis* as a natural human pleasure, originating as musical imitation of bird song, and so defined tragedy as a representation of a plausible (not an actual) human action. In the early Hellenistic age, however, there developed an aesthetic preference, in both poetry and the visual arts, for a *mimēsis* that was a close representation of the perceivable world. The modern term for this phenomenon is realism. Ancient critical terminology commonly used to define realistic *mimēsis* in literature and art included *alētheia*, or "truth," which in this context refers to the accurate representation of the appearance of a thing, and *enargeia*, or "vividness," which refers to the impression of living reality that representation provides the audience. As the author of *On Style* (219) says, "all *mimēsis* has some vividness in it." The representation of ordinary objects and actions in the contemporary world – such as in the newly renovated genre of mime, in accurate description of recent historical events, or in images of old women, destitute fishermen, children, and animals in art – is an example of this realistic trend.

Because of the conceptual link between literature and art as mimetic forms, Hellenistic authors often used literary treatments of art works, called ecphrases, to express, through the analogy of art to poetry, their aesthetic principles. One way of calling attention to the mimetic realism of their own poetry was to represent characters admiring the lifelike quality of an artistic work. Ecphrases thus introduce what might be called a "meta-poetic" element into realistic literature. In Theocritus' "Women Who Attend the Adonis Festival," Praxinoa is amazed at the "accurate drawings" of the painters who decorated woven figures of Aphrodite and Adonis: "how realistically they stand and how realistically they revolve, living, not woven" (15.81–3), she says to her companion. In Herodas' *Mimiambus* 4, Cynno and Phile react in a similar way to the statues and paintings adorning Asclepius' temple (Ch. 3.7). The flesh of a naked boy would suffer a wound if scratched, an ox looks so ferocious that Phile almost cries out, and the hands of the famous painter Apelles are "truthful" (*alēthinai*, 72) in every line drawn. Another important example of this "metapoetic" use of art in Hellenistic poetry is the sequence of nine epigrams on statues (entitled "On Statue-Making") in Posidippus' epigram collection. The sequence opens with the poet speaking in his own voice: "Imitate (*mimēsasthe*) these works, and pass by the archaic rules for making large sculpted images, yes do, sculptors" (62.1–2 Austin and Bastianini). The remainder of the poem makes it clear that the modern statues to be imitated are those of Lysippus; here Posidippus was perhaps following a third-century treatise on art history by Xenocrates, which presented Lysippus as the pinnacle of the development toward naturalism in sculpture. The other epigrams in the section celebrate Lysippus' predecessors (Myron, Cresilas, and Theodoridas) and his successors (Chares who made the Colossus of Rhodes and Hecataeus who sculpted Philitas for Ptolemy Philadelphus) in sculptural naturalism. The connection between lifelike representation in sculpture and poetic realism is made explicit in the second poem in the sequence, on the poet Philitas, who is depicted altogether accurately in his veristic humanness (quoted in Ch. 2.1).

One problem with the critical concept of *mimēsis* was how to represent what cannot be perceived. In art the problem was often posed in terms of how to image the gods in their divine nature. The fifth-century sculptor considered most successful at representing divinity was Phidias, who made the cult statue of Zeus at Olympia and the cult statue of Athena for the Parthenon, both gigantic images in gold and ivory. Phidian majesty offers a natural analogy for the grand style in literature. When asked what model he would use for the Zeus statue, Phidias reportedly quoted a description of the god from the *Iliad* (1.528–30), an anecdote suggesting that only the great Homer could adequately depict Zeus in words,[12] and Dionysius of Halicarnassus (*Isocrates* 3) compares the august dignity of Phidias' statues to the grand style of Isocrates' oratory. Callimachus, no friend of the elevated, weighty style, brings the grandeur of Phidias' Zeus down to size in *Iambus* 6 (fr. 196). For an acquaintance traveling to Elis to view the famous statue, Callimachus describes the length, height, and width of the pedestal, throne, and footstool, reports how much the statue cost, and names the sculptor as Phidias of Athens. The point of these details was perhaps to reduce the statue to what could actually be known in the observable world and so to undercut the claim that it conveyed to the viewer the true majesty of Zeus. The fourth-century sculptor Praxiteles found other solutions to the problem of representing the divine. For the cult statue of Aphrodite at Cnidus, the first nude statue of the goddess, he used as a model his mistress, the courtesan Phryne. Literary interest in the statue and the issue it raises about *mimēsis* is indicated by epigrams (*Planudean Anthology* 160, 162) in which Aphrodite asks, upon first viewing the statue, "Where did Praxiteles see me naked?" In addition to celebrating the success of Praxiteles' achievement, the epigrams also suggest, to the reader aware of Phryne's role as model, that extraordinary humans are indeed godlike, or that divinity is a conceptual projection of human excellence.

For his statue of the god Eros, Praxiteles used a different type of model, namely the *erōs*, "passion," for Phryne that he felt in his own heart. This story points toward the developing concept of *phantasia*, "imagination," which by the end of the Hellenistic era had come to supplement the idea of *mimēsis*. An important passage about *phantasia* comes from Flavius Philostratus' *Life of Apollonius of Tyana* (6.19), a work of the late second or early third century AD. There Apollonius explains how artists like Phidias and Praxiteles learned to represent the gods in art by means of "an action full of wisdom":

Imagination (*phantasia*) made these images, a wiser artist than imitation (*mimēsis*). For imitation will reproduce what it sees, but imagination what it doesn't see, since it will conceive its subject through reference to reality. Feelings of awe often drive away imitation but not imagination, since it proceeds without awe toward the goal of its subject.

A passage in *On the Sublime*, by an unknown author of the imperial period referred to as "Longinus," indicates that *phantasia* was understood somewhat differently when referring to literary matters: *phantasia* in both oratory and poetry is defined as a mental picture productive of speech. Addressing the composer, "Longinus" explains that "under the influence of inspiration and strong feeling you seem to see what you say and bring it before the eyes of your audience" (15.2). For the orator, he says, the goal of provoking these visualizations is to persuade by vividness (*enargeia*), while in poetry the intended effect is the emotional one of enthrallment (*psychagōgia*), something like a combination of apprehension, attraction, and amazement. A complex and evolving concept, then, in the imperial period, *phantasia* had already within the Hellenistic age come to refer to a mental image described by the author so effectively and vividly that the audience is rendered capable of a similar visualization.

While realism dominated in third-century poetry, passages that describe what is not part of the observable world can be interpreted as examples of *phantasia*. Callimachus' description of how the goddess Leto tries to find a place to give birth to Apollo in the "Hymn to Delos" is one of these: in response to Hera's threats, cities, hills, and islands all flee as Leto approaches, until finally the wandering island of Asteria (afterwards called Delos) offers herself as the birthplace for the god. While the Greeks thought of the landscape as inhabited by heroic and quasi-divine spirits, here Callimachus asks us to visualize a fantasy world, in which these places as places, rather than as personified deities, perform the human actions of movement and speech. In the *Argonautica*, Apollonius tends to keep what is perceived by the Argonauts separate from the realm in which the gods move and speak, so that the narrator, in describing divine action, involves the reader in picturing scenes of action superimposed on the world accessible to his mythical heroes. A good example is the passing of the Symplegades, which is successful because Athena holds apart the rocks and shoves through the Argo. We as readers see it in our mind's eye, through the aid of the narrator. But the helmsman Tithys does not, since he supposes that the Argo must possess extraordinary powers breathed into it by Athena when she made it (2.598–618). We do not know whether Callimachus and Apollonius were consciously working with the concept of *phantasia* as a contrast to the veristic realism typical of mime. But the epigrammatist Meleager, writing perhaps at the very end of the second century, does signal his awareness of the *phantasia* concept: in one poem (*Palatine Anthology* 12.125), he describes falling in love with a boy who exists only in a dream, while in two others (12.56–7) he explains that the charms of a boy named Praxiteles, like the sculptor, are now modeled by Eros in the poet's own heart. In yet another epigram (12.106) he explains, using the language of *phantasia*, that he is blind to everything but Myiscus, whose form replaces all else in his mind's eye.

One of the most common critical concepts in the Hellenistic and Roman periods, extending to both prose and poetry and independent of the distinction between mimetic and nonmimetic, was that of the "characters" or categories of style. Already in the fifth century, as shown by the debate between Aeschylus and Euripides in Aristophanes' *Frogs*, there existed a dichotomous division into the "grand" (*semnos*) and "thin" (*leptos*) styles (see Ch. 2.1). Theophrastus, apparently in his lost *On Diction*, spoke of a "middle" style, for which the sophist Thrasymachus was an example,[13] and this threefold division, common in the later Greco-Roman rhetorical tradition, likely began through Theophrastus' attempt to define an Aristotelian "mean" between the extremes of the grand and the plain styles. Our best evidence for the further development and application of criticism based on styles during the Hellenistic period comes from an extant work entitled *On Style*, which scholars once attributed to Demetrius of Phalerum but is now thought to be by some later Peripatetic named Demetrius. While the treatise has been dated as early as the third century BC and as late as the early imperial era, it quite likely belongs to the early first century BC; what is clear is that its contents reflect Hellenistic critical thinking about literary styles. Demetrius begins with a basic discussion of prose style, including rhythmic composition and the difference between paratactic and periodic composition (the latter being more controlled with greater subordination of clauses). Here he compares the older paratactic style (with little subordination of clauses) to archaic statues, which exhibit succinctness and spareness (*ischotēs*), and the more complex periodic style to the grand but polished statues of Phidias (14). The bulk of the treatise is devoted to a discussion of four types of style – the grand, the elegant, the plain, and the forceful. Demetrius is unique in adding a fourth style, and it has been supposed that he does so to create a category especially suited to the fourth-century orator Demosthenes. The discussion of the styles includes examples from both prose and poetry, selected from authors of the archaic and classical periods. Each style has a proper content, diction, and arrangement, and a defective counterpart to each is more briefly analyzed. Demetrius' division of the styles is descriptive rather than prescriptive, since he maintains that, apart from the antithetical grand and plain, any of the categories can be combined with any other for variety of effect.

Another important development in literary theory, which took place in the early Hellenistic period and shaped the discussion that followed, was the division of "poetic art" into the three categories of poet, *poiēsis*, and *poiēma*. While the category of poet clearly concerns the creative individual who brings to a work his own knowledge, preferences, beliefs, and emotions, the distinction between *poiēsis* and *poiēma* is the crucial and innovative one. In this new division, *poiēsis* concerns plot, characters, and thought, while *poiēma* concerns diction, style, and arrangement of words and phrases. The difference is like that of message to means, or content to form, although *poiēsis* came also to refer to a long thematically connected poem, typically epic, and *poiēma* to a shorter poem or a passage within a larger work. The tripartite division can be traced back as far as Neoptolemus of Parium, a Peripatetic literary critic working sometime in the third century who was a major source for Horace's *Art of Poetry*; it was perhaps developed even earlier by Theophrastus. For Neoptolemus, as later for Horace, audience pleasure, achieved primarily through the various technical aspects that made up the category of *poiēma*, was properly balanced by the moral instruction provided by the poet, accomplished primarily through the elements that characterize *poiēsis*. But the Callimachean movement, often associated with *leptōtes*, "thinness" or "refinement," was focused on the new element in poetic art, that is, *poiēma*, both in the original sense of style and in the sense of the short poem or passage where the poet's poetic precision could be fully demonstrated.

A group of literary theorists, called "the critics" by Philodemus and known to us through the refutation of their views in the five books of his *On Poems* (Ch. 3.8), also focused their attentions on the category of *poiēma*. The term "critics" seems to indicate their interest in broader questions, such as the nature and purpose of poetry, as opposed to the narrower concerns of the grammarians. For these literary theorists, *psychagōgia*, a term that refers etymologically to stirring the soul, was produced by means of the technical skills grouped under the category of *poiēma*. These skills were divided into selection of words (*eklogē*) and composition (*sunthesis*), in the technical sense of the arrangement of sounds, words, phrases, and metrical units. Common to all the critics, according to Philodemus, was an overarching emphasis on beautiful sound, or euphony. It was through the choice of appropriate poetic words and their arrangement that euphony, which produces the particular pleasure of poetry, results. Plato's *Cratylus* shows that analysis of sound was already of interest to the sophists in the fifth century, and Dionysius of Halicarnassus' *On Verbal Composition*, an important literary critical work from the Augustan age, provides a critically astute analysis of how arrangement of words and the resulting sound patterns create poetic effect and define literary styles. The theories of the Hellenistic euphonists fill in the intermediate stages in which philosophical analysis of sound and language was reworked as poetic criticism. Since for the euphonist critics poetic pleasure was produced in a physical way when sound "tickles" the ears, the hearer's reaction is considered purely aesthetic, so that the euphonists provide our first aesthetic theory of literature.

Three of the critics known from Philodemus suggest the range of third-century literary discussion, to which Hellenistic poets surely reacted and likely contributed. Andromenides, who shared with Aristotle an interest in high-style poetry like epic and tragedy, believed that good poetry was dependent on the selection of naturally beautiful or "splendid" words and that such words are well suited to the stories of gods and heroes. Andromenides thus provides a theoretical basis for the work of glossographers, like Philitas, and for the usage of unusual Homeric words in Hellenistic poetry, as in Apollonius' *Argonautica* and elsewhere. Another critic, Heracleodorus, advocated a mixture of generic forms and levels of diction. His views dovetail neatly with Callimachus' defense of his *polyeideia*, or composition in mixed styles, in *Iambus* 13. Another of Heracleodorus' views was that content had nothing to do with the particular nature of poetry, since the same subject matter could be treated in prose or even the visual arts. This claim provides a theoretical support for the phenomenon of reworking prose treatises of a scientific or technical nature into verse, as in the didactic poets Aratus and Nicander. The most extreme of the euphonists was Pausimachus of Miletus, who provided a detailed analysis of sounds at the level of letters and syllables, much like that later found in Dionysius' *On Verbal Composition*. More generally, he argues that sound governs word choice as it moves the reader/auditor to sympathetic engagement even against reason. From birds he draws an analogy to the good poet who is naturally talented and succeeds by becoming like the sounds he produces. Pausimachus' theory of poetry can, then, be viewed as mimetic, in the sense that poetry, as an aesthetic experience of sound, replicates physically in the auditory faculty of the audience the object of representation. Not surprisingly, Hellenistic poets display at times an awareness of euphonist theories by programmatic references to poetic sound. In the *Aetia* prologue, for instance, Callimachus claims that his poetry is appreciated by those who love the "shrill sound of the cicada" rather than the braying of the ass. Another example is Theocritus' programmatic onomatopoeia (the use of words that imitate the sound of their referent) at the opening of *Idyll* 1, where the sweet whispering of the pine is likened to the goatherd's sweet piping and the trickling spring is compared to Thyrsis' flowing song. Since a basic theme of bucolic poetry is the interaction of human music with the sounds of nature, the genre as a whole seems well suited to the critical theories of euphony.

Another important trend in Hellenistic literary criticism is allegory. While the euphonists followed the common Hellenistic view that the purpose of poetry was to give pleasure by stirring the soul, the allegorists continued in the older belief that the purpose of poetry was to instruct by revealing the truth. They got around the difficulties of the apparently immoral actions of gods and fantastic accounts of heroic adventures by reading the texts as broadly symbolic, having one meaning on the surface and another hidden beneath. Allegorical commentary on Homer, interpreting the gods as the physical elements of the universe, began as early as Theagenes of Rhegium in the late sixth century. Allegory had a special appeal to philosophers and moralists, and from the third century on it was closely associated with the Stoics. Cleanthes, who succeeded Zeno as head of the Stoa, believed that philosophical prose was inadequate to express the magnificence of the divine and that language cast in meter and rhythm could better approach the truth that comes from contemplating the divine. His *Hymn to Zeus* (fr. 1 Powell, pp. 227–8) allegorizes that god as the commanding force pervading and ordering the universe. His successor Chrysippus was also interested in finding parables for Stoic beliefs in literary works. For instance, he discussed the myth of Athena's birth from the head of Zeus as an illustration of the Stoic view that reason (= Athena) was located in the region of the heart, and the scene in Euripides' *Medea* in which the lead character decides to murder her children was used by Chrysippus to explain the interaction of reason and passion in decision-making.

One of the most influential Stoic allegorists was Crates of Mallus, a scholar who worked at Pergamum in the second century. With the growing Hellenistic understanding of astronomy and of geography, the Homeric poems seemed more and more obviously to contain mere poetic falsehoods, to be accepted only within their own fictional world; to accommodate this realization, the Alexandrian scholar Aristarchus took as his guiding principle to interpret "Homer from Homer." But the Stoic Crates sought to vindicate Homer as a reliable source of knowledge about the physical universe and geographical location by reading key passages allegorically. Particularly famous was his view that Homer understood what was called *sphairopoiia* ("sphere-making"), the representation of the earth as a sphere at the center of a spherical universe traversed by the sun, moon, and stars. One passage that justified this view of Homer's advanced (but hidden) knowledge of Hellenistic astronomical theory was the depiction of Hephaestus manufacturing the shield of Achilles in *Iliad* 18. Crates apparently interpreted this shield as a "representation of the cosmos." He seems to have explained the shield's production at the request of Achilles' mother Thetis as signifying the creation of the universe through the working of "creative order," as the name Thetis may be translated. While the details of Crates' interpretation have been lost, later Stoic sources interpreted the metals used in making the shield as the four elements that make up the physical entities in the universe, the round shield as the shape of the cosmic sphere, the layers of materials used in it as the zones of heavens, and the contrasting cities depicted on it as the principles of peace and war. A Pompeian painting of Thetis gazing into the newly made shield and seeing there her own reflection likely derives from Hellenistic artistic representations influenced by this type of allegorical interpretation, since it suggests the reflected likeness of the physical world and its creative force in accordance with Stoic doctrine (figure 4.2).

Stoic thought was massively influential throughout the Hellenistic period, and scholars are now realizing that allegorical reading was a commonplace interpretive technique from the third century onward. As a result, certain Hellenistic texts, apparently produced in this atmosphere of *allegorēsis*, require translation into different words in order to be understood. The technopaegnia are deliberately riddling (see Ch. 4.2), just as an epigram found on a potsherd offers a "guess-what-I-am" riddle describing an oyster (983–4 Lloyd-Jones and Parsons).[14] Likewise, comprehending Lycophron's *Alexandra* requires puzzling out meaning from knowledge of myriad little-known mythical facts. Clement of Alexandria (*Stromata* 5.50.3) even insisted that the difficult poetry of Euphorion of Calchis (see Ch. 4.5), Callimachus, and Lycophron was written as an exercise for schoolboys, who could, for instance, have learned rare Homeric words from these Hellenistic authors. A series of enigmatic epitaphs by Leonidas, Alcaeus of Messene, Antipater of Sidon, and Meleager thematize allegorical methods of reading by describing tombs adorned with visual symbols that must be deciphered in order to understand the identity or character of the deceased (*Palatine Anthology* 7.421–9). In the last of these, by Alcaeus, the successful interpreter praises himself as an Oedipus who "has solved the riddle of the Sphinx."

Other passages as well, especially ecphrastic ones, seem intended, on the model of Homeric interpretations like Crates', to invite allegorical readings by more educated, or savvy, readers. Some are fairly obvious. For instance, the basket that Europa's mother has given her in Moschus' epyllion is clearly intended to prefigure, through symbol, the girl's mating with Zeus in bull form. Originally a gift to Libya when she married

Figure 4.2 *Hephaestus showing Thetis the shield of Achilles, depicted in a painting from Pompeii. Naples, Museo Nazionale.*

Poseidon, the golden basket has carved on it scenes of Io wandering in cow form and of Zeus simultaneously restoring her to human form and impregnating her with his touch. The naïve Europa fails to understand the hidden message so obvious to the reader (which includes the migration of ethnic groups to new continents, since Libya stands for Africa and the Phoenician princess Europa for Europe). Just as the scenes depicted on Achilles' shield in the *Iliad* – of peace and war, city and country, as well as the heavenly bodies and ocean – represent the physical and social universe of Homer's world, so the three scenes on the goatherd's cup in Theocritus' *Idyll* 1 – of youths in love, an old man, and a boy – represent three stages of a human life. The narrowing of focus from the form of the cosmos and the societies in it to the cycle of a person's life is indicative of Theocritus' smaller-scale poetic program.

More complex is the description of the cloak that Jason wears when he meets the Lemnian queen Hypsipyle (1.721–68). Clearly parallel, again, to the shield that Hephaestus makes for Achilles, the cloak as the work of Athena is a *hyphos*, a woven garment that prepares Jason for victory through love-making, rather than through fighting. But *hyphos* was also a common literary critical term for a longer poem like epic, that is, a *poiēsis* in which theme, plot, and character had to be woven into complicated patterns of interaction and unity. In this way, Apollonius signals that Jason's cloak is to be read as an allegory of his epic poem, and reading so, the scholiasts explain that the cloak represents "cosmic order and the deeds of men." The first scene of the Cyclopes' manufacturing a thunder-bolt for Zeus signifies the divine realm, while the second one of the brothers Amphion and Zethus, the founders of Thebes, signifies all that happens in cities, namely, peace and war, signified as well by the next scene of Aphrodite bringing the shield of Ares. The remaining four scenes of myths are interpreted by the scholiasts as foreshadowing the plot of the *Argonautica*, involving contests and marriages, sacrilege and revenge, and finally salvation. Interestingly, here Aphrodite, like Thetis in the Pompeian painting, sees her reflection in the shiny surface of Ares' shield, as her garment slips off her shoulder. The allegorical suggestion is that in Apollonius the goddess of love controls the epic world and all that happens in it.

With his summaries and refutations of Hellenistic literary critics in *On Poems*, Philodemus, who was writing for Roman intellectuals in the middle decades of the first century, represents a final phase of the critical impulse in this era. His purpose was to defend Epicurean views of poetry against the attacks of the Stoics. That he reads the euphonists through lost works by Crates of Mallus, who applied Stoic principles of physics, logic, and psychology to literary studies, confirms this interpret-ation. Because of the extensive difficulties with the fragile papyri and Philodemus' habit of making his points by refuting others, it is difficult to establish the full range of his views. He agreed with the euphonists against the allegorists that the goal of poetry was enthrallment, not instruction, but he believed that meaningful content, not just beautiful sound, was necessary for good poetry. The excellence of poetry thus lay in the conjunction of content with the aural features that were particular to poetry. He espoused the Epicurean belief in a criterion for the judgment of good and bad poetry based on perceptions and understandings common to all, not just known to intellectual elites or those who set out strict rules for poetic genres. While it has sometimes been believed that Epicurus rejected poetry, it now seems that his position was somewhat different. In the Epicurean system of thought, poetry was apparently neither harmful nor beneficial. It may supply some mild pleasure in the form of entertainment, which is not necessary for human happiness and not harmful either. Philodemus' own epigrams, mostly on erotic and sympotic themes, show that he found poetic practice congenial to his philosophical style of life.

4.5   Reception in Rome

From nearly its beginning, Latin literature was a blend of Greek and Roman. Horace said it best: "Conquered Greece conquered its fierce victor and introduced the arts to rustic Latium" (*Epistle* 2.1.156–7). The culture encountered by the Romans when they began to assert their military dominance over southern Italy and Sicily, mainland Greece, and then Asia Minor and Egypt was the diverse amalgam of Hellenism and native traditions that characterized the kingdoms of Alexander's successors. In some ways, Rome can be viewed as yet another of these Hellenistic kingdoms, the most successful of them, since the Romans finally achieved the Diadochs' goal of ruling all the main areas of Alexander's empire. The crucial difference, however, was that in this new Romanized world the culture of the subjugators was utterly transformed by the intellectual and literary tradition of their Greek subjects. Roman literature was, in a sense, started anew through this process. The meters of Latin poetry were borrowed from Greek poetry, Roman orators trained by studying the techniques developed by Attic orators, and Latin poets adopted the genres and conventions of Greek poetry to Roman topics and mores.

The paths of this influence were numerous and varied. From earliest times Roman culture was shaped by contact with their Italian neighbors – early on the more advanced Etruscans who had absorbed many elements of Greek culture and then later the native Italic peoples of the southern peninsula who lived in proximity, spatially and culturally, to the Greek colonial cities in southern Italy and Sicily. The myth of Rome's founding, the story of the exposed twins Romulus and Remus, utilized a Greek paradigm for city foundation (such as the story of the twins Amphion and Zethus who built the walls of Thebes), and the Romans accommodated themselves within the mythical cycle of the Homeric epics by taking up the Trojan hero Aeneas as their ancestor. The myth as it appears in Vergil's *Aeneid* was in many ways shaped by the politics of the second century (though it had even earlier forms), as the Romans formed an alliance with the Attalids, whose kingdom incorporated the site of old Troy. Callimachus already thought of the Romans as one of those civilized peoples whose legends belonged in his *Aetia*, since he included the story of one Gaius who was wounded defending the walls of Rome; in an illustration of Roman character, Gaius' mother rebuked him by pointing out that his limp would remind him of his heroism (frs. 106–7). Even more dramatically, Lycophron's *Alexandra* offers a celebration of Roman hegemony, presented through typically Hellenistic literary practices such as obscure prophecy and recounting of lesser-known myths.

The second century saw the adaptation of Greek meters, genres, and literary motifs to the Latin language. This happened with the model of third-century Hellenistic aesthetics firmly in view. The major figure in the transformation was Quintus Ennius (239–169), a native of the Messapian region in the heel of the Italian boot, who, as a result of the cultural synthesis present in his homeland, was fluent in Greek, Latin, and the Italic dialect of Oscan. He was brought by Cato the Elder to Rome where he served throughout his life as schoolmaster for upper-class Romans. The influence of Hellenistic literature appears at key points in his Latin compositions. His great *Annales*, a chronological account of Roman history in hexameters, began with a dream in which Homer appeared to him to provide knowledge of the physical universe and to explain that his soul had now migrated (through a peacock!) to Ennius. This direct claim to be the Roman Homer, through a form of metempsychosis that was popular with the Pythagorean sect of southern Italy, follows the example set by Callimachus in his dream near the opening of his *Aetia*. For later Latin writers as well, allusions to Greek models often have this layered character, as a canonical Greek author of the archaic or classical era is claimed for the Latin context through a Hellenistic intermediary. Other works by Ennius descended directly from the innovative genres of the Hellenistic period – his *Hedyphagetica* (*On Pleasant Dining*) imitated Archestratus' gastronomical parody (Ch. 3.8), his *Euhemerus* presented the humanizing theology of Euhemerus (Ch. 4.3), his *Sota* apparently adapted the meter and mocking, often obscene subject matter of Sotades (Ch. 3.8), and his *Saturae* (a genre, satire, later declared by Quintilian to be "wholly ours," *Training in Oratory* 10.1.93), written in six books and variable meters, seems indebted to Callimachus' *Iambi*. His self-epitaph (fr. 46 Courtney) is modeled on Posidippus' "Seal" (118 Austin and Bastianini), an elegiac poem that likely closed an epigram collection, perhaps even the one on the Milan papyrus: Ennius, like Posidippus, makes a request for no tears at his death, since his poetic fame will fly through the mouths of men. Gaius Lucilius (ca. 180–102/1), a Roman of the equestrian class who moved in the circle of Laelius and Scipio Aemilianus, followed Ennius in writing *Saturae*, in thirty books, which displayed within its invective a firm grasp of Hellenistic critical theory. Also a development of the second-century importation of Greek culture into Rome, the comedies of Plautus and Terence are direct adaptations of Attic New Comedy, especially the plays of Menander and Philemon, though sometimes with sections from different plays patched together to form a new plot structure. Greek names and settings were maintained, but the humor was recast, often in a slapstick way, for a Roman audience, who apparently enjoyed seeing the authority figures in the plays, especially the obstructionist fathers, tricked by clever slaves. While many other adaptations of Greek literature to foreign languages and cultural traditions during the Hellenistic period have perished with the demise of pagan civilization, the Latin literature that took form in a Hellenistic environment was the primary route by which knowledge of ancient Greek culture was transmitted in western Europe, until the rediscovery of Greek texts in the Renaissance.

Several key figures from the Greek east were instrumental in introducing the Romans to aspects of Hellenistic thought and literature, although it is important to keep in mind that myriad other contacts have simply escaped the historical record. In 155 the philosopher Carneades, serving in an embassy of intellectuals from Athens, offered Roman audiences a display of oratorical argument for and against justice, which was designed to illustrate the skeptical approach to knowledge that characterized the New Academy. The elder Cato was so shocked by the ethical bankruptcy of Carneades' contradictory arguments that he insisted upon expelling the philosophers. This pattern of fascination with Hellenistic culture and resistance to the implications of its intellectual freedom becomes typical of the emerging Roman synthesis with the Hellenic world. In many cases, educated members of the Roman aristocracy sponsored Greek literati in Italy. Though technically a hostage, Polybius surely had significant influence on the Roman elites gathered around his friend Scipio Aemilianus, just as he found Roman moral standards and devotion to military excellence congenial to his own standards. In the late second century the epigrammatist Antipater of Sidon, an important model for Meleager, lived in Rome; he moved in the same circles as Quintus Lutatius Catulus (Cicero, *On the Orator* 3.194), who adapted Antipater's competence at variation to composing Latin versions of Hellenistic epigrams. Another poet who composed epigram variations in Greek, Licinius Archias, was resident in Rome from about 102 to 62, when Cicero defended him in court against a challenge to his Roman citizenship. This extant speech, called *For Archias*, is famous for its passionate defense of humanist endeavor. Archias also wrote praise poetry for the Roman generals Marius and Licinius Lucullus, although Cicero's hope for the same for his consulship never materialized.

Of particular importance was Parthenius of Nicaea (or Myrleia) in Bithynia, who was brought to Rome as a war captive in the late 70s or 60s, and enslaved in the household of Helvius Cinna, a poet and friend of Catullus. Parthenius taught a generation of young Romans to appreciate the poetic style of Callimachus and Euphorion, and among them was Vergil, who had Parthenius as his instructor in Greek. Like Callimachus, Parthenius was particularly focused on poetic technique, as shown by his use of rare words, play with sound patterns, and the balanced structure of his lines, and on lesser-known myths, especially those of an erotic nature. His one surviving work, entitled *Erotic Stories*, is a prose summary of thirty-six rare myths and legends, written as a source book of Greek romantic material for Cornelius Gallus, who is credited with the invention of Roman love elegy. Parthenius was known for his own elegiac poetry, which included a work entitled *Aphrodite*, a lament for his wife Arete, and an *Encomium for Arete* in three books. His poetry acquired a reputation for obscurity, and some degree of difficulty is suggested by the existence of a commentary on the Arete material found on papyrus (609–14 Lloyd-Jones and Parsons). He wrote in other meters as well, and in one of the *Erotic Stories* (11) he quotes six rather elegant hexameters on the suicide of Byblis, who had conceived a passion for her brother. In a display of technical virtuosity, showing how Greek mythical names can be flawlessly integrated into Latin verse, Vergil composed a hexameter that closely resembled a line of Parthenius consisting of the names of three Greek sea deities: *Glauco et Panopeae et Inoo Melicertae* (*Georgics* 1.437). While Parthenius was surely not the only source for the transmission of the Callimachean manner to Rome, he does seem to have influenced a key group of important and innovative Latin poets.

Equally important to the Roman literati who came of age during the last years of the Republic was the Epicurean philosopher Philodemus (Ch. 3.8). Brought to Rome as a result of the First Mithridatic War about 75, he became attached to the prominent family of the Pisones, who settled him, as it seems, in a luxurious villa at Herculaneum. As more and more of his writings from the Herculaneum papyri are issued in good editions, the more evident becomes his influence on Latin authors. Catullus likely knew his erotic epigrams, and although we have no evidence to connect Philodemus with Lucretius, the Latin poet's remarkable achievement of incorporating Epicurus' physics and moral thought into six books of didactic poetry (*On the Nature of Things*) reflects the same cultural atmosphere of interest in Epicureanism in the final years of the Republic. Vergil's youthful poetry confirms that he studied with an Epicurean philosopher named Siro who lived on the bay of Naples, and it is now clear that he must also have known Philodemus and his philosophical ideas. Papyrus fragments from Herculaneum reveal that Philodemus dedicated certain of his treatises on ethics to Vergil and three of his literary friends. Horace too, who dedicated his *Art of Poetry* to the members of Piso's family, spent time with the Greek and Roman Epicureans living in or near Herculaneum. If Parthenius taught Roman poets technical precision, Philodemus inculcated the importance of meaningful content even in compositions produced to delight rather than instruct. Through Philodemus' influence, as it seems, both Vergil and Horace developed a taste for combining the best of Hellenistic poetic practice with serious subject matter. For instance, the quality of "piety" that Vergil so significantly grants to Aeneas bears resemblance to the description of reverent behavior presented in the fragments of Philodemus' *On Piety* (although adapted from the philosophical sage to the man of action), and the anger that compels Aeneas to kill his Italian enemy Turnus in the final scene of the *Aeneid* can be analyzed within the framework of *On Anger*, where Philodemus presents the Epicurean viewpoint on the proper use of this natural but intense emotion. In addition, Horace's *Art of Poetry*, a verse treatise on poetic criticism, contains paraphrases of views on poetry now found in Philodemus' writings. As more textual material by Philodemus becomes known, we will likely understand even better how much the masterpieces of Augustan literature, especially those of Vergil and Horace, are indebted to the synthesis of Hellenistic philosophical thought produced on the bay of Naples.

In the last decades of the Republic, in the 60s and 50s, a group of young Latin poets attempted to develop a technically precise style with subject matter of a personal, emotional, and often erotic nature. In other words, their goal was to reproduce the early Hellenistic aesthetic revolution in Latin verse and, like third-century Alexandrian poets, their focus was on the stylistic aspects evident in a shorter *poiēma* rather than the sweeping themes of a longer *poiēsis* (see Ch. 4.4). Cicero, who was decidedly ambivalent about this movement (although his own verse, such as his translation of Aratus, was in much the same manner), gave them an enduring name. He calls them *neoteroi* or neoterics (*Epistles to Atticus* 7.2.1), a Greek word meaning "moderns," and in doing so he illustrates the neoteric tendency to mimic certain Hellenistic poets by composing an unusually heavy form of the dactylic hexameter containing an obscure Greek name transliterated into Latin. Elsewhere he speaks of *poetae novi*, "new poets," a Latin phrase apparently synonymous with neoteric; we learn from this passage that the "new poets" attempted to refine Latin spelling and usage by following certain formal grammatical rules, all in the manner of Hellenistic "art and learning" (*Orator* 161). In yet another passage (*Tusculan Disputations* 3.45), Cicero refers to perhaps the same group as *cantores Euphorionis*, "singers of Euphorion," and mocks their dislike of Ennius' forceful but old-fashioned style. Euphorion of Chalcis was a poet of the second half of the third century who continued Callimachus' interest in obscure myths and oblique narrative. Cicero's reason for linking the neoterics with Euphorion rather than Callimachus is unclear, but it is possible that, whereas Callimachus was a model for Latin poets already in the second century, Euphorion, who worked at Athens and then Antioch, became well known in Rome only in the late Republic. Poets like Antipater of Sidon and Archias, also from Antioch, would have been acquainted with this earlier scholar and poet who served the Seleucid Antiochus III. Euphorion was most famous for his hexameter poetry on unusual mythical topics, only fragments of which remain. Known titles are *Hesiod*, *Mopsopia* or *Miscellaneous*, which consisted of miscellaneous stories about Attica, and five books of *Chiliades*, which contained curse poetry directed at thieves of the poet's property. Callimachus' lost *Ibis*, imitated in Ovid's poem of the same name, provided a model for the type of curse poetry written by Euphorion; the curse format seems largely an excuse to narrate briefly a series of mythical stories, which function as models for the harm that the poet wishes on his enemies. In the *Eclogues* (6.64–73, 10.50–1), Vergil links the elegiac love poet Cornelius Gallus to Euphorion, whose poem on the Grynean grove sacred to Apollo was adapted to Latin by Gallus. Although the emperor Tiberius wrote Greek poetry in the manner of Euphorion and Parthenius, their style, emphasizing poetic technique and relatively unknown Greek myths, was too esoteric and intellectual for Roman tastes in the long term. Cicero's sneer fits a tradition of criticism in which Euphorion and Parthenius are commonly grouped with Callimachus (and sometimes Lycophron) as pedantic and obscure poets.[15]

Of the neoterics the only poet whose verse substantively survives is Catullus (ca. 84–54). In several poems he mentions other members of his literary circle, such as his friend Gaius Licinius Calvus, with whom he practiced writing short poetry, Quintus Cornificius, who wrote an epyllion *Glaucus* (about a young man who became a sea god, also the subject of a Greek epyllion entitled *Fisherman* by Alexander Aetolus), and Gaius Helvius Cinna, whose epyllion *Zmyrna* on the incestuous conception and birth of Adonis is celebrated in poem 95 of the Catullan corpus. There, in a statement often taken as exemplary of the neoteric creed, Cinna is praised for the nine years' labor that went into perfecting his little narrative epic, in contrast to the hastily composed historical *Annales* of Volusius, good only as fish wrapping. Catullus' poetry remains our principal source for the genres and technical style favored by the neoterics. His subject matter is primarily his own personal relationships, with male friends and enemies who share his literary and political interests and with the women who attract or repel him sexually. Most prominent among the women subjects is Lesbia, a pseudonym (recalling Sappho from the island of Lesbos) for the aristocratic matron Clodia who was the love of his short life. These relationships were explored in a variety of lyric meters (1–60), which preserve the metrical forms in which the Alexandrians (especially Ascle-piades in lost poetry and Theocritus in *Idylls* 28–30) adapted song meters to lyric verse written for the book, and in epigrams (69–116) that continue Meleager's art of varying epigrammatic predecessors and extend Melea-ger's innovative practice of writing a cycle of love poems for one individual. Seven longer poems, in lyric meters (61, 63) and hexameters (62, 64–8), illustrate the neoteric preference for convoluted structure within brief nar-rative and for myths involving extreme, sometimes bizarre, emotional situations. His translation of Callimachus' "Lock of Berenice" (66), which he offers as a substitute for an original composition after his brother's death (65), marks the enormous debt that neoteric poetry owes to Callima-chean poetics and Callimachean development of personal, emotive voices. Just as the *Hecale* supposedly demonstrated the possibility of composing a unified narrative poem within the Callimachean style, so Catullus, like the other neoterics, showed off his poetic sophistication by composing an epyllion (64). Though ostensibly about the marriage of Peleus and Thetis, the narrative of this epyllion quickly veers, in the elliptical style common to the form, into an elaborate ecphrasis of a coverlet made for the marriage bed. In contrast to the happy occasion of the wedding, the coverlet is adorned with a depiction of Theseus' desertion of Ariadne on the island of Naxos, a scene that comes alive as the abandoned girl utters a lament for her betrayal. In this woven web of the mythical past, freighted with the symbolic burdens of earlier Hellenistic ecphrases (Ch. 4.4), Catullus incorporates the emotions of desire, distress, and longing, the very emotions that mark his own poetic persona in his shorter poems.

Although the Latin literature of the Augustan and Silver Ages is char-acterized by confident adaptation of the canonical Greek authors of the archaic-classical period, the great poets of this era nonetheless retain the stylistic refinements of the neoterics with their open acknowledgment of their Hellenistic predecessors. Over the last half-century it has become evident that the one Hellenistic text to which Latin poets were most indebted was the prologue to Callimachus' *Aetia*. After a careful recon-struction of this passage was published by Rudolf Pfeiffer in 1949–51, scholars began to show how Callimachus' presentation of his poetic creed in the prologue and the following scene of his transportation to Helicon in a dream had been used, time and again, by Latin (and later Greek) poets to make programmatic statements of their own poetic principles. For instance, even though Theocritus was the primary model for the *Eclogues*, Vergil opens the sixth poem, precisely the beginning of the second half of his poetry book, with a reworking of Apollo's appearance to Callimachus in the *Aetia* introduction (6.3–5):

> When I was starting to sing of kings and battles, the Cynthian
> plucked my ear and admonished me: "A shepherd, Tityrus,
> must pasture sheep to be fat but utter poetry that is refined."

Here Vergil adapts to pastoral poetry Callimachus' image of the fat sacrificial victim and slender Muse by blending his own persona as poet with a herdsman named Tityrus from Theocritus' first *Idyll* and by converting the sacrificial animal to the sheep tended by Tityrus. It is a fascinating combination of two major Hellenistic passages, establishing an interconnection of imagery and thought that functions as Vergil's own reading of his source texts. Since the "kings and battles" that are the potential subject for Tityrus/Vergil refer to the military exploits of one Varus, the passage as a whole forms a gracious refusal to celebrate such topics. This kind of friendly refusal, called a *recusatio*, became one of the primary uses of the *Aetia* prologue for Latin authors. Another example is Propertius 3.3, where the elegiac love poet combines motifs from the *Aetia* prologue with Callimachus' dream of Helicon. Propertius, also dreaming, imagines that he is reclining on that mountain, about to taste the water of the Hippocrene fountain "where thirsty father Ennius once drank" (3.3.6), so that he too can sing about the great moments in Roman military history. Just then Apollo appears to warn him away from heroic song, to write a poetry book that "a girl may read as she waits alone for her lover" (3.3.10). Apollo then points to a decorated cave where stand the Muses, one of whom again warns the poet to avoid warlike topics and to write of love. The programmatic *recusatio* ends with Propertius drinking from a spring by the cave and wetting his lips "with Philitean water" (3.3.52). Here the imagery of the prologue is reworked in a complicated scenario to place Propertius as love poet directly in the tradition of the most famous Hellenistic elegists, Callimachus and Philitas. Later in his fourth book Propertius casts himself as the "Roman Callimachus" (4.1.64) for a different reason, because in this last poetry book he turns from love poetry to relating aetiological stories about Roman history and culture, created on the model of the *Aetia* episodes.

The Roman reception of Hellenistic literature has a puzzling, contra-dictory quality because of the gap between the observable influence of

Hellenistic authors on Latin texts and stated opinions about the worth of these same Greek writers. Literary critics of the imperial era rank Hellenistic writers lower than the masters of earlier Greek literature. The purpose of the criticism must, however, be taken into account in each case. For instance, Quintilian in his *Training in Oratory* (10.1.46–84) discusses Greek authors by genres for the purpose of defining their utility in the education of future Roman orators. Since the imaginative literature of the Hellenistic age was generally directed toward enchantment rather than instruction, it will obviously be of less value for the orator. Even though Apollonius was not included in the canon of epic poets (because the Alexandrian scholar/editors did not include anyone of their era), Quintilian recognizes the standing of the *Argonautica* within the "middle" (as opposed to "grand" or "low") stylistic category, to which Hesiod also belonged. His statement that Aratus' poem has no movement, and so lacks diversity, emotion, and personal voice, does not mean he considered it a bad poem, just not a useful model for oratory. Likewise, Theocritus, "admirable in his own genre" (10.1.55), is said to contain nothing pertaining to the forum and to urban life (indicating that Quintilian is thinking only of the rustic poems). Nicander and Euphorion must have some worth, Quintilian suggests, because Vergil imitated them. While epic has the most to offer the aspiring orator, lesser genres provide a pleasing change of pace for the convivial setting of dinner parties. Callimachus is the indisputable master in elegy, according to Quintilian, with Philitas second, although in lyric poetry the archaic poets remain foremost. Hellenistic prose writers are hardly mentioned. In historical writings, the period between Clitarchus, who wrote an eyewitness but unreliable account of the expedition of Alexander the Great, and the universal historian Timagenes of the Augustan age is blank; Quintilian's survey of rhetoricians ends with Demetrius of Phalerum, said to be "almost the last of the Athenians who could be called an orator" (10.1.80); the latest philosopher mentioned by name is Theophrastus, although the "old Stoics," who lack eloquence, are granted some contribution through their strength in argumentation (10.1.84). Quintilian's survey of Greek literature, then, attempts to tack major Hellenistic authors onto the canon of pre-Alexander writers, but he finds that Hellenistic aesthetic sensibilities are little congenial to the active, restless temperament of most Romans.

The Greek author of *On the Sublime* known as "Longinus" also finds Hellenistic authors lacking in the quality that he recommends, namely, the ability to move deeply or exalt the soul through sublimity in subject matter and style (33.4–5). As a result, he counts the perfection of Apollonius and Theocritus against them because the poet who soars aloft or rushes in a torrent must necessarily at times fall flat (as they do not). He names the *Erigone*, a lost elegiac narrative by Eratosthenes that perhaps offered an *aition* for the origin of tragedy, "a blameless little poem," but he also argues that Eratosthenes is not therefore a greater poet than the archaic Archilochus, who sweeps forward in a flood a great body of unordered matter under the force of divine inspiration. It was just this model of the rushing river carrying much garbage in its torrent that Callimachus so vehemently rejected in his *Hymn to Apollo* (2.108–9, translated in Ch. 3.2).

The assessment of Hellenistic literature given by imperial writers long dominated modern critical views. But with the twentieth-century discovery of a wider variety of texts, scholars began an important reevaluation of Hellenistic literature based on its internal principles. Current advances in our knowledge of Hellenistic literary criticism are also proving crucial in uncovering the intellectual paradigms within which Hellenistic authors worked and which they likely helped to develop. And as new Hellenistic texts continue to be discovered, we see more clearly the literary structures on which Latin literature was built. The new collection of Posidippan epigrams, for instance, has revealed how the geographical references in Latin authors, universalizing the power of the Roman empire, have a precedent in the poetic definition of the Ptolemaic territory as coextensive with Alexander's empire. Even if this epigram collection was never transmitted to Rome, it was surely from texts of this sort that Roman poets learned to make political and ideological points of expansive scope within the confines of a refined poetry focused on the human and contemporary.

Notes

1 History and Culture

1. The account of the Athenians' flattery was told in the nearly contemporary history of Demochares and the full text of the hymn, composed by one Hermocles in competition with other poets, was preserved by the early third-century historian Duris of Samos, both of which were excerpted by Athenaeus 6.252f–253f.

2. Described in Athenaeus 5.194c–195f.
3. Pollitt (1986) 235.
4. Fr. 104 Gow and Scholfield (1953).
5. Excerpted by Athenaeus 5.196a–203b from Callixenus of Rhodes, who wrote *On Alexandria* in at least four books.
6. As, for instance, in a series of epigrams: *Palatine Anthology* 11.130, 11.321, 11.322, 11.347.

2 Aesthetics and Style

1. Demetrius, *On Style* 193.
2. The papyrus was initially published by Bastianini and Gallazzi (2001). A more accessible edition with English and Italian translations is Austin and Bastianini (2002).
3. Pliny, *Natural History* 34.65.
4. Strabo 14.2.19 calls him "both critic and poet."

5. See, for instance, the assessment of Antimachus by Quintilian, *Training in Oratory* 10.1.53.
6. In the Hellenistic manual *On Style*, ascribed to one Demetrius, the word for "thunder," *bronta*, is cited as an example of the breadth, length, and roughness of sound that produce the "weighty" style (177).

7. M. L. West, "The New Sappho," *Zeitschrift für Papyrologie und Epigraphik* 151 (2005) 3–6.

8. Dionysius of Halicarnassus' *On Composition*, a work of the Augustan age, develops Hellenistic critical ideas on *synthesis*.

9. For the historical context in which the paean was performed, see Plutarch, *Life of Titus Flamininus* 16.

10. The controversy is discussed in Athenaeus 11.476f–77e.

11. A. Lindsell, "Was Theocritus a Botanist?" *Greece & Rome* 6 (1937) 78–93.

12. E.g., W. Schubart and U. von Wilamowitz-Moellendorff, eds., *Berliner Klassikertexte* (Berlin, 1907), Heft 5.1, pp. 75–6 (1st c. AD), a papyrus roll only about two inches high, containing erotic epigrams by Meleager.

13. The *Sikyonian* is primarily known from P. Sorbonne 72, 2272, 2273, published by A. Blanchard and A. Bataille, *Recherches de Papyrologie* 3 (1964) 103–76, Pl. VI–XIII. The text of Herodas is from British Library, Pap. 135 (2nd c. AD), first published by F. G. Kenyon, *Classical Texts from Papyri in the British Museum* (London, 1891) 1–41.

14. *P. Oxy.* 2211, fr. 1 v. 9, fr. 1 r. 9 = E. Lobel et al., eds., *The Oxyrhynchus Papyri, Part XIX* (London, 1948).

15. P. Lille inv. 76d, 78–9, 82, 84 = C. Meillier, *Cahiers de recherches de l'Institut de Papyrologie et d'Égyptologie de Lille* 4 (1977) 261–86; partially illustrated by Turner and Parsons (1987) no. 75; text in Lloyd-Jones and Parsons (1983) nos. 254–63.

16. P. Med. 18 = *Papiri della R. Università di Milano*, ed. A. Vogliano, I (1937).

17. A tenth-century manuscript (Cod. Parisinus suppl. gr. 247) of Nicander's *Alexipharmaca*, which is about poisons and their remedies, contains botanical drawings that may descend from ancient illustrations; see Gow and Scholfield (1953) 222–3; Weitzmann (1959) 14, fig. 16.

18. Kramer (2001).

19. P. Louvre 7172 = H. Weil, *Un papyrus inédit de la bibliothèque de M. Ambroise Firmin-Didot* (Paris, 1879). See the discussion of D. Thompson, "Ptolemaios and the 'Lighthouse,' " *Proceedings of the Cambridge Philological Society* 213 = New Series 33 (1987) 105–21.

20. P. Berol. 9865 = U. von Wilamowitz-Moellendorff, ed., *Timotheos, Die Perser* (Leipzig, 1903).

21. Cited in note 15 above.

3 Authors and Genres

1. Phaedrus 5.1.

2. Sérafim Charitonidis, Lilly Kahil, and René Ginouvès, *Les Mosaïques de la maison du Ménandre à Mytilène* (*Antike Kunst*, Beiheft 6, Bern, 1970).

3. Herodotus 4.155.

4. The ancient source is Athenaeus 13.597b–599c.

5. Prominent among these sources is the claim in the *Suda* biography of Callimachus that Callimachus' *Ibis*,

a lost poem disparaging some rival poet, concerned Apollonius.

6. Pseudo-Acro on Horace, *Art of Poetry* 357.

7. Athenaeus 5.206d–209e preserves Moschion's description and Archimelus' poem.

8. Papyrus Vindobonensis Rainer 29801 (Gow [1952a] pp. 168–70).

9. *Commentary on the Phaenomena of Aratus and of Eudoxus* 1.1.4.

10. Prose translation in Long and Sedley (1987) 326–7.

11. *Syll.*³ 452 = W. Dittenberger, *Sylloge inscriptionum Graecarum*, 3rd ed. (Leipzig, 1915, reprinted Hildesheim, 1960).

12. *P. Oxy.* 2221, in E. Lobel et al., eds., *The Oxyrhynchus Papyri, Part XIV* (London, 1948), and P. Milan. 608, in I. Cazzaniga, "Nuovo frammento di scholion a Nicandro, Theriaka vv. 526–29," *Studi Italiani Filologia Classica* 27–8 (1956) 83–101.

13. P. Mil. Vogl. VIII 309 = Bastianini and Gallazzi (2001).

14. *Inscriptiones Graecae* IX 1² I, 17A = T 3 Austin and Bastianini.

15. Epitaphs for a dog named Tauron are known from a third-century papyrus (977 Lloyd-Jones and Parsons).

16. *Palatine Anthology* 7.410–11, 7.37, 7.707–8.

17. *Palatine Anthology* 7.247, 9.518–19, 11.12.

18. P. Grenfell 1ᵛ, in B. P. Grenfell, *An Alexandrian Erotic Fragment and Other Greek Papyri* (Oxford, 1896).

19. This is the definition given by the musical expert Aristoxenus, as reported by Athenaeus 14.620e.

20. British Library, Pap. 135, published by F. G. Kenyon, *Classical Texts from Papyri in the British Museum* (London, 1891).

21. Although an adult male's desire for an adolescent boy was considered acceptable in the Greek world, an adult male's *passive* acceptance of a male sexual partner was perceived as shameful.

22. Aristotle, *Poetics* 2.5 calls him the "first writer of parodies." The main source for the history of Greek parody is Athenaeus 15.698a–699c.

23. P. Mich. inv. 6946, edited by H. S. Schibli, "Fragments of a Weasel and Mouse War," *Zeitschrift für Papyrologie und Epigraphik* 53 (1983) 1–25.

24. For the life of Crates, see Diogenes Laertius 6.85–93 and, for Hipparchia, 6.96–8.

25. For his life, see Diogenes Laertius 9.109–16, who used a commentary on the *Silli* by Apollonides of Nicaea.

26. *P. Oxy.* 1082 = Arthur S. Hunt, ed., *The Oxyrhynchus Papyri, Part VIII* (London, 1911).

27. *P. Oxy.* 1176 = Arthur S. Hunt, ed., *The Oxyrhynchus Papyri, Part IX* (London, 1912).

28. See Agatharchides, *On the Erythraean Sea* fr. 21, Cicero, *Brutus* 286, Dionysius of Halicarnassus, *On Literary Composition* 4, 18, and "Longinus," *On the Sublime* 3.2. At the same time, Dionysius in *On Literary Composition* 4 considered Polybius and other Hellenistic historians (including Phylarchus, Duris, and Hieronymus of Cardia, an important lost historian of the Diadochs) and philosophers (especially the Stoic Chrysippus) to have written with

such disinterest in attractive stylistic arrangement that "they have left behind such compositions as no one can bear to read through to the final *corōnis.*" The imperial focus on good style in prose works helps explain why so much of Hellenistic prose, focused on accurate content, has been lost.

29. Diogenes Laertius 7.156; J. von Arnim, *Stoicorum veterum fragmenta* I, fr. 73 (Leipzig, 1903–24).

30. Also extant in Greek is *Data* and in Arabic translation *On Divisions*

(of Figures). Of disputed authorship, in Greek, are *Phaenomena* (on geometrical astronomy), *Optics,* and *Catoptrics* (on the optics of reflection).

31. Heath (1921) 1.402.

32. *Vaticanus Graecus* 204.

33. Preserved by Athenaeus 11.497d.

34. Kramer (2001).

35. Steven Jackson, *Myrsilus of Methymna: Hellenistic Paradoxographer* (Amsterdam, 1995) 6.

36. Codex Palatinus Graecus 398.

4   Topics in Hellenistic Literature

1. W. Rhys Roberts in his introduction to "Demetrius," *On Style* in the Loeb edition of Aristotle, *The Poetics,* "Longinus," *On the Sublime,* both translated by W. Hamilton Fyfe, and "Demetrius," *On Style,* translated by W. R. Roberts (Cambridge, MA: Harvard University Press, 1927) 263.

2. Of particular importance are Pfeiffer's edition of Callimachus (1949–51), Gow's edition of Theocritus (1952b), and Gow and Page (1965) on Hellenistic epigrams.

3. The term is that of Harold Bloom, *The Anxiety of Influence: A Theory of Poetry* (New York: Oxford University Press, 1973; 2nd ed., 1997).

4. See Susan Stephens and John Winkler, eds. and trans., *Ancient Greek Novels: The Fragments* (Princeton: Princeton University Press, 1995) 11–17 for discussion of the multiple factors in the development of the novel form, including possible influences from non-Greek cultures.

5. The term originated with Wilhelm Kroll, *Studien zum Verständnis der römischen Literatur* (Stuttgart, 1924, reprinted 1964).

6. Marcotte (2000) 35.

7. Bing (1988) 20.

8. Principally, in Cameron (1995).

9. A statue of a seated poet holding a bookroll, housed in the Vatican Museum, is labeled on its base Posidippus, but it is disputed whether this is the epigrammatist or a comic poet of the same name.

10. *P. Oxy.* 1011 = Arthur Hunt, ed., *The Oxyrhynchus Papyri, Part VII* (London, 1910).

11. Among the earlier literary accounts preserved in Parthenius' *Erotic Stories,* sibling passion occurs in 2 (from Philitas' *Hermes*), 5 (from Hermesianax's *Leontion*), 11 (from Apollonius' *Foundation of Caunus*), and 31 (from the historian Phylarchus). The sources for the stories in Parthenius are indicated in marginal notes.

12. Strabo 8.3.30.

13. Reported by Dionysius of Halicarnassus, *Demosthenes* 3.
14. Preserved on a papyrus of the second century (P. Louvre inv. 7733 = F. Lasserre, "L'élégie de l'huître," *Quaderni Urbinati di Cultura Classica* 19 [1975] 145–76); it has an explanatory commentary.
15. Euphorion was criticized already by Crates of Mallus (*Palatine Anthology* 11.218) for his excessive use of Homeric glosses. For criticism of Parthenius, see Erycius (*Palatine Anthology* 7.377) and Pollianus (*Palatine Anthology* 11.130). Lucian (*How to Write History* 57) contrasts Homer's simple effectiveness with the verbosity of Parthenius, Euphorion, and Callimachus.

Chronological Tables with Dates of Kingship

The Argeads

Philip II (m. Olympias) (ca. 359–336)
Alexander the Great (m. Rhoxane) (336–323)
Philip III Arrhidaeus (m. Eurydice) (323–317)
Alexander IV (323–310)

The Antigonids

Antigonus I the One-Eyed (323–301)
Demetrius I Poliorcetes (m. Phila I, d. of Antipater) (301–283)
Antigonus II Gonatas (m. Phila II, d. of Seleucus I) (276–239)
Demetrius II (239–229)
Antigonus III Doson (229–221)
Philip V (221–179)
Perseus (179–168)

The Seleucids

Seleucus I Nicator (m. Apama; m. Stratonice, d. Demetrius I of Macedon)
(321–281)

Antiochus I Soter (m. Stratonice I) (281–261)
Antiochus II Theos (m. Laodice I, d. Seleucus I; m. Berenice,
    d. Ptolemy II) (261–246)
Seleucus II Callinicus (246–225)
Seleucus III Ceraunus (225–223)
Antiochus III "the Great" (m. Laodice II, d. Mithradates II of Pontus)
    (223–187)
Seleucus IV Philopator (187–175)
Antiochus IV Epiphanes (175–164)
Antiochus V Eupator (164–162)
Demetrius I of Syria (162–150)

The Attalids

Philetaerus (283–263)
Eumenes I (263–241)
Attalus I (m. Apollonis) (241–197)
Eumenes II (m. Stratonice) (197–158)
Attalus II Philadelphus (also m. Stratonice) (158–138)
Attalus III Philometor (138–133)

The Ptolemies

Ptolemy I Soter (m. Eurydice I; m. Berenice I) (323–282)
Ptolemy II Philadelphus (m. Arsinoe I, d. Lysimachus; m. Arsinoe II,
    d. Ptolemy I) (282–246)
Ptolemy III Euergetes (m. Berenice II, d. Magas of Cyrene) (246–221)
Ptolemy IV Philopator (m. Arsinoe III, d. Ptolemy III) (221–205)
Ptolemy V Epiphanes (205–180)
Ptolemy VI Philometor (180–164, 163–145)
Ptolemy VII Neos Philopator (145)
Ptolemy VIII "Physcon" (170–163, 145–116)
Cleopatra VII (51–31)

Suggested Reading

1 History and Culture

Recent general histories of the Hellenistic period include Green (1990), a lively and detailed account of Hellenistic history and culture, often idiosyncratic in interpretation, and Shipley (2000), a balanced and readable account connecting political events with cultural change. Both Austin (1981) and Bagnall and Derow (2004) provide a selection of historical sources in translation. The essays in Erskine (2003) balance history with culture. For the interaction of Rome with Hellenistic culture, see Gruen (1984).

1.2 Macedonia and Greece. For Macedonia, see Andronicos (1984) with illustrations of the tombs at Vergina, Ginouvès (1994), an illustrated discussion emphasizing the archaeological finds, and Carney (2000) on Macedonian royal women. For Hellenistic Athens, see Habicht (1997); for Hellenistic Sparta, Cartledge and Spawforth (2002) Part I offers a general account.

The best summary of Hellenistic philosophy is Algra et al. (1999); also invaluable is Long and Sedley (1987), which contains select sources for Hellenistic philosophy (Greek and Latin texts in vol. 2, English translation and discussion in vol. 1). Briefer general treatments are given in Long (1986) and Sharples (1996); for a readable introduction to Stoicism, see Rist (1969) and, for Epicureanism, Rist (1972). Nussbaum (1994) provides an excellent discussion of Hellenistic approaches to achieving contentment. On the conventional values of nonelites, see the essays in

Bilde et al. (1997). Bibliography for individual philosophers is listed under Ch. 3.8 below.

1.3 Seleucid Asia. For a revisionist history of the Seleucid empire, emphasizing the cultural influence of the eastern (and non-Greek) portions of the kingdom in its formation, see Sherwin-White and Kuhrt (1993); Downey (1963) provides a good account of ancient Antioch for the nonspecialist.

1.4 Attalid Pergamum. Still useful, though dated, is Hansen (1971), especially Ch. 9 on Attalid patronage of learning; more recent essays on archaeology, culture, and religion can be found in Koester (1998). For Pergamene art, see Pollitt (1986) Ch. 4 and the essays in Grummond and Ridgway (2000), especially Gruen on Attalid use of culture for dynastic purposes.

1.5 Ptolemaic Egypt. For Ptolemaic history in the context of its Greek and Egyptian heritage, see Chauveau (2000) and Hölbl (2001). Fraser (1972) is an unsurpassed, massively documented account of cultural history of Hellenistic Alexandria, for the serious reader. For the archaeological remains in Alexandria, see Empereur (1998), a sumptuously photographed account including the recent discoveries from the harbor, and Venit (2002) on the architecture and painted decorations in the monumental tombs of Hellenistic and Roman Alexandria. Rice (1983) is useful for a sense of Ptolemaic opulence, and Walker and Higgs (2001) is a good resource for the visual culture that surrounded Cleopatra. For glimpses into the lives of nonelite members of Ptolemaic culture, see Pomeroy (1984) on women, Bowman (1986), and Lewis (1986).

The standard work on Hellenistic scholarship is Pfeiffer (1968); see too Fraser (1972) Ch. 8. For a succinct discussion of the Ptolemies' establishment of the Museum, see Maehler (2004); Blum (1991) provides a rich resource on the Library at Alexandria; on the role of the Alexandrian scholars in the transmission of Homer, see Nagy (1996) Part II. For a concise, though now dated, summary of what is known about Hellenistic literary criticism, see Kennedy (1989) Ch. 6; additional bibliography on this topic is listed under Ch. 4.4 below.

2 Aesthetics and Style

Our knowledge and understanding of Hellenistic literature, especially poetry, was revolutionized in the twentieth century by the discovery of a large number of new texts and by important editions of major authors and genres. The older fragments, in Greek without translation, are mostly in Powell (1925), the newer ones in Lloyd-Jones and Parsons (1983) and Lloyd-Jones (2005). As a result, only in the last three decades or so have scholars begun to present the same kind of literary-cultural evaluation that more canonical Greek and Latin literature earlier received. The number of general accounts that synthesize this new material remains quite small. Accounts of major authors can be found in Bulloch (1985a) and Hutchinson (1988). Cameron (1995), despite his polemical tone, provides an important revisionary reading of Callimachus and his contemporaries. Fantuzzi and Hunter (2004) offer expert readings of major authors and genres, with much recent bibliography. Selection of Greek texts for major and some minor poets with commentary can be found in Hopkinson (1988); Fowler (1990) offers an anthology of poetry in translation.

2.1 Aesthetic Principles. On the Hellenistic aesthetic, see Fowler (1989). For the fragments and testimonia of Philitas, see Spanoudakis (2002) and for discussion of his writings, Bing (2003); for translation and discussion of Erinna's *Distaff*, see Gutzwiller (1997) 202–11; on Callimachus' antipathy to Antimachus, see Krevans (1993). For a rare literary reading of the prologue to the *Aetia*, see Acosta-Hughes and Stephens (2002).

2.2 Meter, Dialect, and Diction. A comprehensive treatment of the style of Hellenistic poets has yet to be written, but Fantuzzi and Hunter (2004) Ch. 6 offer a stylistic analysis of Hellenistic epic. The most complete resources remain the major commentaries on individual poets and works, which are listed under Ch. 3. For the innovations in Hellenistic metrics, see West (1987) Ch. 6 or the more detailed account in West (1982) Ch. 4. On acrostics, see Courtney (1990).

2.3 Literature as Artefact. A good general account of the materials and circumstances of book production, as well as the survival of texts, is found in Easterling and Knox (1985a). Turner (1980) offers a readable and reliable account of Greek papyri; Turner and Parsons (1987), written for the nonspecialist, provides a wealth of illustrations of papyri; and Sider (2005) presents an attractively illustrated introduction to the library of Greek papyri recovered from Herculaneum. Johnson (2004), a detailed study of thousands of Roman-era papyri from Oxyrhynchus in Egypt, is readable, though directed at specialists. A comparable study of Ptolemaic-era literary papyri is yet to be done, but Cribiore (1996) discusses the evidence for school exercises in Greco-Roman Egypt. For a general account of the transmission of ancient texts, with an emphasis on textual criticism, see Reynolds and Wilson (1991).

3   Authors and Genres

3.1 Menander. Greek text and English translation are available in the excellent Loeb edition by Arnott (1979–2000), in vol. 1, *Shield, Grouch*

(= *Peevish Fellow*), *Men at Arbitration*; in vol. 2, *Hated Man, Girl with Cut Hair*, in vol. 3, *Samian Woman, Sikyonian(s)*. The standard commentary on the Greek text is Gomme and Sandbach (1973). For the genre of New Comedy in Athens and Rome, see Hunter (1985). For general interpretation of Menander's dramatic art, see Webster (1974), Goldberg (1980), Zagagi (1994), Walton and Arnott (1996), and Fantuzzi and Hunter (2004) 404–32; on metatheatricality in Menander, Gutzwiller (2000); for performance and use of the mask in Menander, Wiles (1991); and for connections between New Comedy and Athenian political and social life, Konstan (1995), Scafuro (1997), and Lape (2004).

3.2 Callimachus. There currently exists no complete Greek edition or English translation of all the known poems and fragments of Callimachus. Callimachus occupies two different volumes in the Loeb series, with Greek text and English translation: the *Hymns* and *Epigrams* are in Mair (1921) and the fragments, though excluding newer pieces such as the "Victory of Berenice" and some bits of the *Hecale*, are in Trypanis (1958). Good, though selective, translations in Lombardo and Rayor (1988), Fowler (1990) 41–69, and Nisetich (2001). The standard Greek text, with Latin notes, is Pfeiffer (1949–51), with newer fragments in Lloyd-Jones and Parsons (1983) and Lloyd-Jones (2005). On Callimachus as a bibliographer, see Blum (1991). General interpretation in Fraser (1972) 1.717–93, Bulloch (1985a) 549–70, and Hutchinson (1988) Ch. 2; Cameron (1995) provides a revisionary, sometimes too dogmatic account, and Selden (1998) argues for a coherence of vision in Callimachus' poetry through the theme of displacement. On the *Aetia*, see Fantuzzi and Hunter (2004) Ch. 2; on the *Iambi*, Clayman (1980), Kerkhecker (1999), and Acosta-Hughes (2002); on the *Hecale*, Hollis (1990); and on the epigrams, Gutzwiller (1998) Ch. 5. For individual *Hymns*, see McLennan (1977) on "Zeus," Williams (1978) on "Apollo," Bing (1988) 91–143 on "Delos," McKay (1962b) and Bulloch (1985b) on "Bath of Pallas," and McKay (1962a) on "Demeter."

3.3 Apollonius of Rhodes. The standard text is Fränkel (1961); a good commentary on Book 3 is provided by Hunter (1989). Modern translations of the *Argonautica* include Fowler (1990) 73–231, Hunter (1993b), and Green (1997). For interpretation, see Beye (1982), Bulloch (1985a) 586–98, Hutchinson (1988) Ch. 3, Clauss (1993), Hunter (1993a), and Fantuzzi and Hunter (2004) Ch. 3. Feeney (1991) 57–98 provides an excellent discussion of the problematic nature of the gods in Apollonius. Nelis (2001) offers an important study of Vergil's use of Homer through Apollonius.

3.4 Theocritus and the Other Bucolic Poets. The standard text of all the bucolic poets is Gow (1952a). The standard commentary for Theocritus, with translation, is Gow (1952b); for select poems (*Idylls* 1, 3, 4, 6, 7, 10, 11, and 13), Hunter (1999) is excellent. For commentary on Bion, see Reed (1997). Wells (1988) provides a good modern translation of Theocritus, and translation of the other bucolic poets can be found in Edmonds (1928). For general interpretation of Theocritus, see Bulloch (1985a) 570–86 and Hutchinson (1988) Ch. 4. For interpretation of his pastoral poems, see Halperin (1983), Gutzwiller (1991), Fantuzzi and Hunter (2004) 133–90, and the essays on Greek bucolic in Fantuzzi and Papanghelis (2006); on the meaning of the word *bucolic*, see Gutzwiller (2006). On the urban mimes, see Burton (1995), on court poetry, Griffiths (1979) and Hunter (2003), and on Theocritus' use of archaic poetry, Hunter (1996). Kerlin (1910) provides information about Theocritus' influence on English literature.

3.5 Didactic Poetry. For an overview of Hellenistic didactic poetry, see Bulloch (1985a) 598–606 and Toohey (1996) Ch. 3. Greek text and English translation of Aratus are available in Kidd (1997) and in G. R. Mair's edition in Mair (1921). Those with a serious interest in Aratus or his astronomy should supplement Kidd's commentary with Martin's edition (1998), which has, in French, an excellent introduction, translation, commentary, and star charts. For interpretation of Aratus, consult Hutchinson (1988) 214–36, Gee (2000) Ch. 3 with discussion of Aratus' influence on Ovid's *Fasti*, and Fantuzzi and Hunter (2004) 224–45. On Aratus' carefully honed style, particularly with regard to euphony, see Pendergraft (1995). Greek text and English translation of Nicander are in Gow and Scholfield (1953); recent discussion of the dating problem, with differing conclusions, in Cameron (1995) 194–208 and Massimilla (2000, in Italian).

3.6 Epigrams. Complete translation with text of the *Greek Anthology* is in Paton (1916–18). The standard text and commentary for Hellenistic epigrams is Gow and Page (1965) and for Philodemus and Archias, together with other Greek epigrammatists down to Nero, Gow and Page (1968). The more detailed commentary on Philodemus by Sider (1997) is excellent. Cameron (1993) has produced a remarkably learned but dense study of the history of the anthology. For general interpretation, see Fraser (1972) 1.553–617, Gutzwiller (1998), and Fantuzzi and Hunter (2004) Ch. 7. Text and translation of the Posidippus papyrus can be found in Austin and Bastianini (2002); interpretive essays are offered in Acosta-Hughes et al. (2004) and Gutzwiller (2005).

3.7 Dramatic Poetry. See, generally, Fraser (1972) 1.618–21 and Fantuzzi and Hunter (2004) 432–43. Sifakis (1967) discusses the epigraphical and archaeological evidence for lost Hellenistic drama; Jacobson (1983) offers text, translation, and discussion of Ezechiel's *Exagoge*. The most accessible text and translation of Lycophron's *Alexandra*, with explanatory notes from the scholia, is still Mair (1921); for a literary view, see Hutchinson (1988) 257–64 and for discussion of the genre, West (2000). For text, translation, and commentary on the "Maiden's Lament," see Bing (2002). Text and translation of Herodas, together with Sophron and fragments of popular mime, are now conveniently published by Cunningham in Rusten (2002). Text of Sophron with translation and commentary is in Hordern (2004). Commentary on Herodas can be found in Cunningham (1971), and for interpretation, see Mastromarco (1984) who argues for performance, Hutchinson (1988) 236–57 on the connection between lowness and dramatic form, and Skinner (2001) on the treatment of women.

3.8 Parodic and Philosophical Literature. Text, translation, and commentary for Archestratus are found in Olson and Sens (2000) and for Matro, see Olson and Sens (1999); both works discuss the history of Greek parody. For the *Battle of the Weasel and Mice*, see West (2003) 229–32 with text and translation at 259–63. Greek text and commentary for Machon are in Gow (1965), while for translation the reader should follow Gow's references to the Loeb edition of Athenaeus by Gulick (1951–71); for interpretation of Machon as politically subversive, see Kurke (2002). Knox's text and (stilted) translation of Phoenix and Cercidas are found in Rusten (1993). For discussion of the influence of satiric and philosophical poets, especially Timon, on Callimachus' *Aetia* prologue, see Andrews (1998). Text and translation for Theophrastus' *Characters* can be found in Rusten (2002) and, with full commentary, in Diggle (2004). The fragments of Posidonius, in Greek, are published by Edelstein and Kidd (1989), with commentary in Kidd (1988) and translation in Kidd (1999). For the texts of Epicurus with translation and commentary, see Bailey (1926). Asmis (1990) and Sider (2005) 78–97 provide summaries of Philodemus' surviving texts; for interpretation, see the essays in Obbink (1995), Fitzgerald et al. (2004), and Armstrong et al. (2004).

3.9 Polybius. Text and translation are available in Paton (1922–7). Walbank's historical commentary (1957–79) is indispensable for serious study. General interpretation in Walbank (1972); Sacks (1981) studies the uniqueness of Polybius' historiographical vision; Eckstein (1995) discusses his moral vision; Champion (2004) examines cultural ideology. On Polybius' use of geography, see Clarke (1999) Ch 2.

3.10 Technical Prose Writing. A good source book for Greek science, with passages in translation from Hellenistic and imperial writers, is Irby-Massie and Keyser (2002). Cuomo (2001) Chs. 3–4 provides an accessible introduction to Hellenistic mathematics, with emphasis on practice; more detailed history in Heath (1921); Fraser (1972) 1.376–434 discusses mathematics and science in Alexandria. Euclid's *Elements* is available in a translation by Heath (1926). Archimedes' *On the Sphere and the Cylinder* has received an excellent and faithful translation by Netz (2004b), with commentary; for the other works, the standard translation is Heath (1897). Dijksterhuis (1987) provides discussion of Archimedes' life and works. For the *Conics* of Apollonius of Perge, see Heath (1896) and, for Book 4, Fried (2002); for Diocles' text, see Toomer (1976). Important cognitive and cultural studies of Greek mathematics are offered by Netz (1999) and (2004a). Heath (1932) provides a good short history of Greek astronomy, with translation of key Hellenistic documents; Evans (1998) offers an accessible history of practice, while a more detailed and specialized analysis is in Neugebauer (1975). On Aristarchus, see Heath (1913). For the texts of Biton and Philo, see Marsden (1971); for a history of the development of Greek and Roman artillery, Marsden (1969). For a good introduction to ancient medicine, including the Hellenistic period, see Nutton (2004); for medicine in Alexandria, see Fraser (1972) 1.338–76. Staden (1989) offers an excellent study of Herophilus in the context of early Hellenistic medicine, and Staden (1996) an intriguing essay on the relationship of medicine to other sciences. For Greek text of Apollonius of Citium's commentary, with German translation and the manuscript illustrations, see Kollesch and Kudlien (1965). On the Alexandrian geographical writers, see Fraser (1972) 1.525–53; fragments and discussion of Agatharchides are in Burstein (1989). On paradoxography, see Fraser (1972) 1.770–4 and Schepens and Delcroix (1996).

4 Topics in Hellenistic Literature

4.1 Learning and Innovation. General discussions of allusion in Hellenistic poetry include Giangrande (1967) and Hopkinson (1988) 6–11; the details are documented in many commentaries, such as Hunter (1993a) on Apollonius and Sens (1997) on Theocritus' *Idyll* 22. For the role of *hapax legomena* in Hellenistic allusion, see (in French) Cusset (1999) and, for Apollonius, Kyriakou (1995). For the Hellenistic epyllion, see Gutzwiller (1981) and, more selectively, Merriam (2001). For recent treatments of genre-marking and mixing of genres, see the essays in Harder et al. (1998). For Archimedes' *Cattle Problem*, see Fraser (1972) 1.407–9 and Dijksterhuis (1987) 398–401. For Eratosthenes' "Duplication of the Cube," see Heath (1921) 1.244–60 with translation of the epigram and Fraser (1972) 1.410–13, and on the mathematical problem Cuomo (2001) 57–60. On Eratosthenes' *Hermes*, see Fraser (1972) 1.623–4, 641 and Pfeiffer (1968) 168–9. For Apollodorus of Athens, see Pfeiffer (1968) 253–66. Marcotte

(2000) offers text of the anonymous author of *Circuit of the Earth* (called Pseudo-Scymnus), with translation, notes, and detailed introduction in French.

4.2 Book Culture and Performance. The fundamental work on Hellenistic book culture is Bing (1988), while Cameron (1995) provides a vigorous argument for the continuing importance of inscription and performance. While thorough studies of the structure of Callimachus' *Aetia* and his book of *Hymns* are yet to be published, Clayman (1980) provides a good discussion of the *Iambi* as a collection. On Hellenistic epigram collections, see Gutzwiller (1998) and the essays in Gutzwiller (2005); on the evidence for Theocritean poetry books, see Gutzwiller (1996).

4.3 Social and Political Background. For ideology in New Comedy, see Konstan (1995) and Lape (2004). On Euhemerus see Fraser (1972) 1.289–95; the best source for Dionysius Scytobrachion, though lacking translation of the fragments, is Rusten (1982). On Theocritus' strategies in his court poetry, see Griffiths (1979), and for a reading of the "Lock of Berenice" as Ptolemaic court poetry, see Gutzwiller (1992). Discussions of Egyptianizing elements in Alexandrian poetry can be found in Bing (1988) 91–143, Koenen (1993), Selden (1998), and Stephens (2003); Hunter (2003) 46–53 provides a more questioning analysis. On the courtier Callicrates, see Bing (2002/3). Text and translation of the *Letter of Aristeas* can be found in Hadas (1951); interpretation in Honigman (2003). On women writers and gender issues, see Snyder (1989), Skinner (1991), (2001), (2005), Gutzwiller (1997), (1998) 54–88, and Manwell (2005). For text and translation of the *Megara*, see Vaughn (1976), and on women as subjects in epyllia, Merriam (2001). On gender and social mobility, see Burton (1995) and Selden (1998).

4.4 The Critical Impulse in Literature and Art. Since scholars are now in the process of recovering the broad trends that shaped Hellenistic literary criticism, there is as yet no general treatment of the subject. For the relationship of literature and art, see Onians (1979), Fowler (1989), and Zanker (2004), and for the philosophical basis of Hellenistic viewing, Goldhill (1994). On Hellenistic theories of mimeticism, see Halliwell (2002) Chs. 9–10; on poetic realism, see Zanker (1987). Text and translation of Demetrius, *On Style* in Roberts (1902); brief discussion in Kennedy (1989) 196–8. The basic source for the euphonist critics and Philodemus is Janko (2000), although this edition is intended for classical scholars. Fantuzzi and Hunter (2004) 449–61 provides a summary of the euphonists. The introduction to Sider's edition of his epigrams (1997) offers a readable account of Philodemus and his theories of poetry.

4.5 Reception in Rome. For a recent account of Hellenistic poetry in Rome, see Fantuzzi and Hunter (2004) 461–85. Fragments of Ennius

and minor Latin poets, including neoterics, with commentary but no
translations, are in Courtney (2003); translation of Ennius' fragments is
available in Warmington I (1935–40). The fragments of Parthenius, with
translation, commentary, and an excellent introduction, are in Lightfoot
(1999); for Parthenius' influence on Roman authors, see Francese (2001).
The fragments of Euphorion, with commentary in French, are in Groningen (1977); on Hellenistic curse poetry, see Watson (1991). For a
summary of the influence of the *Aetia* prologue on Roman literature, see
Hopkinson (1988) 98–101. For Vergil's intertextual use of Hellenistic
poetry, see Thomas (1999) and Nelis (2001).

Bibliography

Acosta-Hughes, Benjamin. 2002. *Polyeideia: The "Iambi" of Callimachus and the Archaic Iambic Tradition*. Berkeley, Los Angeles, London: University of California Press.

Acosta-Hughes, Benjamin, Kosmetatou, Elizabeth, and Baumbach, Manuel, eds. 2004. *Labored in Papyrus Leaves: Perspectives on an Epigram Collection Attributed to Posidippus*. Washington, DC: Center for Hellenic Studies.

Acosta-Hughes, Benjamin and Stephens, Susan. 2002. "Rereading Callimachus' *Aetia* Fragment 1." *Classical Philology* 97: 238–55.

Algra, Keimpe, Barnes, J., Mansfeld, J., and Schofield, M., eds. 1999. *The Cambridge History of Hellenistic Philosophy*. Cambridge: Cambridge University Press.

Andrews, N. E. 1998. "Philosophical Satire in the *Aetia* Prologue." In Harder et al. pp. 1–19.

Andronicos, Manolis. 1984. *Vergina: The Royal Tombs and the Ancient City*. Athens: Ekdotike Athenon SA.

Armstrong, David, Fish, J., Johnston, P. A., and Skinner, M. B., eds. 2004. *Vergil, Philodemus, and the Augustans*. Austin: University of Texas Press.

Arnott, W. G., ed. and trans. 1979–2000. *Menander*. 3 vols. Cambridge, MA: Harvard University Press.

Asmis, Elizabeth. 1990. "Philodemus' Epicureanism." In *Aufstieg und Niedergang der römischen Welt: Geschichte und Kultur Roms im Spiegel der neueren Forschung*, Teil II, Band 36.4. Edited by Wolfgang Haase. Berlin and New York: Walter de Gruyter. pp. 2369–406.

Austin, C. and Bastianini, G., eds. 2002. *Posidippi Pellaei quae supersunt omnia*. Milan: LED (= Edizioni Universitarie di Lettere Economia Diritto).

Austin, M. M. 1981. *The Hellenistic World from Alexander to the Roman Conquest: A Selection of Ancient Sources in Translation*. Cambridge: Cambridge University Press.

Bagnall, Roger and Derow, Peter. 2004. *The Hellenistic Period: Historical Sources in Translation*. New ed. Oxford: Blackwell Publishing.

Bailey, Cyril, ed. and trans. 1926. *Epicurus: The Extant Remains*. Oxford: Clarendon Press.

Bastianini, Guido and Gallazzi, Claudio, with Austin, Colin, eds. 2001. *Posidippo di Pella: Epigrammi (P. Mil. Vogl. VIII 309)*. In Papiri dell'Università degli Studi di Milano, 8. Milan: LED (= Edizioni Universitarie di Lettere Economia Diritto).

Beye, Charles R. 1982. *Epic and Romance in the "Argonautica" of Apollonius*. Carbondale: Southern Illinois University Press.

Bilde, Per, Engberg-Pedersen, Troels, Hannestad, Lise, and Zahle, Jan, eds. 1997. *Conventional Values of the Hellenistic Greeks*. Aarhus: Aarhus University Press.

Bing, Peter. 1988. *The Well-Read Muse: Present and Past in Callimachus and the Hellenistic Poets* (Hypomnemata 90). Göttingen: Vandenhoeck & Ruprecht.

Bing, Peter. 2002. "The 'Alexandrian Erotic Fragment' or 'Maedchens Klage.' " In *The Bilingual Family Archive of Dryton, His Wife Apollonia and Their Daughter Senmouthis (P. Dryton)*. Edited by Katelijn Vandorpe. Brussels: Koninklijke Vlaamse Academie van België. pp. 381–90.

Bing, Peter. 2002/3. "Posidippus and the Admiral: Kallikrates of Samos in the Milan Epigrams." *Greek, Roman, and Byzantine Studies* 43: 243–66.

Bing, Peter. 2003. "The Unruly Tongue: Philitas of Cos as Scholar and Poet." *Classical Philology* 98: 330–48.

Blum, Rudolf. 1991. *Kallimachos: The Alexandrian Library and the Origins of Bibliography*. Translated by Hans H. Wellisch. Madison: University of Wisconsin Press.

Bowman, Alan K. 1986. *Egypt after the Pharaohs, 332 BC–AD 642*. Berkeley: University of California Press.

Bulloch, A. W. 1985a. "Hellenistic Poetry." In Easterling and Knox, eds. pp. 541–621.

Bulloch, A. W., ed. 1985b. *Callimachus: The Fifth Hymn*. Cambridge: Cambridge University Press.

Burstein, Stanley M., ed. and trans. 1989. *Agatharchides of Cnidus: On the Erythraean Sea*. London: Hakluyt Society.

Burton, Joan B. 1995. *Theocritus's Urban Mimes: Mobility, Gender, and Patronage*. Berkeley, Los Angeles, London: University of California Press.

Cameron, Alan. 1993. *The Greek Anthology from Meleager to Planudes*. Oxford: Clarendon Press; New York: Oxford University Press.

Cameron, Alan. 1995. *Callimachus and His Critics*. Princeton: Princeton University Press.

Carney, Elizabeth D. 2000. *Women and Monarchy in Macedonia*. Norman: University of Oklahoma Press.

Cartledge, Paul and Spawforth, Antony. 2002. *Hellenistic and Roman Sparta: A Tale of Two Cities*. 2nd ed. London and New York: Routledge.

Champion, Craige B. 2004. *Cultural Politics in Polybius's "Histories."* Berkeley, Los Angeles, London: University of California Press.

Chauveau, Michel. 2000. *Egypt in the Age of Cleopatra: History and Society under the Ptolemies*. Translated by David Lorton. Ithaca and London: Cornell University Press.

Clarke, Katherine. 1999. *Between Geography and History: Hellenistic Constructions of the Roman World*. Oxford: Clarendon Press.

Clauss, James J. 1993. *The Best of the Argonauts: The Redefinition of the Epic Hero in Book 1 of Apollonius's "Argonautica."* Berkeley, Los Angeles, Oxford: University of California Press.

Clayman, D. L. 1980. *Callimachus' "Iambi."* Leiden: E. J. Brill.

Courtney, Edward. 1990. "Greek and Latin Acrostichs." *Philologus* 134: 3–13.

Courtney, Edward, ed. 2003. *The Fragmentary Latin Poets*. Paperback edition with Addenda. Oxford and New York: Oxford University Press.

Cribiore, Raffaella. 1996. *Writing, Teachers, and Students in Graeco-Roman Egypt* (American Studies in Papyrology 36). Atlanta: Scholars Press.

Cunningham, I. C., ed. 1971. *Herodas: Mimiambi*. Oxford: Clarendon Press.

Cuomo, S. 2001. *Ancient Mathematics*. London and New York: Routledge.

Cusset, Christophe. 1999. *La Muse dans la Bibliothèque: Réécriture et intertextualité dans la poésie alexandrine*. Paris: CNRS.

Diggle, James, ed. and trans. 2004. *Theophrastus: Characters*. Cambridge: Cambridge University Press.

Dijksterhuis, E. J. 1987. *Archimedes*. Translated by C. Dikshoorn. 2nd ed. Princeton: Princeton University Press.

Downey, Glanville. 1963. *Ancient Antioch*. Princeton: Princeton University Press.

Easterling, P. E. and Knox, B. M. W. 1985a. "Books and Readers in the Greek World." In Easterling and Knox, eds. pp. 1–41.

Easterling, P. E. and Knox, B. M. W., eds. 1985b. *The Cambridge History of Classical Literature I: Greek Literature*. Cambridge: Cambridge University Press.

Eckstein, Arthur M. 1995. *Moral Vision in "The Histories" of Polybius*. Berkeley, Los Angeles, London: University of California Press.

Edelstein, L. and Kidd, I. G., eds. 1989. *Posidonius I: The Fragments*. 2nd ed. Cambridge and New York: Cambridge University Press.

Edmonds, J. M., trans. 1928. *The Greek Bucolic Poets*. Rev. ed. Cambridge, MA: Harvard University Press.

Empereur, Jean-Yves. 1998. *Alexandria Rediscovered*. Translated by Margaret Maehler. London: British Museum Press.

Erskine, Andrew, ed. 2003. *A Companion to the Hellenistic World*. Malden, MA and Oxford: Blackwell Publishing.

Evans, James. 1998. *The History and Practice of Ancient Astronomy*. New York and Oxford: Oxford University Press.

Fantuzzi, Marco and Hunter, Richard. 2004. *Tradition and Innovation in Hellenistic Poetry*. Cambridge: Cambridge University Press.

Fantuzzi, Marco and Papanghelis, Theodore, eds. 2006. *Brill's Companion to Greek and Latin Pastoral*. Leiden: E. J. Brill.

Feeney, D. C. 1991. *The Gods in Epic: Poets and Critics of the Classical Tradition*. Oxford: Clarendon Press; New York: Oxford University Press.

Fitzgerald, John T., Obbink, Dirk, and Holland, Glenn, eds. 2004. *Philodemus and the New Testament World*. Leiden and Boston: E. J. Brill.

Fowler, Barbara H. 1989. *The Hellenistic Aesthetic*. Madison: University of Wisconsin Press.

Fowler, Barbara H., trans. 1990. *Hellenistic Poetry: An Anthology*. Madison: University of Wisconsin Press.

Francese, Christopher. 2001. *Parthenius of Nicaea and Roman Poetry* (Studien zur klassischen Philologie 126). Frankfurt am Main: Peter Lang.

Fränkel, Hermann, ed. 1961. *Apollonii Rhodii Argonautica*. Oxford: Clarendon Press.

Fraser, P. M. 1972. *Ptolemaic Alexandria*. 3 vols. Oxford: Clarendon Press.

Fried, Michael N., trans. 2002. *Apollonius of Perga: Conics, Book IV*. Santa Fe: Green Lion Press.

Gee, Emma. 2000. *Ovid, Aratus and Augustus: Astronomy in Ovid's "Fasti."* Cambridge: Cambridge University Press.

Gerber, Douglas, ed. and trans. 1999. *Greek Elegiac Poetry from the Seventh to the Fifth Centuries BC*. Cambridge, MA and London: Harvard University Press.

Giangrande, G. 1967. "*Arte allusiva* and Alexandrian Epic Poetry." *Classical Quarterly* 17: 85–97.

Ginouvès, René, ed. 1994. *Macedonia from Philip II to the Roman Conquest*. Princeton: Princeton University Press.

Goldberg, Sander M. 1980. *The Making of Menander's Comedy*. Berkeley and Los Angeles: University of California Press.

Goldhill, Simon. 1994. "The Naive and Knowing Eye: Ecphrasis and the Culture of Viewing in the Hellenistic World." In *Art and Text in Ancient Greek Culture*. Edited by Simon Goldhill and Robin Osborne. Cambridge: Cambridge University Press. pp. 197–223.

Gomme, A. W. and Sandbach, F. H. 1973. *Menander: A Commentary*. Oxford: Oxford University Press.

Gow, A. S. F., ed. 1952a. *Bucolici Graeci*. Oxford: Clarendon Press.

Gow, A. S. F., ed. and trans. 1952b. *Theocritus*. 2 vols. 2nd ed. Cambridge: Cambridge University Press.

Gow, A. S. F., ed. 1965. *Machon: The Fragments*. Cambridge: Cambridge University Press.

Gow, A. S. F. and Page, D. L., eds. 1965. *The Greek Anthology: Hellenistic Epigrams*. 2 vols. Cambridge: Cambridge University Press.

Gow, A. S. F. and Page, D. L., eds. 1968. *The Greek Anthology: The Garland of Philip*. 2 vols. Cambridge: Cambridge University Press.

Gow, A. S. F. and Scholfield, A. F., eds. and trans. 1953. *Nicander: The Poems and Poetical Fragments*. Cambridge: Cambridge University Press.

Green, Peter. 1990. *Alexander to Actium: The Historical Evolution of the Hellenistic Age*. Berkeley and Los Angeles: University of California Press.

Green, Peter, trans. 1997. *The Argonautika, by Apollonios Rhodios*. Berkeley, Los Angeles, London: University of California Press.

Greene, Ellen, ed. 2005. *Women Poets in Ancient Greece and Rome.* Norman: University of Oklahoma Press.

Griffiths, Frederick T. 1979. *Theocritus at Court* (Mnemosyne Supplement 55). Leiden: E. J. Brill.

Groningen, B. A. van, ed. 1977. *Euphorion.* Amsterdam: Adolf Hakkert.

Gruen, Erich S. 1984. *The Hellenistic World and the Coming of Rome.* 2 vols. Berkeley, Los Angeles, London: University of California Press.

Grummond, Nancy T. de and Ridgway, Brunilde S., eds. 2000. *From Pergamon to Sperlonga: Sculpture and Context.* Berkeley: University of California Press.

Gulick, Charles B., ed. and trans. 1951–71. *Athenaeus: The Deipnosophists.* 7 vols. Rev. ed. Cambridge, MA and London: Harvard University Press.

Gutzwiller, Kathryn. 1981. *Studies in the Hellenistic Epyllion* (Beiträge zur klassischen Philologie 114). Meisenheim am Glan: Anton Hain.

Gutzwiller, Kathryn. 1991. *Theocritus' Pastoral Analogies: The Formation of a Genre.* Madison: University of Wisconsin Press.

Gutzwiller, Kathryn. 1992. "Callimachus' "Lock of Berenice": Fantasy, Romance, and Propaganda." *American Journal of Philology* 113: 361–85. Reprinted in *Greek Literature 7: Greek Literature in the Hellenistic Period.* Edited by Gregory Nagy. London. pp. 305–31.

Gutzwiller, Kathryn. 1996. "The Evidence for Theocritean Poetry Books." In *Theocritus* (Hellenistica Groningana 2). Edited by M. A. Harder, R. F. Regtuit, and G. C. Wakker. Groningen: Egbert Forsten. pp. 119–49.

Gutzwiller, Kathryn. 1997. "Genre Development and Gendered Voices in Nossis and Erinna." In *Dwelling in Possibility: Women Poets and Critics on Poetry.* Edited by Yopie Prins and Maeera Shreiber. Ithaca and London: Cornell University Press. pp. 202–22.

Gutzwiller, Kathryn. 1998. *Poetic Garlands: Hellenistic Epigrams in Context.* Berkeley, Los Angeles, London: University of California Press.

Gutzwiller, Kathryn. 2000. "The Tragic Mask of Comedy: Metatheatricality in Menander." *Classical Antiquity* 19: 102–37.

Gutzwiller, Kathryn, ed. 2005. *The New Posidippus: A Hellenistic Poetry Book.* Oxford: Oxford University Press.

Gutzwiller, Kathryn. 2006. "The Bucolic Problem." *Classical Philology* 101.

Habicht, Christian. 1997. *Athens from Alexander to Antony.* Translated by Deborah Schneider. Cambridge, MA: Harvard University Press.

Hadas, Moses, ed. and trans. 1951. *Aristeas to Philocrates (Letter of Aristeas).* New York: Harper & Brothers.

Halliwell, Stephen. 2002. *The Aesthetics of Mimesis: Ancient Texts and Modern Problems.* Princeton and Oxford: Princeton University Press.

Halperin, David M. 1983. *Before Pastoral: Theocritus and the Ancient Tradition of Bucolic Poetry.* New Haven and London: Yale University Press.

Hansen, Esther V. 1971. *The Attalids of Pergamon.* 2nd ed. Ithaca and London: Cornell University Press.

Harder, M. A., Regtuit, R. F., and Wakker, G. C., eds. 1998. *Genre in Hellenistic Poetry* (Hellenistica Groningana 3). Groningen: Egbert Forsten.

Heath, Thomas. 1896. *Apollonius of Perga: Treatise on Conic Sections*. Cambridge: Cambridge University Press.

Heath, Thomas, trans. 1897. *The Works of Archimedes*. Cambridge: Cambridge University Press.

Heath, Thomas. 1913. *Aristarchus of Samos: The Ancient Copernicus*. Oxford: Clarendon Press. Reprint ed., New York: Dover, 1981.

Heath, Thomas. 1921. *A History of Greek Mathematics*. 2 vols. Oxford: Clarendon Press.

Heath, Thomas, trans. 1926. *Euclid's Elements*. 2nd ed. Cambridge: Cambridge University Press. Reprint ed., Santa Fe: Green Lion Press, 2002.

Heath, Thomas. 1932. *Greek Astronomy*. London and Toronto: J. M. Dent & Sons; New York: E. P. Dutton. Reprint ed., New York: Dover, 1991.

Hölbl, Günther. 2001. *A History of the Ptolemaic Empire*. Translated by Tina Saavedra. London and New York: Routledge.

Hollis, A. S., ed. 1990. *Callimachus: "Hecale."* Oxford: Clarendon Press.

Honigman, Sylvie. 2003. *The Septuagint and Homeric Scholarship in Alexandria: A Study in the Narrative of the "Letter of Aristeas."* London and New York: Routledge.

Hopkinson, Neil, ed. 1988. *A Hellenistic Anthology*. Cambridge: Cambridge University Press.

Hordern, J. H. 2004. *Sophron's Mimes: Text, Translation, and Commentary*. Oxford: Oxford University Press.

Hunter, R. L. 1985. *The New Comedy of Greece and Rome*. Cambridge: Cambridge University Press.

Hunter, R. L., ed. 1989. *Apollonius of Rhodes: Argonautica, Book III*. Cambridge: Cambridge University Press.

Hunter, R. L. 1993a. *The "Argonautica" of Apollonius: Literary Studies*. Cambridge: Cambridge University Press.

Hunter, R. L., trans. 1993b. *Apollonius of Rhodes: Jason and the Golden Fleece (The Argonautica)*. Oxford: Clarendon Press; New York: Oxford University Press.

Hunter, R. L. 1996. *Theocritus and the Archaeology of Greek Poetry*. Cambridge: Cambridge University Press.

Hunter, R. L., ed. 1999. *Theocritus: A Selection*. Cambridge: Cambridge University Press.

Hunter, R. L. 2003. *Theocritus: Encomium of Ptolemy Philadelphus*. Berkeley, Los Angeles, London: University of California Press.

Hutchinson, G. O. 1988. *Hellenistic Poetry*. Oxford: Clarendon Press.

Irby-Massie, Georgia and Keyser, Paul. 2002. *Greek Science of the Hellenistic Era: A Sourcebook*. London and New York: Routledge.

Jacobson, Howard. 1983. *The "Exagoge" of Ezekiel*. Cambridge: Cambridge University Press.

Janko, Richard, ed. and trans. 2000. *Philodemus: On Poems, Book 1*. Oxford and New York: Oxford University Press.

Johnson, William A. 2004. *Bookrolls and Scribes in Oxyrhynchus*. Toronto, Buffalo, London: University of Toronto Press.

Kennedy, George A., ed. 1989. *The Cambridge History of Literary Criticism I: Classical Criticism*. Cambridge: Cambridge University Press.

Kerkhecker, Arnd. 1999. *Callimachus' Book of "Iambi."* Oxford: Clarendon Press.

Kerlin, Robert T. 1910. *Theocritus in English Literature*. Lynchburg, VA: J. P. Bell.

Kidd, Douglas, ed. and trans. 1997. *Aratus: Phaenomena*. Cambridge: Cambridge University Press.

Kidd, I. G. 1988. *Posidonius II: The Commentary*. Cambridge and New York: Cambridge University Press.

Kidd, I. G. 1999. *Posidonius III: The Translation of the Fragments*. Cambridge: Cambridge University Press.

Koenen, Ludwig. 1993. "The Ptolemaic King as a Religious Figure." In *Images and Ideologies: Self-Definition in the Hellenistic World*. Edited by Anthony Bulloch, E. S. Gruen, A. A. Long, and A. Stewart. Berkeley, Los Angeles, London: University of California Press. pp. 25–115.

Koester, Helmut, ed. 1998. *Pergamon: Citadel of the Gods*. Harrisburg, PA: Trinity Press International.

Kollesch, Jutta and Kudlien, Fridolf, eds. 1965. *Apollonii Citiensis in Hippocratis de articulis commentarius*. Translated into German by J. Kollesch and D. Nickel. Berlin: Academia Scientiarum.

Konstan, David. 1995. *Greek Comedy and Ideology*. New York and Oxford: Oxford University Press.

Kramer, Bärbel. 2001. "The Earliest Known Map of Spain (?) and the Geography of Artemidorus of Ephesus on Papyrus." *Imago Mundi* 53: 115–20.

Krevans, Nita. 1993. "Fighting Against Antimachus: The *Lyde* and the *Aetia* Reconsidered." In *Callimachus* (Hellenistica Groningana 1). Edited by M. A. Harder, R. F. Regtuit, and G. C. Wakker. Groningen: Egbert Forsten. pp. 149–60.

Kurke, Leslie. 2002. "Gender, Politics and Subversion in the *Chreiai* of Machon." *Proceedings of the Cambridge Philological Society* 48: 20–65.

Kyriakou, Poulheria. 1995. *Homeric Hapax Legomena in the "Argonautica" of Apollonius Rhodius: A Literary Study*. Stuttgart: Franz Steiner.

Lape, Susan. 2004. *Reproducing Athens: Menander's Comedy, Democratic Culture, and the Hellenistic City*. Princeton and Oxford: Princeton University Press.

Lewis, Naphtali. 1986. *Greeks in Ptolemaic Egypt: Case Studies in the Social History of the Hellenistic World*. Oxford: Clarendon Press.

Lightfoot, J. L., ed. 1999. *Parthenius of Nicaea: The Poetical Fragments and the Ἐρωτικὰ Παθήματα*. Oxford, New York: Oxford University Press.

Lloyd-Jones, Hugh, ed. 2005. *Supplementum supplementi Hellenistici*. Berlin: Walter de Gruyter.

Lloyd-Jones, Hugh and Parsons, Peter, eds. 1983. *Supplementum Hellenisticum*. Berlin: Walter de Gruyter.

Lombardo, Stanley and Rayor, Diane, trans. 1988. *Callimachus: Hymns, Epigrams, Select Fragments*. Baltimore and London: Johns Hopkins University Press.

Long, A. A. 1986. *Hellenistic Philosophy: Stoics, Epicureans, Sceptics*. 2nd ed. Berkeley and Los Angeles: University of California Press.

Long, A. A. and Sedley, D. N. 1987. *The Hellenistic Philosophers*. 2 vols. Cambridge: Cambridge University Press.

McKay, K. J. 1962a. *Erysichthon: A Callimachean Comedy* (Mnemosyne Supplementum 7). Leiden: E. J. Brill.

McKay, K. J. 1962b. *The Poet at Play: Kallimachos, the Bath of Pallas* (Mnemosyne Supplementum 6). Leiden: E. J. Brill.

McLennan, G. R. 1977. *Callimachus: Hymn to Zeus, Introduction and Commentary*. Rome: Ateneo & Bizarri.

Maehler, Herwig. 2004. "Alexandria, the Mouseion, and Cultural Identity." In *Alexandria, Real and Imagined*. Edited by Anthony Hirst and Michael Silk. Aldershot: Ashgate Publishing. pp. 1–14.

Mair, A. W., trans. 1921. *Callimachus: Hymns, Epigrams. Lycophron: Alexandra*. G. R. Mair, trans. *Aratus: Phaenomena*. London: W. Heinemann. Reprint ed., Cambridge, MA: Harvard University Press, 1969.

Manwell, Elizabeth. 2005. "Dico ergo sum: Erinna's Voice and Poetic Reality." In Greene. pp. 72–90.

Marcotte, Didier, ed. and trans. 2000. *Géographes grecs, Tome I: Introduction générale, Ps.-Scymnos: Circuit de la Terre*. Paris: Les Belles Lettres.

Marsden, E. W. 1969. *Greek and Roman Artillery: Historical Development*. Oxford: Clarendon Press.

Marsden, E. W. 1971. *Greek and Roman Artillery: Technical Treatises*. Oxford: Clarendon Press.

Martin, Jean, ed. and trans. 1998. *Aratos: Phénomènes*. 2 vols. Paris: Les Belles Lettres.

Massimilla, Giulio. 2000. "Nuovi elementi per la cronologia di Nicandro." In *La letteratura ellenistica: Problemi e prospettive di ricerca* (Atti del Colloquio Internazionale, Università di Roma "Tor Vergata," April 29–30, 1997). Edited by Roberto Pretagostini. Rome: Quasar. pp. 127–37.

Mastromarco, Giuseppe. 1984. *The Public of Herodas*. Amsterdam: J. C. Gieben.

Merkelbach, Reinhold and Strauber, Josef, eds. 1998–2004. *Steinepigramme aus dem griechischen Osten*. 5 vols. Stuttgart and Leipzig: Teubner; Munich and Leipzig: K. G. Saur.

Merriam, Carol. 2001. *The Development of the Epyllion Genre through the Hellenistic and Roman Periods*. Lewiston, NY: Edwin Mellen Press.

Nagy, Gregory. 1996. *Poetry as Performance: Homer and Beyond*. Cambridge: Cambridge University Press.

Nelis, Damien. 2001. *Vergil's "Aeneid" and the "Argonautica" of Apollonius Rhodius*. Leeds: Francis Cairns.

Netz, Reviel. 1999. *The Shaping of Deduction in Greek Mathematics: A Study in Cognitive History*. Cambridge: Cambridge University Press.

Netz, Reviel. 2004a. *The Transformation of Mathematics in the Early Mediterranean World: From Problems to Equations*. Cambridge: Cambridge University Press.

Netz, Reviel, trans. 2004b. *The Works of Archimedes* I. Cambridge: Cambridge University Press.

Neugebauer, O. 1975. *A History of Ancient Mathematical Astronomy*. 2 vols. Berlin, Heidelberg, New York: Springer-Verlag.

Nisetich, Frank, trans. 2001. *The Poems of Callimachus*. Oxford and New York: Oxford University Press.

Nussbaum, Martha. 1994. *The Therapy of Desire: Theory and Practice in Hellenistic Ethics*. Princeton: Princeton University Press.

Nutton, Vivian. 2004. *Ancient Medicine*. London and New York: Routledge.

Obbink, Dirk, ed. 1995. *Philodemus and Poetry: Poetic Theory and Practice in Lucretius, Philodemus, and Horace*. New York: Oxford University Press.

Olson, S. Douglas and Sens, Alexander, eds. 1999. *Matro of Pitane and the Tradition of Epic Parody in the Fourth Century BCE*. Atlanta: Scholars Press.

Olson, S. Douglas and Sens, Alexander, eds. 2000. *Archestratos of Gela: Greek Culture and Cuisine in the Fourth Century BCE*. Oxford: Oxford University Press.

Onians, John. 1979. *Art and Thought in the Hellenistic Age: The Greek World View 350–50 BC*. London: Thames & Hudson.

Page, D. L., ed. 1981. *Further Greek Epigrams*. Cambridge: Cambridge University Press.

Paton, W. R., ed. and trans. 1916–18. *The Greek Anthology*. 5 vols. Cambridge, MA: Harvard University Press.

Paton, W. R., ed. and trans. 1922–7. *Polybius: The Histories*. 6 vols. Cambridge, MA: Harvard University Press.

Pendergraft, Mary. 1995. "Euphony and Etymology: Aratus' *Phaenomena*." *Syllecta Classica* 6: 43–67.

Pfeiffer, Rudolf, ed. 1949–51. *Callimachus*. 2 vols. Oxford: Clarendon Press.

Pfeiffer, Rudolf. 1968. *History of Classical Scholarship from the Beginnings to the End of the Hellenistic Age*. Oxford: Clarendon Press.

Pollitt, J. J. 1986. *Art in the Hellenistic Age*. Cambridge: Cambridge University Press.

Pomeroy, Sarah B. 1984. *Women in Hellenistic Egypt from Alexander to Cleopatra*. New York: Schocken Books. Reprint ed., Detroit: Wayne State University Press, 1990.

Powell, J. U. 1925. *Collectanea Alexandrina: reliquiae minores poetarum Graecorum aetatis Ptolemaicae*. Oxford: Clarendon Press. Reprint ed., Chicago: Ares, 1981.

Reed, J. D. 1997. *Bion of Smyrna: The Fragments and the "Adonis."* Cambridge: Cambridge University Press.

Reynolds, L. D. and Wilson, N. G. 1991. *Scribes and Scholars: A Guide to the Transmission of Greek and Latin Literature*. 3rd ed. Oxford: Clarendon Press; New York: Oxford University Press.

Rice, E. E. 1983. *The Grand Procession of Ptolemy Philadelphia*. London: Oxford University Press.

Rist, J. M. 1969. *Stoic Philosophy*. Cambridge: Cambridge University Press.

Rist, J. M. 1972. *Epicurus: An Introduction*. Cambridge: Cambridge University Press.

Roberts, W. Rhys, ed. and trans. 1902. *Demetrius: On Style*. Cambridge: Cambridge University Press.

Rusten, Jeffrey. 1982. *Dionysius Scytobrachion* (Papyrologica Coloniensia 10). Opladen: Westdeutscher Verlag.

Rusten, Jeffrey. 1993. *Theophrastus: Characters.* Cunningham, I. C. *Herodas: Mimes.* Knox, A. D. *Cercidas and the Choliambic Poets.* Cambridge, MA: Harvard University Press.

Rusten, Jeffrey. 2002. *Theophrastus: Characters.* Cunningham, I. C. *Herodas: Mimes, Sophron and Other Mime Fragments.* Cambridge, MA and London: Harvard University Press.

Sacks, Kenneth. 1981. *Polybius on the Writing of History* (University of California Publications in Classical Studies 24). Berkeley, Los Angeles, London: University of California Press.

Scafuro, Adele C. 1997. *The Forensic Stage: Settling Disputes in Graeco-Roman New Comedy.* Cambridge: Cambridge University Press.

Schepens, Guido and Delcroix, Kris. 1996. "Ancient Paradoxography: Origin, Evolution, Production and Reception." In *La letteratura di consumo nel mondo Greco-Latino* (Atti del Convegno Internazionale, Cassino, September 14–17, 1994). Edited by Oronzo Pecere and Antonio Stramaglia. Cassino: Università degli Studi di Cassino. pp. 373–460.

Selden, Daniel. 1998. "Alibis." *Classical Antiquity* 17: 289–412.

Sens, Alexander. 1997. *Theocritus, Dioscuri (Idyll 22): Introduction, Text, and Commentary.* Göttingen: Vandenhoeck & Ruprecht.

Sharples, R. W. 1996. *Stoics, Epicureans and Sceptics: An Introduction to Hellenistic Philosophy.* London and New York: Routledge.

Sherwin-White, Susan and Kuhrt, Amélie. 1993. *From Samarkhand to Sardis: A New Approach to the Seleucid Empire.* London: Duckworth.

Shipley, Graham. 2000. *The Greek World after Alexander, 323–30 BC.* London and New York: Routledge.

Sider, David, ed. 1997. *The Epigrams of Philodemos: Introduction, Text, and Commentary.* New York and Oxford: Oxford University Press.

Sider, David. 2005. *The Library of the Villa dei Papiri at Herculaneum.* Los Angeles: J. Paul Getty Museum.

Sifakis, G. M. 1967. *Studies in the History of Hellenistic Drama.* Athlone Press: University of London.

Skinner, Marilyn. 1991. "Nossis *Thēlyglōssos:* The Private Text and the Public Book." In *Women's History and Ancient History.* Edited by Sarah B. Pomeroy. Chapel Hill and London: University of North Carolina Press. pp. 20–47. Reprinted in Greene. pp. 112–38.

Skinner, Marilyn. 2001. "Ladies' Day at the Art Institute: Theocritus, Herodas, and the Gendered Gaze." In *Making Silence Speak: Women's Voices in Greek Literature and Society.* Edited by André Lardinois and Laura McClure. Princeton and Oxford: Princeton University Press. pp. 201–23.

Skinner, Marilyn. 2005. "Homer's Mother." In Greene. pp. 91–111.

Snyder, Jane M. 1989. *The Woman and the Lyre: Women Writers in Classical Greece and Rome.* Carbondale: Southern Illinois University Press.

Spanoudakis, Konstantinos. 2002. *Philitas of Cos.* Leiden: E. J. Brill.

Staden, Heinrich von, ed. and trans. 1989. *Herophilus: The Art of Medicine in Early Alexandria*. Cambridge: Cambridge University Press.

Staden, Heinrich von. 1996. "Body and Machine: Interactions between Medicine, Mechanics, and Philosophy in Early Alexandria." In *Alexandria and Alexandrianism*. Malibu: J. Paul Getty Museum. pp. 85–106.

Stephens, Susan A. 2003. *Seeing Double: Intercultural Poetics in Ptolemaic Alexandria*. Berkeley, Los Angeles, London: University of California Press.

Thomas, Richard. 1999. *Reading Virgil and his Texts: Studies in Intertextuality*. Ann Arbor: University of Michigan Press.

Toohey, Peter. 1996. *Epic Lessons: An Introduction to Ancient Didactic Poetry*. London and New York: Routledge.

Toomer, G. J., ed. and trans. 1976. *Diocles On Burning Mirrors: The Arabic Translation of the Lost Greek Original*. Berlin, Heidelberg, New York: Springer-Verlag.

Trypanis, C. A., ed. and trans. 1958. *Callimachus: "Aetia," "Iambi," Lyric Poems, "Hecale," Minor Epic and Elegiac Poems, and other Fragments*. Cambridge, MA: Harvard University Press.

Turner, E. G. 1980. *Greek Papyri: An Introduction*. 2nd ed. Oxford: Clarendon Press; New York: Oxford University Press.

Turner, E. G. and Parsons, P. J. 1987. *Greek Manuscripts of the Ancient World* (Bulletin Supplement 46). 2nd ed. London: Institute of Classical Studies.

Vaughn, John W. 1976. *The Megara (Moschus IV): Text, Translation and Commentary* (Noctes Romanae 14). Bern and Stuttgart: Paul Haupt.

Venit, Margorie S. 2002. *Monumental Tombs of Ancient Alexandria: The Theater of the Dead*. Cambridge: Cambridge University Press.

Walbank, F. W. 1957–79. *A Historical Commentary on Polybius*. 3 vols. Oxford: Clarendon Press.

Walbank, F. W. 1972. *Polybius*. Berkeley, Los Angeles, London: University of California Press.

Walker, Susan and Higgs, Peter, eds. 2001. *Cleopatra of Egypt: From History to Myth*. London: British Museum Press; Princeton: Princeton University Press.

Walton, J. Michael and Arnott, Peter D. 1996. *Menander and the Making of Comedy*. Westport, CT and London: Greenwood Press.

Warmington, E. H. 1935–40. *Remains of Old Latin*. 4 vols. Cambridge, MA: Harvard University Press.

Watson, Lindsay. 1991. *Arae: The Curse Poetry of Antiquity*. Leeds: Francis Cairns.

Webster, T. L. B. 1974. *An Introduction to Menander*. Manchester: Manchester University Press; New York: Barnes & Noble.

Weitzmann, Kurt. 1959. *Ancient Book Illumination*. Cambridge, MA: Harvard University Press.

Wells, Robert, trans. 1988. *The Idylls of Theocritus*. Manchester and New York: Carcanet.

West, M. L. 1982. *Greek Metre*. Oxford: Clarendon Press.

West, M. L. 1987. *Introduction to Greek Metre*. Oxford: Clarendon Press.

West, M. L. 2003. *Homeric Hymns, Homeric Apocrypha, Lives of Homer*. Cambridge, MA and London: Harvard University Press.

West, Stephanie. 2000. "Lycophron's *Alexandra*: 'Hindsight as Foresight Makes No Sense'?" In *Matrices of Genre: Authors, Canons, and Society*. Edited by Mary Depew and Dirk Obbink. Cambridge, MA: Harvard University Press. pp. 153–66.

Wiles, David. 1991. *The Masks of Menander: Sign and Meaning in Greek and Roman Performance*. Cambridge: Cambridge University Press.

Williams, Frederick. 1978. *Callimachus: Hymn to Apollo, A Commentary*. Oxford: Clarendon Press.

Zagagi, Netta. 1994. *The Comedy of Menander: Convention, Variation and Originality*. London: Duckworth.

Zanker, Graham. 1987. *Realism in Alexandrian Poetry: A Literature and its Audience*. London and Sydney: Croom Helm.

Zanker, Graham. 2004. *Modes of Viewing in Hellenistic Poetry and Art*. Madison: University of Wisconsin Press.

Index